The
Proactive Health
Solution

Nadia Yacoub Cavallini

authorHOUSE®

AuthorHouse™ LLC
1663 Liberty Drive
Bloomington, IN 47403
www.authorhouse.com
Phone: 1-800-839-8640

Published by AuthorHouse   02/27/2014

ISBN: 978-1-4817-5882-6 (sc)
ISBN: 978-1-4817-5881-9 (hc)
ISBN: 978-1-4817-5883-3 (e)

Library of Congress Control Number: 2013910136

Any people depicted in stock imagery provided by Thinkstock are models, and such images are being used for illustrative purposes only. Certain stock imagery © Thinkstock.

Photography by: Fit Forever Photography/www.fitforeverphotography. com and Masserman Photography/www.massermanphotography.com

Cover by: Boomerang Design and Advertising.

This book is printed on acid-free paper.

Because of the dynamic nature of the Internet, any web addresses or links contained in this book may have changed since publication and may no longer be valid. The views expressed in this work are solely those of the author and do not necessarily reflect the views of the publisher, and the publisher hereby disclaims any responsibility for them.

Throughout this book, most names have been changed to protect privacy.

This book is dedicated to all the people who have lost hope in their battle to become healthy and fit.

Contents

Acknowledgments

Let me begin by thanking the founder and CEO of Life Time Fitness, Mr. Bahram Akradi, who over twenty years ago envisioned and created more than just a "gym." With his foresight and ingenuity, he engineered a mecca. Life Time Fitness (LTF) is indeed a one-of-a-kind experience. It offers superior quality and leading-edge services in all dimensions of health and fitness. It's a social hub for the community and a family recreation center all in one. At Life Time, there's something for everyone. As stated in their motto, it's truly an organizational empire committed to a "Healthy Way of Life." This outstanding organization continues to make a positive impact on our nation's health and for this, I am grateful. Thanks to all the members and my former clients from Life Time who helped me to recognize the need for this type of book. I deeply appreciate everyone who has significantly influenced my life by allowing me to change theirs.

Thanks to all the hard-working personal trainers who are committed to positively changing lives; because of them countless people have been inspired to break barriers and make significant improvements in their health. I've built numerous friendships through Life Time, some I've known for many years and others for only a short period. Whether within my social circle or working together as part of a dedicated team, each and all have touched my life in a unique way. Though I can only provide a few highlights, I'd like to start by thanking a few people from the LTF management team; in particular, Chris Seiler, Meghan Taylor Brandyberry, and Nina Del Tora for their tremendous leadership skills and directing team effort to achieve success. With his straightforward approach, Chris is a true leader in every sense of the word. Meghan has always been an inspiration by managing to bring out the best in people, while Nina was the super-glue keeping it altogether with her relentless energy and patience.

Next, I'd like to recognize and thank those who've been part of the same LTF Personal Training Team, starting with my always helpful, multitalented, and beautiful friend Angela Harrigan. Angela's commitment to excellence, her team spirit, and hard work are unparalleled; she's a mighty weapon in any arsenal and has the heart of a real trooper. Thanks to Jason Tillinger for being a diamond in the rough—calm, reliable, and so generous with his time in helping others. Thanks to Dave Pankow for being steady and cool in the midst of the storms and for the exhilaration of early morning boot camp. Thanks to the original and dynamic trio of Justin Grey, Alex Gruin, and Pierre Binandeh; the exceptional Pilates professionals, Cheryl Maher, Carly McPhail, and Erica Autio; the team leader extraordinaire, Jen Jenson, along with the mighty team rock stars, Rosemary Scranton and Missie McSweeney; and the bustling, always-in-sync dietitian, Erica Wasser.

Thanks to all my good friends and colleagues for their support and the positive impact they've made on my life. This includes: Dawn Kott Williams, Lisa Welch, Vanessa Poota, Megan Slaven, Stacey Cerroni, Donna and John McPherson, Dan Fell, Kristen Pierce, Marilyn Natchez, Scott Keil, Sean Cassar, Wendy Yates, Grant Elias, Michelle and Nick Faranso, Shawn Saba, Julia Stevens, Jeff Siegel, Steve Palms, John Jones, Sean Dick, Shehzad "Shaz" Sheikh, Steve Fine, Brian Grzyb, Anjanette Curry, Steve and Shelia Simmons, Chris Stepping, Andy Elliott, Lo Robert, Lea Clelland, Ellen Dittmer, Sherri Robinson, Pam Kouza, Frank Gamez, Joshua Kline, Ron Keller, Heather Frayne, Ray Powell, Stephanie Blouin, Jason Beckman, Ashley Sellman, Saro Avakian, and Jenny Kolb. Also, from the former LTF front desk, Michelle White, Crystal Williams, Brett Gerken, and André Halabu—thanks for many hearty laughs!

It is hard to convey enough thanks to my parents and family: my mom, Elaine Yacoub, in particular, who helped immensely during my time of career transition—this book wouldn't have been possible without her; my dad, Fuad Yacoub, who by his very nature is a remarkable leader and who taught me many lessons in life that are incorporated throughout this book; my sister, Nancy Yacoub, who offered some great suggestions and has shed a unique perspective from different parts of the world through her global travels; my brother, Michael Yacoub, MD, whose unwavering faith in me and comical nature has always brought tremendous encouragement and a smile to my face. Thanks to his wife Jennifer, Diane and Eric Crawford and Marvin and Leah Yacoub, for their ongoing encouragement and moral support, and to all the extended members of my family for blessing my life in so many ways.

Most of all, thanks to my absolutely wonderful, husband Keith Cavallini—the love of my life and best friend who never ceases to amaze me with the greatness of his heart. He has patiently supported me every step of the way, offering valuable input and helping out wherever possible. I'm truly blessed and grateful to have such a treasured jewel in my life.

Big thanks must go to Stas Glick, who helped me find my dream job at Fitness 19; I couldn't ask to work for a better organization. Thanks to all the outstanding Fitness 19 team members and personal trainers whom I've been privileged to work with, including Derrick Ritenour, Janna Turk, Russell Yerge, Franco Santariga, Robin Morgan, Rosa Bradley, Cyd Croft, Ross Terrasi, Jesse Williams, Ryan Carlson, Christian Lemieux, Ryan Trainor, Jackie Gearhart, Claire Beer and Rajeev Shahani.

I would also like to thank Richard Nascimento, an angel, who briefly crossed my path and brought incredible hope, enlightenment, and inspiration to my life.

Thanks to each of my clients and everyone who has allowed me to share their stories of how the Proactive Health Solution has helped to transform their lives and health. Above all, thanks to God, whose divine spirit guided me while writing this book. I'm confident that anyone who begins this journey toward optimal health will also be blessed by the same sovereign Spirit.

Introduction:
The Proactive Health Solution

Developing a Proactive Mind-Set

Inherent in human nature is a universal desire to be healthy and fit. People everywhere love to talk it up, professing they want to lose weight and get "in shape." That sounds impressive except for one problem; the greater majority don't actually do anything about it. Why is this so? Most people claim they don't have any motivation or that there's just not enough time in the day. The desire to be healthy, however, is innate, so the motivation is still there; it's just lying dormant. Furthermore, making the time for a health regimen would be a lot easier if people accessed their God-given privilege to proactively manage their life. What does all this mean? Well, this book isn't only about learning *what* to do to lose weight, eat right, and exercise. Plenty of people already know what to do, but they still don't do it. So while gaining knowledge is certainly important, learning *how* to develop a healthy lifestyle should take precedence.

The **Proactive Health Solution (PHS)** is a guide to help you make the important changes necessary to live a healthy lifestyle. It will teach you how to apply fundamental principles to honor your body and nurture all aspects of your well-being. If you've reached your wit's end and are fed up with being out of shape and unhealthy, then it's time to open your mind to another way of thinking. The PHS allows you to see through a different lens. It will help you claim a new lease on your life and health.

Facts to Consider

- ***Taking care of your health is a fundamental personal privilege.***

If you don't take care of your health, you forfeit your own personal power. This is something you need to do for yourself—no one can do it for you. Unfortunately, for many people this fundamental privilege has turned into a seemingly unobtainable mission. That's because their lifestyle and health issues have snowballed out of control, but it doesn't have to be that way. It's your personal privilege to be healthy, and you alone can reclaim this power starting right now.

- ***Your physical body is the only vehicle you have to take you through this life.***

You only get one body—one vehicle—for the rest of your life. Just like a car needs regular maintenance to run smoothly, so does your physical body. If you don't maintain your car, eventually the parts break down, and there's a cost to pay. Similarly, when you don't take care of physical body, this will takes its toll. Muscles atrophy, metabolism slows down, weight creeps on; you lose strength and flexibility and develop postural distortions. Before you know it, everything seems to be falling apart. When you barely have enough energy to get through the day, this is the price you pay. Poor health will slow you down and affect the quality of your life.

- ***Commitment fuels the motivation needed to be proactive with your health.***

When you make a commitment to be proactive with your health, this is unequivocally a wise decision. It's never too late and out of all the decisions you'll ever make in this lifetime, rest assured, that's a keeper! Being healthy speaks for itself by providing many natural incentives, but sustained motivation can't precede this commitment. In other words, the starting point to building and maintaining motivation is to make this commitment to yourself. This doesn't mean you should stop going to the doctor and refuse conventional medicine. It means you willingly take responsibility for your health and all aspects of your well-being. By becoming proactive this commitment puts *you* in control. Think about it; in a personal health crisis, you might decide to seek the opinions of two or three doctors. Ultimately however, the way you decide to proceed is still up to you. You can capitalize on this notion by being proactive with your health right now. This serves as preventive maintenance. Genetics aside, you have within you, the power to transform your health and drastically improve the quality of your life.

Of course, there's no magic bullet. To keep your commitment, you'll need to put forth the effort by backing up your words with action—that requires discipline. In order to become disciplined, you'll need to sustain motivation. The Proactive Health Solution will be your guide as you do the work. It will lead you from the moment you make this important lifestyle management decision up toward "discipline" which is the pinnacle of the PHS Pyramid. Your mission is to climb the pyramid until you reach the top.

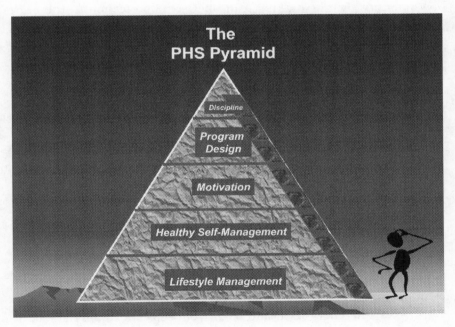

Reality Check

Health insurance companies are finally providing incentives for healthy behaviors by offering lower costs or deductibles. So if taking a proactive approach to health is definitely worthwhile, it's time to ask yourself some important questions: Do I eat in a health conscious way? Do I make time to exercise regularly? Do I manage stress? Do I deal with my emotions constructively? Do I have any inner peace or balance in my life? If the answer to these questions is no, then this is your reality check!

Realistically, most people become disillusioned because they know that developing healthy habits is the right thing to do, but time and again, they fail to do it. This is quite unfortunate, because our daily actions—simple measures—can have profound outcomes. For instance, you probably know someone who has experienced some form of heart trouble. Statistically, the majority of those who fall into this category could've averted this risk through preventive measures, simply by doing cardiovascular exercise on a consistent basis. They don't need to run a marathon! No, just a few months of regular cardiovascular exercise, even low intensity such as walking, can offer some protection to the heart and lungs. Consistent bouts of cardiovascular exercise can provide many long-term benefits. It lowers blood pressure and cholesterol, improves aerobic endurance, and reduces the risk of heart disease. In fact, research has proven that walking helps to prevent or control heart attack and stroke. Of course when physical activity is combined with a heart-healthy diet this makes an even more favorable impact. A good-quality exercise and nutrition program provides us with a strategy; it empowers us to make significant improvements in our health.

When we take advantage of this tremendous opportunity, we gain the power to prevent or manage a host of health issues such as Type II diabetes; colon, prostate, breast, and other cancers; anxiety; depression; dementia; obesity; and more. Consider that just walking for half an hour each day, four to five times per week, will significantly reduce the risk of heart disease. Similarly, if we consumed more fresh fruits and vegetables, which have natural healing powers, this would do wonders to cleanse our bodies and renew our health. Plenty of people are aware that taking these measures is beneficial, but how many act on it? Remember, it's not only important to know *what to do*, but we must learn *how to do it*. Most individuals need a road map to help them navigate toward optimal health. The Proactive Health Solution paves the way.

What exactly is the Proactive Health Solution?

The Proactive Health Solution is a self-empowering, educational process that will *help you to help yourself,* for when it comes to your health, this is the goal: to be proactive and develop the lifestyle habits that help to serve you along your life journey. Unlike the standard cookie-cutter approach to many health and fitness programs, it doesn't promise simply a means to "get in shape" or attain the perfect body. Rather, the PHS provides a conceptual and practical methodology that incorporates components and principles that help you to manage your life and health. It provides a link between knowing what to do and actually doing it.

The distinct advantage of the PHS is that while in pursuit of this mission, you're the one in control. *You choose* the way that benefits you the most. It's a journey of self-discovery and personal empowerment. The PHS provides the basic structure and guidelines, but you hold the power and can go at your own pace. If you're ever going to proactively manage your life and health, you must understand that the greater part of this process—the personal choices you make and the outcomes that follow—will rest in your own hands.

On a larger scale, societies worldwide can certainly benefit by gaining some common ground in this arena. Currently, however, the concept of the PHS is somewhat of a novelty—nothing quite like it has been fully cultivated. That's because the conceptual process itself is still in the pioneering stage. Within any society, there are different views about the development of healthy habits, but nothing has been adopted that clearly resonates with all. People in China, for example, may have a completely different idea from those living in England or Brazil. Consequently, this is a subject matter that is still evolving and it needs much molding across the globe. In any case, no society will be able to adopt a basic process until it recognizes what has been missing in the first place. Indeed, there are many avenues to health, yet if it's only health gurus who are enlightened; this won't make a significant impact upon the lives of whose health suffers the most.

Remember, there are two points to consider here; the individual and the collective. On an individual basis, anybody can benefit by implementing the PHS; it has already helped many of my clients. Executing and measuring such a process collectively within society, however, only becomes feasible at a later stage. Typically, trials and testing can take many years, but what happens today will affect the future and course of every generation.

The PHS presents a paradigm shift, to be ahead of the game in terms of managing health, not back-pedaling. Consider, however, that some people only accept change when it becomes imperative. Just as when new technologies are introduced into society, some catch on right away and others struggle, because they remain behind the times. Similarly, when any society has suffered enough, when the repercussions of an unhealthy lifestyle has taken its toll on enough lives, eventually a common process for the development of healthy habits will begin to unfold. Although there's still more that needs to be refined within this evolving and significant matter, the PHS is a cutting-edge model that attempts to provide this essential structure.

What's the purpose of the Proactive Health Solution?

There are two main objectives behind the PHS. The first is to empower individuals to become proactive with all aspects of their health and well-being. Within this process, each individual must climb the five building blocks of the PHS Pyramid. While each block serves a specific function, the primary goal is to reach the top of the pyramid—the height of discipline. The second objective is purely educational; it's to help guide societies and children alike with a model; a collective, fundamental process that leads to a healthy lifestyle.

How can the PHS objectives be achieved?

The PHS provides a basic yet highly integrated methodology. Five main components or building blocks govern this growth process: *Lifestyle Management, Healthy Self-Management, Motivation, Program Design,* and *Discipline.* These components are supported by accompanying principles that essentially represent the "how-to" steps. By applying the PHS principles throughout your lifestyle choices and behaviors, you can activate the components. (The principles will be discussed in separate chapters.) This methodology is designed to work in conjunction with any viable health and fitness program.

CHAPTER 1

A Vision of Hope for Health Care Reform

What is optimal health? There could be a wide range of descriptions, depending upon whom we ask. Biologically, the human body is incredibly fascinating, with its intricate blend of parts and systems. From a medical standpoint, an oncologist would describe it as a body that is cancer-free, whereas a cardiologist would focus primarily on the criteria for a healthy heart. Aside from the substantial physical considerations, however, there are numerous other viewpoints. A psychotherapist is mainly concerned with evaluating and raising a consciousness of mental and emotional wellness, while a preacher is called to help save and bolster mankind's spiritual condition in hopes of promoting greater world peace.

Indeed, optimal health appears to be a conglomeration of unique and numerous sorts. For all practical purposes, however, we can summarize optimal health as a healthy mind, body, and spirit. This fundamental concept shouldn't be grasped only by holistic gurus. If individuals from all walks of life could quickly identify this notion, surely that would mark the path into a revolutionary era. For many people, an adjustment of perception is necessary. Optimal health does in fact, encompass more than the physical body, and to this extent, we're all a work in progress. A new paradigm is underway. It's time for a change, and many strides are yet to be made within the health arena, both individually and collectively.

Faith and Truth

The crusade toward optimal health requires some faith, so the first juncture of this journey begins by gaining a vision of hope. Don't believe that you

1

have to see it to believe it. You have to believe it to see it! Lose the demons of despair and discouragement. Instead, start envisioning and believing that it's possible to transform your body and to receive restoration and healing in every aspect of your health. When you keep a vision that's filled with hope, you'll gain the faith necessary to believe in the best. "Faith is being sure of what we *hope* for and certain of what we do not see."[1]

Of course, your faith (or lack thereof) may be a private matter, from both a personal and religious perspective, yet it can have a profound impact on your life and well-being. What we each personally believe could very well be independent of our so-called faith in God per se. While nobody wants to miss the mark, our beliefs and thought processes may or may not be aligned with the truth. Just consider the offbeat, organized faith-based religions that have fallen prey to deception. There have been enough people victimized or brainwashed, all in the name of their fanatical faith. Historically, we can observe the devastating effects of such religious fanaticism. For instance, the Jonestown massacre, led by Jim Jones on November 18, 1978, destroyed 918 lives (276 of whom were children). Before the terrorist attacks on September 11, 2001, this deadly tragedy marked the single largest loss of U.S. civilian life in a non-natural disaster.

On the other hand, some people have no professed faith at all, yet they live by goodwill and bring no harm to others. Certainly, there will always be plenty of differences and extremes regarding matters of faith. Whether you're a religious scholar or a religious skeptic, this is irrelevant; you're still entitled to your own opinion. You're always free to choose what to think and believe. However, good faith that provides hope, healing, and restoration to your mind, body, and spirit can only come from God, the source of all sovereign power and truth. "For it is by grace you have been saved, through faith—and this is not from yourselves, it is the gift of God—not by works, so that no one can boast."[2]

So amid the spectrum of human free will and much traditionalism, can we find some common ground? Yes, it is possible, for aside from any particular ideology or lofty religious doctrine, the truth is universal; it is a supreme reality that carries tremendous power. The more enlightened you are by the truth, the more power you'll have to transform your life and health. Knowing the truth can help you release chains of bondage and improve well-being on many levels—mental, spiritual, or physical. For instance, have you ever noticed that when you finally forgive someone who has caused you deep-rooted bitterness, this actually makes *you* feel better? If you've never done so, you should try it. There is tremendous power in forgiveness. When you release toxic emotions that have been long bottled up, this is for your benefit—it improves *your* entire health and well-being. Whenever you discover the truth, whatever the truth may be, you'll find freedom in its power. "Then you will know the truth and the truth shall set you free."[3]

Many people struggle to improve their health because they haven't yet come to terms with the truth. Instead, the self-imposed limitations of fear have kept them stuck in a cycle of doubt and negativity. Going through the motions of a fitness routine doesn't exactly count. Why? It doesn't necessarily lead to a healthy lifestyle transformation. If we truly want to live a healthier lifestyle, inevitably changes will need to take place. Psychological barriers, personal hang-ups, and bad habits need to be broken, yet left to our own devices this may not occur. That's because each of us, in our own human capacity, has limited strength; our tactics and coping mechanisms fail. However, when we approach our desire for change by placing faith in something greater than ourselves, we open a new path for personal transformation. With God, miracles are possible.

Whatever name you use, a higher power is available to help you transform your life and health for the best. "'For I know the plans I have for you,' declares the Lord, 'plans to prosper you and not to harm you, plans to give you *hope* and a future. Then you will call upon me, and come and pray to me, and I will listen to you. You will seek me and find me when you seek me with all your heart. I will be found by you.'"[4] This isn't about being religious. It's about whether you personally choose to seek a higher source of power to help you transform for the better, all the way around—in mind, body, and spirit. When the time is right, you'll just know. The reality is that if you're ever going to experience optimal health, then you need to nourish not only your physical body in a proper way, but your mind and spirit as well. Make no mistake; they're all connected.

Your emotions tend to follow your thoughts. If you think negatively, how does that make you feel? Although depression can be triggered by a biochemical imbalance; sometimes it's your own discouraging thoughts that create chronic depression. Everybody feels down occasionally, but ultimately, how does one cope? What are the telltale signs of healthy versus unhealthy behaviors? Alcohol and drugs have long been common vices, and nowadays it's no secret that people use food much in the same way to try to escape from their emotional pain. When obesity becomes the result, a cycle of neurotic behavior will follow, which only makes matters worse. It should be clear that these types of coping mechanisms are bound to fail. So how in the world does anyone get out of this funk? Again, in order to break such unhealthy behavior, we must each be willing to face our own moment of truth.

The truth will clear your head and set you straight from the inside, out. It can free you from unhealthy addictions and steer you to make better decisions. When your thoughts are aligned with the truth, this helps you get a grip on your emotions. Besides, who really enjoys being around a drama queen (or king)? It's true that sometimes our emotions can get the best of us; we're only human. In order to be healthy, however, we need to direct our thoughts and energy toward what's constructive, not what's destructive. If your mind is always flooded with negative thoughts of discouragement, then it's time to prepare for a mental battle. This battlefield takes place in your own mind—nobody can think for you. You must discover your own truth to fight off thoughts of deception and discouragement. The Bible says this is a battle you must fight with faith: "Fight the good fight of the faith."[5] If you seek and meditate on God's word, this can cleanse your mind with the truth. "Sanctify them by the truth; your word is truth."[6] "Jesus answered, 'I am the way, the truth and the life.'"[7] "For this reason I was born, and for this I came into the world, to testify to the truth. Everyone on the side of truth listens to me."[8] When the truth pierces your heart, it's an experience that can change you forever on many levels.

In time, you'll discover that striving to reach optimal health is an integration process. The progress you make along this journey will strike a healthier balance between your mind, body, and spirit. Each of these dimensions is interconnected and if one is out of sync, this can indeed affect another. Consider, getting a deep-tissue massage. Relaxing your mind during the massage deepens the rejuvenating effect upon your body and calms your spirit. When you have peace of mind, this will have quite a different effect on your body than an anxious mind-set. If your mind is consumed by worry, you may stay up all night, tossing and turning. Or perhaps all that mental anxiety will trigger an overeating impulse, which certainly takes a toll on you physically. One dimension of health (the mind) has had an effect on another (the body). Initially, you may find it unrealistic to gain any sense of balance, but as you become more aware of these connections, it will get easier. For now, just understand that the closer you are to reaching and maintaining this ideal balanced state, the healthier you'll be.

This is viewing the broad scale of how your mind is integrated with your body and spirit, but it's certainly nothing new. Ancient wisdom pointed to this reality long ago, through the study and practice of yoga, which helps to balance the chakras. A "chakra" is a system of energy that runs throughout your body. There are at least seven main chakras, sometimes referred to as energy meridians, present in the human body, and every part of the body has an associated chakra. Each chakra has a connection with one of the endocrine glands, as well as with a certain group of nerves called a *plexus*. The chakras regulate the flow of energy throughout your consciousness and each vibrates at a different frequency. The state of flow of the energy is determined, therefore, by what you decide to think and feel and the way you choose to experience the world around you. When these energy systems flow smoothly, you experience wholeness, but when the energy is blocked, you experience tension. If the tension continues to mount, it could eventually manifest physically as a symptom. In yoga, when we hold certain poses, this helps to release tension in different parts of the body and brings balance back to the individual chakras.

Whenever we experience health setbacks of any sort, we should take a moment to observe our mind-set. If we want to experience optimal health then we must focus our thoughts on life and wellness, not on death and disease. Regardless of our circumstance, we can begin to affirm and believe it's possible to be healthy. God can heal our infirmities. "Finally, brothers, whatever is true, whatever is noble, whatever is right, whatever is pure, whatever is lovely, what is excellent or praiseworthy, think about such things."[9] It stands to reason that if optimal health includes the mental, physical, and spiritual aspects of our well-being, then we need more than just a "nutrition and exercise" program.

Yet in the midst of trying to adopt an integrated approach toward optimal health, we also need to learn how to proactively manage our lifestyle. Shockingly, Western society, as a whole, still hasn't fully grasped either concept. That is, most people are so far off base when it comes to proactively managing their lifestyle that they barely can muster the time to entertain the idea of *basic* physical health, let alone optimal or holistic health. Collectively, we've failed miserably in both of these areas, and nationally, we're facing a health care crisis for a reason. If we stay on this beaten path and continue to neglect the root causes behind our health issues, then we're only going to dig ourselves deeper into a bottomless pit. Trying to solve this massive problem in a fragmented way is not the answer. Managing our lifestyle and health calls for a great deal more. We need something that is innovative, comprehensive and upheld within a reliable structure.

What's Health Care Reform?

There has been much confusion in the United States about health care reform in recent years. As soon as we hear those words "health care reform," it's likely that a political debate will follow. However, we shouldn't confuse health care reform with politics, insurance policies, pre-existing medical conditions, or a public option. There will always be different debates and pros and cons regarding these types of matters. The reality is that health care reform has been necessary for a long time on a global scale, not solely in the United States. The health care crisis is absolutely massive; it's now a global problem. We must change our perception, however, about what we consider health care reform. It should not be viewed merely as the allocation of insurance dollars and the forcing of insurance coverage upon the millions of currently uninsured.

Stipulations, regulations, and public policy regarding insurance coverage should not be misconstrued as "health care reform," per se. While those are certainly important matters to consider, if we only refer to health care reform in this regard, it leaves us with a fragmented view. Division and frustration are sure to follow. Most people can sense something is not right but can't seem to put their finger on it. There's a reason. At the grassroots level, it's just not realistic to put that much power into any bureaucratic system. As individuals and citizens of any country, we're still personally responsible for our own health. If any society is ever going to make significant strides regarding health care matters, it must teach the development of healthy habits to empower all individuals—this lies at the heart of true health care reform.

That doesn't mean that government shouldn't intervene where needed. There's no doubt that people can benefit from an organized system, but we need clear-cut direction, education, and expertise. In the end, however, we must never lose sight of our personal responsibility. We, as individuals, hold many answers to our health issues, and this will always be our personal privilege, regardless of any jurisdiction. Within the Obama administration, the United States has taken a historic step to try to fix the health care system. In the process, however, it has overlooked many elements of health care reform by being *reactive* instead of *proactive*. Administered by itself, it lacks the proper groundwork for a successful health care overhaul, not because some people won't benefit from it, but because it's mostly concerned with *paying* for the consequences of poor lifestyle habits, rather than *preventing* them in the first place. There are repercussions, individually and collectively. We're still in dire need of so much more, in spite of how many visits we make to the doctor's office.

The real reason behind this health care dilemma is not that people don't have the proper coverage or can't afford health insurance, although that could certainly contribute partially to some problems. This issue has a significantly wider and deeper magnitude. If people were proactive in adopting a healthy lifestyle, we wouldn't be faced with the health care predicament of this era. A sensibly revised health care system requires a great deal of education about the development of healthy habits. We need a revolutionary solution—an educational tool, that will help guide and empower all individuals—and we need it now.

Today, we can begin to alter the health of our future. The Proactive Health Solution (PHS) is an intervention that can stop the worsening health cycle. It offers a comprehensive, practical way to help pull societies out of the downward spiral by empowering each of us individually and teaching the development of healthy habits to all. My practical experience of working as a personal trainer was the inspiration behind the design of the PHS. After consulting with many people of diverse backgrounds, ages, and professions, I recognized a common need. Although everyone came to me with different fitness objectives and a unique life story, each struggled with similar lifestyle issues. I discovered that aside from any fitness program, it was this dimension of developing healthy behaviors and discipline that people needed the most, yet the basic direction to do this was missing. I knew it was necessary to create something simple yet powerful enough to help guide, motivate, and empower all individuals to become proactive with their health.

The PHS utilizes a self-empowering methodology. It allows anyone to transform the broad dimensions of his or her life and health, with all its ambiguous complexities, by merging them within a reliable solution-oriented format. The program design of nutrition and exercise works in conjunction with powerful principles. This provides an ideal structure for personal growth as it guides people to proactively manage their lives and health. It's a set of health education tools that was never taught in school.

Gain a Vision of Hope

Did you know that it takes courage to have *hope*? Think about the 9/11 fireman who went into a burning building to save a life. The odds didn't look very good, yet he went in because he believed and *hoped* for the best. That took a lot of courage! It's cowardly to give up and think negatively. It takes a person of character with passion and courage to do what needs to be done. Sometimes, life will test your courage to see if you will step up with that last bit of *hope*.

Quench Your Mind and Spirit

- "If anyone is thirsty, let him come to me and drink. Whoever believes in me, as the Scripture has said, streams of living water will flow from within him."[10]

- "I have food to eat you know nothing about."[11]

- "I am the bread of life. He who comes to me will never go hungry and he who believes in me will never be thirsty."[12]

- "For you are God's temple, the home of the living God."[13]

- "Having such great promises as these, dear friends, let us turn away from everything wrong, whether of *body or spirit,* and purify ourselves, living in the wholesome fear of God, giving ourselves to him alone."[14]

- "With this news bring cheer to all discouraged ones. Encourage those who are afraid. Tell them, "Be strong, fear not, for your God is coming to destroy your enemies. He is coming to save you. And when he comes, he will open the eyes of the blind, and unstop the ears of the deaf. The lame man will leap up like a deer and those who could not speak will shout and sing!"[15]

- "So take a new grip with your tired hands, stand firm on your shaky legs, and mark out a straight, smooth path for your feet so that those who follow you, though weak and lame, will not fall and hurt themselves, but become strong."[16]

CHAPTER 2

The Downward Spiral into
the Health Care Crisis

Before going any farther, we must consider what's happening today in society. Is the health care crisis really just an obesity crisis? Approximately 65 percent of American adults are either overweight or obese. In February 2006, *USA Today* reported, "More than 60 million adults are considered obese—up 77 percent since 1987."[1] Despite wide-reaching public and private efforts to curb the overweight and obesity epidemic in America, the trend continues to worsen. In the first week of July 2008, the US Centers for Disease Control (CDC) released statistics indicating 26.1 percent of Americans are obese—that's one out of every four people! This represented an increase of ½ percent over the previous year, 2007.[2] A report in 2010 by the Organization of Economic Cooperation and Development (OECD) claimed that 75 percent of all Americans will be overweight or obese by 2020.[3] "Obesity is a growing threat to public health in all the advanced countries throughout the world. We have to find the most effective and cost-efficient way to deal with the problem,"[4] OECD spokesman Matthias Rumpf said.

We can't maintain healthy behaviors if we don't even know how to develop them. According to a survey released by the American Psychological Association (APA), when it comes to dealing with stress, a number of Americans turn to unhealthy behaviors such as overeating and smoking for relief, and they don't exercise.[5] Despite the numbers of adults who are very concerned about stress, only 55 percent are making an effort to manage it—a trend that could have long-term consequences for the health of Americans, Newman said.[6] Adults who experience stress are less likely to

11

say they are in good health, and they report higher rates of hypertension, depression, and obesity. Rajita Sinha, director of the Research Program on Stress, Addiction, and Psychopathology at Yale University School of Medicine, said that when a person is stressed, the need to feel better 'takes precedence over impulse control.' She stated, "We tend to choose a response based on what we know, based on habit. We will be looking for things that calm us down, but they may not be the best thing for us. She recommends trying to start good habits early on and paying close attention to 'why we do one thing over the other' to be more aware of long-term consequences." [7]

The Costs of Unhealthy Behaviors

As long as we neglect teaching *how* to develop healthy habits, we'll fail to make any significant economic progress. The overweight and obesity trend will give rise to many health issues, and we'll face even greater long-term challenges. Obesity increases the risk of heart disease, diabetes, several types of cancer, and other diseases. The costs associated with being notably overweight or obese are at an all-time high. "Americans who are thirty or more pounds over a healthy weight cost the country an estimated $147 billion in weight-related medical bills in 2008, double the amount a decade ago, according to a study by government scientists and the non-profit research group RTI International. Obesity is the single biggest reason for the increase in health care costs," said Eric Finkelstein, a health economist with RTI and lead researcher on the study.[8] Fortunately, "the data about what's driving costs higher are becoming more developed and succinct", said Richard Chaifetz, ComPysch CEO.[9]

The Centers for Disease Control (CDC) in Atlanta identified five chronic diseases that cause more than two-thirds of all deaths each year. According to this 2003 CDC report, "The Power of Prevention," the main five diseases include heart disease, cancer, stroke, chronic obstructive pulmonary disease (COPD, such as asthma and emphysema), and diabetes. Chronic diseases account for about 75 percent of annual health care costs and often can be traced back to tobacco use, poor eating habits, or lack of physical activity. "These three modifiable health-damaging behaviors are responsible for much of the inordinate suffering and early death of millions of Americans,"[10] the report noted.

Additional findings in the annual report of the journal *Health Affairs* stated, "The nation will spend $4 trillion on health care—or about $12,320 per person annually—by 2015."[11] Furthermore, the federal government has determined that within a decade one dollar out of every five dollars spent in the US economy will go for health care, with annual spending consistently growing faster than the overall economy. The cost to employers for insurance resulting from the obesity crisis is staggering. Not only does the employer medical insurance cost rise, but it costs tremendously in time off and lost productivity. A fall 2005 report in the *American Journal of Health Promotion* compared the sick days of normal-weight men and women to obese men and women. They discovered that normal-weight men and women took, on average, three and three and a half sick days, respectively. For obese men and women, those numbers are significantly higher. Men more than sixty pounds overweight missed an average of five days annually; women more than one hundred pounds overweight missed an average of eight days. According to the CDC, these extra days contributed to $56 billion a year in obesity-related productivity losses.[12]

Savvy companies are quick to recognize the benefits of providing a small gym for their employees. They operate with a win/win strategy by tying wellness objectives to the corporate mission. Microsoft, for example, supplies locker rooms and showers for its walking, running, and biking employees. It's among many organizations that have taken corporate wellness programs to the next level. Not only do these types of employers save big on medical insurance, but they also recognize that healthier employees become more productive and valuable to the organization.

"Wellness managers and directors say the long—and short-term benefits realized by company wellness plans range from a decline in medical claims and sick days to an overall boost in production." —Working up sweat pays off: Companies' bottom lines healthier so are employees. *The Detroit News,* 1997.

The Quick-Fix Snares: Mishaps of Diets

We can hardly address this escalating obesity trend and decline of health without first gaining some insight into the mishaps of diets. These days, nearly everyone wants to lose weight, and they'll try just about anything to do it. For a great majority, this is their first line of thought: "I'm going to try the new XYZ diet, and this will help me to lose weight *fast*." People have gotten so carried away by the quick-fix that they've lost their ability to focus on anything else that pertains to health. We must deal immediately with this subject, for such hastiness is front and center of society's health dilemma. Countless individuals haven't learned how to develop healthy behaviors *proactively,* because they've been too busy *reacting* to many quick-fix schemes. Most contemporary strategies for weight loss grab our attention with a unique appeal and a convincing cure-all concept. Couple these messages with extreme before-and-after pictures, and people get hooked. As a result, much of society has been sidetracked, consumed by information overload and trying frantically to keep up with the latest diet.

Every year, a new trend emerges, promising to solve the weight-loss dilemma. Historically, we've been inundated with all kinds of diets—the Grapefruit Diet, Seaweed Diet, Protein Diet, Fruit Diet, Liquid Diet, Vegetarian Diet. Today, the variations are almost as unique as the individuals that follow them—the Fast Food Diet, the Cheater's Diet, the Personality Type Diet, just to name a few. Most diets are contained within an assortment of trends, including no-fat, high-carb, low-protein, low-fat, no-protein, high-protein, no-carb, high-fat, and low-carb. These patterns continue and may repeat in different combinations and guises.

The modern concept of dieting to lose weight began in the early 19th century. Since then, we can draw some valid conclusions, but we must slow down our pace to make such observations. One conclusion, in particular, is that a diet that eliminates all fat—is *not* the answer to combating obesity. It is not *fat* that makes us *fat.* Yet many people have gotten so hung up or lost in the fad-diet craze that they've failed to grasp this basic information. When scientific studies revealed that a low-fat diet wasn't any better than a high-fat diet, with the exception of limiting saturated fat, some misinterpreted this to mean they could eat as much fat as desired; while those who remained in the anti-fat era, still believe that all fat is evil. If we stopped to get our facts straight, we'd see the grain of truth in the matter: we should include fat in our diet, but put a limit on *saturated fat*—stuff like lard, butter, and high-fat meat and cheese. To differentiate between saturated fat and any other kind, we only need to read the labels! (As a general rule, daily saturated fat intake shouldn't exceed 22 grams.) So while it's necessary to recognize this distinction in fat; this is still easy enough for a nutrition dummy. Again, this doesn't mean you can't have *some* saturated fat, so don't start dumping out everything in your refrigerator. Just look at it another way: add butter to your bread, not bread to your butter! Most of us wouldn't think of eating a stick of butter, yet some people think it's perfectly okay to scarf down an entire extra-large double-cheese pizza, completely loaded, followed by a gallon of ice cream.

It might appear that numerous individuals can't make heads or tails out of this barrage of information, but the reality is that most just don't bother to try and separate fact from fiction. Unfortunately, many who are desperate to lose weight will hear only what they want to hear, going from one diet to the next. If a weight-loss trend or diet, regardless of how skewed, receives enough hype, people from all walks of life will inevitably line up like little ducks, ready to follow. If we don't stop chasing the quick-fix, the health of our nation will continue on its downward spiral. It's this very type of personal and societal irresponsibility that will sink us deeper into a health care crisis.

The reality is that weight loss trends come and go, and a fad diet is essentially, nothing more than a marketing scheme designed to pique the interest of people who haven't yet learned how to eat in a normal and healthy way. Usually, we can find two possible points of contention associated with fad diets. The first is with the diet itself, which more than likely misrepresents the facts. This may not be intentional, but any purported diet solution that effectively promotes its ideology still can play on the vulnerabilities of others. Second, the way people perceive and interpret this information may be skewed, resulting from limited knowledge or blatant ignorance. All too often, we find both of these communication antics working against each other. The fad diets can make us many promises, but in the end, most deliver little or nothing.

As consumers, it's time to get smart. We must recognize whether these diet marketing strategies contain any truth or if they entirely misrepresent the facts. Just imagine following one of these fad diets for months, only to discover later that it poses a serious health risk. In the long run, the extremes of dieting never triumph. Most aren't worth the time or effort, but perhaps you've tried one yourself at some point. Ladies, if you've been trying to fit into that dress that just won't zip, or guys, if your beer belly is hanging over your belt, what are you going to do? Let's face it; when people get desperate they resort to desperate measures.

What appears successful with many dieting schemes may not necessarily be so. Just because someone lost weight on a fad diet that doesn't necessarily mean everything is fine. Our physical body is more than what we see on the outside; it's a remarkable and complex piece of biochemical machinery. The foods we eat hold a profound influence on what happens metabolically within our body. If we don't feed it properly, our metabolic system ends up out of whack and creates all sorts of disorders—high blood sugar, hormonal imbalances, high cholesterol, high blood pressure, elevated triglycerides, vitamin and mineral deficiencies, and insulin-related issues that can lead to diabetes. Successful weight loss must go beyond the mere act of shedding pounds in the short term. It means losing weight by following a sound nutrition plan and adopting healthy behaviors. In turn, this will yield many long-term advantages, such as improving overall health, helping us to keep the weight off (there's a concept), making the right food choices, eating small, frequent meals throughout the day to keep metabolism revved up, dealing constructively with emotions instead of resorting to food, managing stress, and staying physically active. Learning how to apply the principles behind the Proactive Health Solution will help you to get healthy the right way—by developing and maintaining these types of behaviors. If you only focus on weight loss, however, you won't necessarily reap any of these lifelong benefits.

Plenty of people lose weight only to gain it back on a yo-yo cycle. Others may even develop adverse side effects, such as a dangerous spike in LDL cholesterol or kidney problems. In fact, according to a prevention health book, *New Foods for Healing,* here's what Michael D. Myers, M.D. a physician in private practice in Los Alamitos, CA says, "Even though losing weight can help prevent gallstones, losing too much too fast can have the opposite effect, because it causes cholesterol levels in the gallbladder to rise. What's more, if you seriously cut back on the amount of food you eat, your gallbladder will naturally be less active, permitting stone-forming sludge to accumulate."[13]

Any number of physical and psychological issues can be triggered if weight loss doesn't occur properly. Unfortunately, the net effect of dieting can create more trouble than it's worth. While this might not always be the case, there's definitely an element of risk, and this should be enough cause for concern. Certainly, it appears wonderful when someone loses weight, but we need to look past the external appearance.

You may be wondering if there's a quick way to determine successful weight loss. Theoretically, since everybody processes food differently, there's no one-size-fits-all diet plan. There are several variables to consider, including a person's current weight, overall physical condition and specific health issues, hormonal status (particularly, insulin and glucagon levels), food intolerances, and activity level. To keep this simple, however, you still can use a good old-fashioned method. A key performance indicator (KPI) of sensible weight loss is eating in a healthy and normal way. Basically, what this means is that while nothing is off limits, the *focus* is primarily on food that are wholesome and unprocessed—fruits and vegetables, lean meats, seafood, whole grains, legumes, nuts and seeds, and organic or farm-fresh dairy (in particular, cage-free eggs or yogurt without additives/grass-fed non-GMO). In other words, feast mostly on foods that are a product of nature versus a product of industry. That's pretty easy!

"Normal" means you're still entitled to your food preferences and favorite snacks—you can eat whatever you want, as long as this is done *in moderation.* For example, if you're at a house party where the host served potato chips as well as raw vegetables and dip, you don't freak out and start preaching the virtues of a no-carb or no-fat diet. You might munch on a few chips, but you load up on the raw veggies, because you know this is definitely a healthy option. This keeps your eating style flexible, healthy, and normal. Again, normal is a good thing—no need for deprivation or extremes. It's okay; you're not going to blow up if you have a small slice of birthday cake.

Though your caloric intake may need to change when losing weight, you don't need to be obsessed with dieting. The Atkins or Cabbage Soup Diet is not required, and there's nothing normal about living on a "baby food" diet. In fact, much of the success behind Weight Watchers can be attributed to such prevailing wisdom. This outstanding organization teaches people how to focus on wholesome foods, but it allows individuals to have any option in their eating plan—within the parameters of their "point system." As a result, Weight Watchers has helped millions of people lose weight effectively, and they continue to be the global leader in weight-management services.

You also must understand that appearance isn't everything. If your skinny friend professes to eat only fast food and doesn't gain a single pound, this doesn't mean he's healthy by other standards. What is the status of his cholesterol level, blood pressure, and cardiovascular condition? Certainly some fast-food options are healthier than others, but if someone continues to go overboard on the consumption of saturated fat and high-cholesterol foods, eventually this will have consequences, usually in clogged arteries. When it comes to weight loss, there's a constructive way to do it, but there are plenty of erratic ways it can be done as well.

If you discover that a particular diet causes some bad or chronic side effects, then it's best to steer clear. Why put your health at risk? Individually, we each have specific nutrition requirements, in addition to potential hormonal imbalances. Many diets will cause more imbalances and wreak havoc on our metabolic system, such as spiking our blood sugar or raising insulin. Always aim to get the facts straight and remember to consider the source. Some diets are recommended for individuals with a specific health condition, so it could possibly work well for some, but not for others. For instance, a diet higher in protein usually will help those with diabetes and related problems by stabilizing blood sugar levels. Some people are allergic to gluten, and this might be a serious cause for concern. Others may have a major issue with dairy because they're lactose intolerant. If you're trying to lose weight, do your own due diligence. If someone you know has lost a significant amount of weight, be sure to ask him/her a lot of questions. The answers could reveal whether that weight loss plan is worth a try. Consider some of the questions on the following page.

- How quick did the weight come off? The safe guideline is one to two pounds per week. (Those morbidly obese can lose more initially.)
- Initially, did you consult with a nutrition expert?
- Were the meals balanced and designed to meet specific needs?
- How long has this healthy weight been maintained?
- Did you have prior health issues? If so, has there been any improvement?
- What if any, side effects have you experienced?
- What were your eating habits like before weight loss? What about during weight loss? What are your eating habits like now?
- Was exercise included in the program?
- In general, how health-conscious are you?

What is the typical outcome associated with a fad diet? Let's consider Jane Doe, who tried the latest high-protein diet and lost a significant amount of weight in just a couple months. After a few more weeks into the diet, however, Jane couldn't seem to stick with it—she was low on energy and began to reintroduce the foods that were off limits. A rough day at the office and a poor performance review sends her into an emotional tailspin. Stressed out and worried about losing her job, she turns to food for comfort. As life's daily pressures continue to mount, Jane starts devouring whatever she can get her hands on. When that yummy pie with whipped cream and chocolate sprinkles calls her name, there's no holding back—she inhales the whole thing! A couple months later and Jane is out of luck; she gained all her weight back. As a result, she gets depressed and becomes more compulsive in her overeating. Soon, she weighs more than before she started the diet in the first place. Frustrated with the scale, she sees no other alternative except to try another diet. Unfortunately, she repeats the cycle.

Obviously, Jane developed all kinds of psychological hang-ups that were tied to her eating habits and this compounded her health issues in more ways than one. That's the classic problem with fad diets; they don't work, because they're not normal or healthy. The extremes of dieting will put those who already have serious emotional-eating issues at a greater psychological disadvantage. Behind the glamorous popularity of fad diets, most don't do any long-term good. Unfortunately, without the expertise of a registered dietitian or nutritionist, some people will continue to tread in dangerous territory.

It's also important to understand the term "diet." If you change your eating patterns by making healthy choices and controlling portion sizes, you can still refer to this as a positive change in your diet. It's not the same thing as "going on a diet." To clarify this distinction, let's consider a diet that completely eliminates a particular macronutrient. It should be clear this choice isn't making a healthy change to your diet; but it's a "fad diet" and a setup for failure. How can you be sure? Well, everybody requires a certain percentage of three essential macronutrients—protein, carbs, and fat. Each of these macronutrients serves its purpose for good health, and if you eliminate one *entirely*, this spells trouble. This is a fundamental concept of nutrition, something that people should readily understand if they expect to gain control over their eating habits. Unfortunately, there are many who don't know what a macronutrient is; let alone why their body needs it. Then after attempting a diet that completely eliminates one, they discover the hard way that it just doesn't work—at least not in the long run. Eventually, when the missing macronutrient is reintroduced, the inevitable takes place. The vast majority gain all the weight back or, just like Jane, end up worse than before they tried the diet in the first place.

The primary reason why people get sucked into these vicious diet cycles is because the "quick-fix" prevails—everybody wants whatever works *now*! Jane didn't gain one hundred pounds in one night, but she wants to take it off "today." When this same type of impulsive behavior is multiplied on a larger scale, it creates a downward spiral of a far greater magnitude— namely, a health care crisis. It's time to put the skids on this frantic pace.

The Need for Restructure in Health Education

Our society needs a real wake-up call. First and foremost, we need to stop getting distracted and stuck in this cycle of quick-fix schemes. Being healthy is not just about losing weight. Certainly, the right nutrition strategy is important, but it doesn't stop there. Remember, when it comes to optimal health, we must consider all aspects of our well-being—the mind, body, and spirit. We need to revamp our entire thought process and understand that this requires more than just a meal planner and exercise schedule. As we strive toward this end, we need a method—some direction and structure to keep it all together. So where in the world do we begin? Just like a judge who calls for "order in the court," our first line of social order is that we need to gain some psychological order in our thoughts when it comes to our health.

In the past, we've relied mostly on physical education (PE) classes for many health answers, yet that has left much to be desired. What is needed to achieve optimal health must go beyond the realm of physical activity, sports, and athletic training. The mental, physical, and spiritual facets of health should also be addressed, but this hasn't been taught in the classroom, at least not in any standardized fashion. Though physical education certainly holds an important place, traditionally it has not drawn a direct correlation toward this bigger picture of optimal health. Unfortunately the concept of optimal health alone; still hasn't been fully grasped by the mainstream. Most people don't have any idea what this entails; instead, they simply focus on weight loss, weight loss, and weight loss. The prevailing narrow viewpoints of health along with its faltering educational structure, is a problem that stems from deep roots.

Historically, we will find that this greater developmental process has been overlooked. Nothing has been officially established within any health curriculum (PE class or otherwise) to provide this cross-functionality of developing healthy behaviors or linking these missing counterparts of optimal health. (Parents haven't necessarily picked up the slack where standard education has failed.) Even in many health and nutrition classes, it's been hit or miss. We must hone in on this missing piece of the puzzle; for it is huge. Currently, anything that is taught within the scope of this subject doesn't plausibly come together, it is only compartmentalized.

We should also keep in mind that any such commonality must go beyond lip service, because most people already know they should eat right and exercise. For long-lasting change to take place, healthy behaviors must become a way of life, but getting the motivation and discipline for this, is an entirely different matter. Certainly, behavior modification can occur in numerous ways, but without any educational direction to lead the way this poses a major problem.

The widespread lack of infrastructure creates tremendous uncertainty, a gridlock that has left many people overwhelmed and thoroughly confused.

Information overload, relentless distractions of marketing and social media can make even the thought of getting healthy seem quite daunting. Utter confusion lies at the root of the growing obesity epidemic. This is a global problem; the United States, Mexico, and England have been leading the pack, with the fastest obesity growth rates, according to the OECD.[14]

Physical education teachers, personal trainers, registered dietitians, health and fitness specialists along with wellness centers, holistic treatment facilities, weight loss clinics, and numerous other organizations have been diligently at work. Yet in recent years, we've only witnessed a steady rise in obesity. Why? It's because all these good efforts are sporadic. That is, the polarity between these various objectives does not directly lead to any clear commonality.

Although we are making a small dent, these initiatives aren't linked within any system that compels them to collaborate. Unfortunately, without the cohesiveness of a collaborated structure, it becomes much less practical to apply on many levels. So while such efforts can be helpful to a certain extent, in many cases, they just won't stick. These endeavors would work more efficiently and make a far greater impact if they were connected to a larger scale; something that rested under one umbrella. We need a comprehensive, uniform model to teach and promote healthy behavior; yet that educational structure must be functional enough to generate worldwide motivation and appeal. This critical portion—the "how-to"; must be consistent in the scope and practice of any health-conscious community service, initiative, or physical education program.

Any feasible system that supports this development of healthy behaviors must also promote all dimensions of well-being—in the mind, body, and spirit. Our youth need exposure to better-quality health education, but they should also be taught informally (at home, health or recreation centers, churches, etc.) to help reinforce what they learn. We need service providers within various health sectors, teachers, parents and numerous organizations to get on the same page. Without a cross-functional system to provide constructive interchange, we can't bring about significant reform in health-care. We don't have a complete agenda—only fragmented pieces.

Where do we start? By establishing a fundamental protocol within the health education arena, we can begin curbing the spiraling obesity problem through preventive measures. The Proactive Health Solution does just that; it's a model that guides people to be proactive, not reactive. It's designed to teach and empower all. Even children can begin learning how to develop healthy behaviors when they're instructed to discover the treasures inside the PHS Pyramid. The Proactive Health Solution is an ideology that can be taught on different levels, in schools and through various educational workshops. It provides a common set of behavior modification principles that can be referenced anywhere—in PE classrooms, in homes, and within any health or fitness program. Without such a link, much of our hard work and organized efforts will go to waste. What happens if we continue to focus only on the physical side of health, while neglecting the psychological?

Let's consider physical education with its initiative of promoting physical activity among children. The main objective is to teach Johnny the benefits of being physically active, so we pluck him from his environment and make him participate in a particular sport. However, if we disregard Johnny's psychological well-being, this can backfire. Why? For starters, we know nothing about Johnny's family life or background. Does he come from an emotionally stable family, a broken home, or a severely dysfunctional environment? Has he developed properly or has his psychological growth been thwarted by domestic violence and verbal abuse? Is he an autistic child and if so, to what degree? These types of considerations are important, particularly since childhood maltreatment, mental illness, and autism have become more prevalent in today's society. We must also take into account that some parents and coaches take sports far too seriously. Striving to win at all costs, they don't know how to properly convey healthy competition and this can seriously intimidate children.

Given enough adverse circumstances, this will only magnify Johnny's problems. In such a case, the expectations placed upon him may have inadvertently become senseless and cruel. Johnny is gripped with fear; he's virtually paralyzed on some level as those underlying conditions that affect his psyche have been neglected. Forcing him to play a sport in this situation wherein he doesn't readily perform up to par will only be adding insult to injury. His teammates are bent on winning and harass him for shoddy performance. This further damages his shaky sense of self-esteem. Self-esteem is not a trivial aspect of health; it's an important dimension of psychological well-being. When a child's self-esteem has been crushed, this opens the floodgates to many long-term psychological issues, dysfunctional behaviors, and unhealthy coping mechanisms, such as overeating. Soon, Johnny begins to develop a negative association with sports and physical activity and instead, he finds more comfort in food. Unknowingly, we've managed to sabotage our good intention of teaching Johnnie how to value physical activity.

Since we can't monitor a child's home environment or spare him from a painful upbringing, it becomes all the more crucial not to overlook this psychological side of health. From an education standpoint, we have an opportunity to make a positive dent in a child's psychological world. At the very least, health education should be redesigned to support both elements: the physical, as well as the psychological. They're interconnected and function synergistically as counterparts of optimal health. Children should be free to develop at their pace. Psychologically, they need to make this connection between athletic training and the benefits of overall health. They should learn to view the challenge of physical activity as a positive experience, one that enhances their entire well-being—not something that scares the living heck out of them. A revised health education curriculum can help them recognize this bigger picture of optimal health, which connects and nurtures all aspects of their well-being.

Let's face it; everybody needs physical activity, but not everyone is cut out for sports. Some children have natural athletic ability; others take longer to develop it. However, taking a child's psychological well-being into account will reduce the pressure and anxiety often associated with athletic performance. A fumble or loss in a sporting event won't shatter his or her world. Win or lose, children can be guided to see the big picture. They should learn that athletic skill takes practice and physical training promotes optimal health. This will help them to value and enjoy physical activity, blunders and all. Physical activity and athletic training, then, becomes a positive outlet for *all* children, not just for those who excel naturally in sports. When education begins to effectively support the psychological side of health, it'll spark a greater desire to improve the physical. Physical activity is inherent to our human nature. If children are educated and coached properly, they'll be naturally motivated to engage in it.

Connecting the psychological to the physical, however, will require a paradigm shift—a progressive change in the mind-set of educators and parents worldwide. In short, we need a revolution to promote optimal health. Health education must become more comprehensive and rise to a higher standard on several levels. It also needs to expand across culture and age.

So many individuals, both young and old, have psychological issues to overcome, but we've only looked at the surface symptoms and failed to address the real problems. This negligence has created a backlash—people who are overweight or obese, yet have no real desire to change. Food becomes an escape. It's merely a coping mechanism to shield them from their real issues. The cycle needs to be stopped. People are eating themselves to death.

It appears that a void originated in the health and physical education system, which dates back centuries. Centuries ago, "health" was mostly viewed in relation to the physical condition and functioning of the body. It wasn't until 1948 that the World Health Organization (WHO) embraced the mental and social aspects of health. At that time, health was defined as *"a state of complete physical, mental, and social well-being and not merely the absence of disease or infirmity."* In 1984, the WHO expanded the definition to include the spiritual dimension of health, as defined in accordance with social and cultural patterns. Finally, another modification was endorsed in 1998 by the WHO executive board to read as follows:

"Health is a dynamic state of complete physical, mental, spiritual, and social well-being and not merely the absence of disease or infirmity."[15]

Recent studies have confirmed that stress, worry, depression, and anger increase the risk of heart disease, heart attack, and stroke. Negative emotions can cause toxins to reside within the physical body and this can lead to all sorts of health problems.

"There are two primary reasons why negative emotions can have such an impact on the heart," says clinical psychologist Barry J. Jacobs, PsyD, a spokesman for the American Heart Association (AHA). "People who are stressed out and depressed are less likely to practice good self-care," says Dr. Jacobs, a faculty member at the Crozer-Keystone Family Medicine Residency Program in Springfield, Pa. "They may eat poorly, indulge in alcohol too much, fail to stick to a prescribed medical regimen, or sleep poorly." According to Dr. Jacobs, there is growing evidence regarding the biological effects of psychological stress. "For example, there's mounting research that when people get stressed

out, their hormonal system produces more cortisol," a hormone released by the adrenal gland, says Dr. Jacobs. "This has been associated with heart disease and diabetes," he says. Continuous stress also affects the circulatory system. "The arteries tend to narrow when people are in situations of very high stress," Dr. Jacobs says. "That causes increased blood pressure "Second, depression can also have a negative effect on the heart. Depression has been linked with increased inflammation, as measured by markers in the blood," Dr. Stewart says. "These markers have been shown to predict future heart attacks. Depression also has an effect on the immune system, which then affects cardiopulmonary health."[16]

Certainly, there are repercussions when we neglect this big picture of optimal health. Everybody needs to grow psychologically to make the integral connections that are unique and in sync with his or her own life experience. The least we can do as parents and educators is to teach children to recognize the consequences of their choices and behaviors. However, there could be a fine line between coaching people out of their comfort zone and allowing them to grow in self-awareness. After a certain stage, we should only point individuals in the right direction, we should not pressure them to behave in a certain way; otherwise this may squash their growth process. We each know what does or doesn't resonate well with us. To empower individuals, we must respect their freedom of choice and allow them to mature at their own pace, but education can guide their choices with plenty of resources. As educators, we must be patient and remember that learning can also occur on a subconscious level. Any good-quality teacher has the ability to make a positive and lasting impact on someone's life even if they don't realize it right away.

Teaching individuals to apply the PHS principles will help them develop the skills necessary to better manage their life and self. This type of education marks the way into personal growth and lends the guidance to navigate, that is, to recognize the right choice when it presents itself. Within the PHS methodology, health education and physical education share a protocol. Without the security of this common thread, many of our organized social programs and personal attempts to get healthy will simply fall apart. It's through a revision of strategy that the PHS is able to bridge these gaps. It's time to sow the seeds into a healthier future.

CHAPTER 3

Debunking the Myths and Identifying Psychological Issues

What it Really Means to Eat Right

Although it sounds quite simple, eating right is a message that can stir fearful connotations in the hearts and minds of many. Some people have this notion that they must live on alpha sprouts, tofu, and celery sticks, with reduced-fat vinaigrette dressing on the side, while others believe they'll be deprived of their favorite foods and feel horrible. Nothing could be farther from the truth. Eating right doesn't deprive you and make you feel horrible; it makes you feel great! But if that's the case, then why don't more people do it? This is largely due to an error in public opinion, so we must clear up this common misconception. Eating right doesn't mean you can't indulge in some of your favorite foods; it just means you need to do it in the right way. There's a fundamental difference between *indulging* and *overindulging*. For instance, *indulging* in a serving or two of ice cream on occasion is quite different from *overindulging* by eating a whole carton every single night. Think of it this way: you can still consume comfort foods, but don't allow those comfort foods to "consume you." It's absolutely natural to be comforted by certain foods, but not to the point that it consumes your life by compromising your health. This same logic applies to exercise. Relaxing on the couch isn't a bad thing, but not to the extreme of becoming a "couch potato." Learn to put things in perspective.

A Principle of Health: Exercise

There are numerous reasons why people don't exercise. Most people recognize that exercise requires them to break out of their comfort zone in some way, but they have no motivation to do so or any idea of how to go about it. Countless people are so overwhelmed with their current responsibilities that finding the time to exercise seems impossible. Others believe they just won't like exercise, so they never bother to try. Many make this presumption that they're not the "exercise type," because they were horrible in sports and don't have an athletic bone in their body. Some individuals have simply become so accustomed to their sedentary lifestyle that the thought of exercise never crosses their mind, or perhaps stepping into a gym scares the living daylights out of them. Then there are those who love going to the gym, but they don't actually exercise—they only go to socialize. Some people profess that they're too depressed to exercise. While we all face different struggles and can have compassion for others, we can't do anything to change this principle of health. Exercise is not optional when it comes to being healthy; it's a primary requirement. Our physical body needs exercise much in the same way it needs food, water, sleep, and proper rest.

The problem is that people don't understand the importance of exercise until they're lying in a cardiac care unit.—Dr. Gerald Fletcher, American Heart Association *(Mayo Clinic, Jacksonville, Florida)*

Research Touts the Benefits of Exercise

Exercise causes the brain to release feel-good endorphins, which are opium-like substances that ease pain and produce a sense of comfort and euphoria. It also encourages the nerve cells in the brain to secrete other neurotransmitters, such as serotonin, dopamine, and norepinephrine, which improve general feeling. Deficiencies of these hormones and enzymes have been linked to symptoms of depression, anxiety, impulsivity, aggression and increased appetite.

So if you think you're too depressed to exercise, understand that *not exercising* may actually be what's keeping you depressed. When people don't exercise, they simply defy a principle of health. Remember, what you value internally will be represented externally. Some people only recognize the value of exercise when their life is at stake, and the doctor orders them to do it. This is unfortunate, because if we continue to view exercise as optional, it becomes unrealistic to make it a good habit. People need to learn the basic principles that govern a healthy lifestyle. These principles don't change based on our feelings or life circumstances. We will always have a choice in the matter, but we still can't change the facts. While this may be tough for some to accept, it should be perfectly clear.

. . . .

To be healthy, exercise is not an option;
it's a requirement. We must learn
to honor this principle of health.

. . . .

Commitment to Exercise—
Develop the Psychological Congruence

You might nod your head and say, "I get it—exercise is important," but this doesn't mean you're personally committed to it. In order to make progress, you must develop some psychological congruence between what you say and what you do. For instance, it's Sunday morning, and you're kicked back, reading the newspaper. Your spouse suggests joining a gym down the street. You look up from the paper and say, "Sure, honey, that sounds great!" Yet that's as far as that conversation goes. In this case, the value of exercise has already been diminished before you ever get a chance to experience the benefits. Likewise, you may go through the motions without any real conviction about it. Let's say your friend, bubbly Betty, twisted your arm to go to the gym for Zumba classes. Then Betty moves out of town and leaves you to go solo. If there was no congruence between your mind and actions, you'll drop out too, because you really weren't committed to it in the first place. This happens all the time; people start fitness programs and drop out for the slightest of reasons. On a personal level, you must value exercise for yourself.

By developing the psychological congruence between knowing what you should do and your willingness to do it, you'll find that committing to an exercise program will happen naturally. As with any law or principle we break, there are consequences. If we don't exercise, we suffer the repercussions—it can diminish the quality of our life, affect the lives of those close to us, and put a huge economic drain on society. On the other hand, if we understand this principle of health and commit to it through action, it's like turning a light switch on and walking in the light.

Exercise is Good Stuff

Allow me to demystify exercise for a moment. It's a lot less ugly than you might think, in spite of how much you may sweat or stink. There's no doubt that physical activity can be challenging, both physically and mentally. Throughout my work experience as a personal trainer, I've found that many people have some initial aversion, resistance to, or fear of exercise. With the proper guidance and encouragement, however, they discover that it can be loads of fun. In time, they begin to welcome the challenge. What they thought would make them feel horrible actually has the opposite effect. In the process, they may grunt and groan, but simultaneously, they release pent-up stress. They get rid of that worn-out, sluggish feeling and replace it with increased energy, strength, and renewed confidence. When toxins are sweated out and the endorphins kick in, people feel wonderful! After experiencing the rejuvenating effects of a great workout, people get hooked—and rightly so. They love the results!

Facing Up: The Psychology of Our Health Issues

On the fitness front, health clubs have sprouted all across the nation. Most offer state-of-the art machines, a cardio section, free weights, and a wide variety of equipment for multidimensional methods of training. Some have a broad range of classes—from the rigors of boot camp to the rejuvenating effects of yoga. Whether we want to join a cycling team, a running club, or train for a triathlon, we have relatively easy access to these opportunities. This might be through a large health and fitness facility, a local sports club, or a perk offered by an employer. We might belong to a private studio or decide to set up a home gym in the comfort of our own basement. Through the Internet, we can obtain virtually any resource to suit our preference. So given the tremendous rise of resources made available, shouldn't we be a nation that's in great shape? Yet nationally and globally, we are hardly making a dent in the battle against obesity. Why is being healthy out of the norm? Who or what's to blame?

An article from *USA Today* states, "Evidence that advertising contributes to the rise in childhood obesity is weak. Sweden banned TV junk-food ads aimed at kids more than fifteen years ago, but its percentage of overweight children is as high as in comparable European countries."[1] Furthermore, it states, "Daily TV watching by American kids has actually dropped more than an hour since 1977, and kids view 12 percent fewer ads, a Federal Trade Commission economist found. Meanwhile obesity among children has tripled."[2]

Let face it; the media isn't the culprit. As a nation and across the globe, various efforts are being made to fight this obesity epidemic. The resources are there, but much of the effort is for naught. Health club memberships and corporate gyms go unused; home exercise equipment collects dust. Money and resources are wasted, and we remain a culture obsessed with weight loss and struggling with health issues. Why have some people neglected themselves to the point that their biggest inspiration is being the "Biggest Loser" in terms of weight loss? When will average people begin to pay homage to their health? As individuals, we must assume our own responsibility in the matter. In order for real transformation to occur, we must identify the underlying psychological issues behind our unhealthy behaviors. We can start by asking ourselves two basic questions: Why do I overeat, and why don't I exercise?

Wrapped within the PHS methodology is our underlying psychological condition—it's no longer shrouded in mystery. Identifying our real issues will prevent us from getting stuck in denial and stagnation. It helps us to recognize up front that we have options aside from self-pity, depression, or the big bag of potato chips and box of sugar cookies. If people had been guided by this psychological process in the first place, many wouldn't have turned to food or other vices to cope. Instead, they'd get to work on identifying and resolving their personal issues. The PHS facilitates this option of personal empowerment—there's no need to drown in hopelessness.

Every individual can begin to activate his or her personal solution. We might need to work on the same PHS component, but we each have our own personal issues to resolve. For example, within the healthy self-management component, emotional eating is a common problem for many. However, the backdrop for this issue varies. Some people eat when they're bored, others when they're anxious or stressed, and some only when they're depressed and lonely. Some individuals can't say no to the pressures of social eating and drinking. Others sabotage their own success due to unresolved fears from the past—their issues could be buried very deep, and that pain may be multifaceted. We don't know what's going on in someone else's subconscious. We each need to face our own truth; yes, even if the truth hurts. If we sugarcoat our issues, we ultimately sugarcoat our health.

CHAPTER 4

Unveiling the Dimensions of the PHS Pyramid

The PHS Components, Principles, and Symbolization

Pyramids are the most ancient and greatest monumental structures in the world. Many pyramids contain legends, geometrical and advanced knowledge of mathematics, profound information, and hidden mysteries. The Great Pyramid of Giza in Egypt is considered one of the Seven Wonders of the World. There was a time when only the holy of holies was allowed inside—the pharaoh and high priest. Today, the pyramid has not lost its power. It's used to share meaning, develop systems, and align people with processes and strategy. Pyramids have long been used to teach and are renowned in the educational arena for solidifying understanding. They're represented in many societal, governmental, and educational capacities, yet no such pyramid has been designed to offer a comprehensive health solution. Some attempts have been made, however, particularly within the nutrition arena.

The US Department of Agriculture (USDA) created the Food Guide Pyramid in 1992. This was followed by a revision in 2005, renamed My Pyramid, which included exercise along with food recommendations and used a vertical color scheme. There was yet another revision in 2008, created by the Department of Nutrition from Harvard School of Public Health, called the Healthy Eating Pyramid. When we evaluate these pyramids from a nutrition standpoint, traditionally they serve a purpose, but they leave much to be desired. The later versions include exercise and while this is progressive in one sense, the processes are missing. None caters to the demands of the times. With the advancements in global technology, we live in a busier day and require a system with clear, practical guidance. We also need something that appeals to human motivation. If healthy behavior modification is depicted correctly, we will find that it's a synergistic process made on several levels—a science like any other. We can certainly benefit from following a system that supports this integration of the mind, body, and spirit.

So today, motivation wanes, in part, because people are confused. There's too much ambiguity. For instance, if we view the Healthy Eating Pyramid, we must be careful to recognize that *exercise* and *weight control* (the ideals at the base) are mutually exclusive concepts. Not everyone has a problem with their weight; some people want to gain weight as part of their fitness objectives. When we focus on recommendations for healthy eating, we shouldn't overlook or misconstrue these distinctions. A healthy diet is not based upon exercise; it's *combined* with it to develop a healthy lifestyle and achieve any fitness goal—weight-related or not. There's definitely a consensus that good nutrition and exercise are important factors at the crux of healthy living, yet the difference with the PHS Pyramid is that it also offers a process to support how this may be done.

Without any lifestyle and self-management skills, all the knowledge about nutrition and exercise won't get us very far. These management skills hold the keys to a vast majority of our health issues—yet we've been stuck in a crossfire. If people across the globe agree that more needs to be done to improve health and wellness, then why does nothing get done? There's no health police. No regulation or accountability thrusts people into the path of least resistance. It sets off a chain reaction of all sorts—everything from escalating health issues to a failing economy. Is there a way to compel people to develop these necessary skills and provide accountability?

Intrinsically, nothing can infringe upon our free will. With free will comes freedom of choice. We're each entitled to stand by our own values and preferences, whatever those may be. If Anna chooses to be a vegetarian, that's her prerogative; if Joe decides to eat pizza, pop, and ice cream every day, that's his choice. People may choose to exercise regularly, sporadically, or never at all. Some people manage stress well; others don't. Some are workaholics; others are alcoholics. Lifestyle choices and behaviors vary.

However, if there was a common theme to developing healthy behaviors that everyone could readily understand, this would grant us the best of both worlds. In other words, some standard instruction can be blended with our own individuality to create a win/win situation. Whether we live in Japan, Africa, or Australia is irrelevant. Whether we are nine years old or ninety, it doesn't matter. From an education standpoint, once we all acquire a greater understanding, it'll set a higher precedence for everyone. This would provide us with a foundation to build skills that are necessary to follow through, while empowering each of us to be resourceful in our own way. It puts us in a better position to consciously decide for ourselves *if* and *how* to proceed. After all, if this is our own responsibility, why not capitalize on it? Ultimately, then, this is how to create accountability. We have no one to answer to but ourselves.

Unfortunately, many people haven't been encouraged to think for themselves, let alone take responsibility for their health. Some countries only focus on education that produces greater competition in high technology, while others discourage autonomy through a repressive regime. Globally, we've neglected this subject. The PHS paradigm bridges these fundamental gaps. By reviewing the components of the PHS Pyramid in schematic progression, we discover a hierarchy that's intrinsic to humankind. Fundamentally, it's based upon the laws of human nature and personal development.

Consider the typical learning curve. Behavioral psychologists often refer to this as an "experience curve" or "improvement curve." Extensive studies have been done on this subject, yet let's consider what comes naturally. Nobody learns to run before learning how to walk. We can hardly be expected to read in a foreign language if we're unfamiliar with its alphabet. Likewise, acquiring the skills to develop healthy behaviors and reach our fitness goals is no different. There are stages—a natural flow to this growth process, whether we realize it or not. For instance, I wouldn't expect my de-conditioned (out of shape) and obese clients who never trained in their life to compete with elite athletes in a triathlon. Initially, that would go against the grain of human nature. Physically and mentally, we need preparation to make this type of progress.

So before expecting to manage our health, we should be proactive and take responsibility for managing our life. These two principles make up the primary component—lifestyle management—on the PHS Pyramid. If our life isn't managed well, it will lack a natural flow, which makes it more challenging to manage our health. We long to be healthy and transform our physical body, but there are conflicts in priorities and time management, and battles between our heart and head. The hierarchical structure of the PHS Pyramid provides the groundwork for some much-needed guidance. It leads us on a path toward discipline—something we all need in order to maintain healthy behaviors—and remember, even children can learn on some level. If you're ready to make a healthy transformation, then start by reviewing the five components on the main PHS Pyramid.

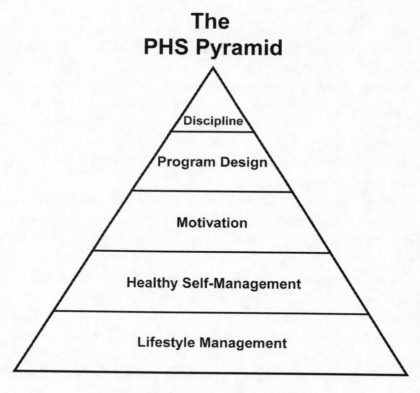

Figure 1: The Main PHS Pyramid

The Five Components of the Proactive Health Solution:
Lifestyle Management—bids you to do it
Healthy Self-Management—frees you to do it
Motivation—inspires you to do it
Program Design—teaches you what to do and how to do it
Discipline—makes you do it

The PHS utilizes these five components to summarize the fundamental growth process. The "do it" stem signifies taking care of your health. These five horizontal distinctions reflect the windows of the PHS Pyramid, yet embedded within are the jewels. That is, each component contains a jewel or subset of jewels. These jewels are the key principles that allow us to develop synergy between our various parts. When we adopt these principles—just like a diamond with a beautiful cut, clarity, and color—so too can we shine with this brilliance. There's much more to us than our physical body. We're powerful entities that exist on different levels—mental, emotional, spiritual, and physical. We also have eternal qualities that extend far beyond the here and now.

If we're greater than the sum of our physical parts, why have we neglected everything that makes us so unique and wonderful? At this deeper level, we're magnificent and infinitely superior to any health issue or setback we ever may encounter. Until we uncover these precious powers within, our struggles with health won't stop. Our consciousness holds much of our power, and we can learn how to tap into this incredible resource in an innovative way. We can uncover timeless and profound truths through our own unique tree of life. We can begin to see parts of ourselves that have been long hidden and marvel at the parallels that each of these areas represents. We can correlate these areas to essential truths that bring us together in mind, body, and spirit. We've been lost at sea; floating on the surface of health remedies, focusing more on the outside than what is deep within our own power.

Next, review the principles to observe how they correlate to the five components.

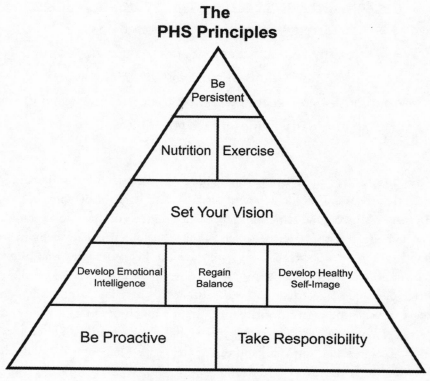

Figure 2: The PHS Principles

Each of these principles corresponds respectively to one of the five components on the main PHS Pyramid. For instance, when you apply the two principles to "*Be Proactive*" and "*Take Responsibility*," you'll be working on the lifestyle management component. Remember, the five components are positioned in a building-block format, reflecting how behavior modification takes place *naturally* in progressive stages. In this regard, the main goal is to reach the top of the pyramid to become disciplined. If you apply the principles from the bottom up, this will help you to climb each block or component on the pyramid. The principles by themselves, however, are universal. Any time you live in harmony with them, they'll lead you to a higher place. These principles can be adopted in this progressive format, simultaneously, or whatever order takes precedence in your life. On the pyramid, this might mean going backward in order to move forward—that's okay. The components and principles are all interconnected.

Basically, the five components compose the outer layers of a health solution. When the inside of these components are unraveled, this methodology becomes even more profound. It's truly an empirical equation that reflects how these higher truths or principles correlate with our health. Each principle or jewel, though basic in nature, has a deeper symbolic significance. This significance only further compounds the alignment of our integration—in mind, spirit, emotions, and body. Perhaps this is where the pyramid reveals part of its mystery. We have great depth, as do the pyramids, yet we too can unravel much of our identity within this systematic formula. We can discover correlations within ourselves as we study the power behind the PHS principles.

On the first tier of the pyramid, *Lifestyle Management*, the principles reflect our free will to make choices, while holding us accountable for our life. The second tier is quite profound in that it illustrates a divine composite of optimal health—the mind, spirit, and emotions, all within the *Healthy Self-Management* component. To elaborate, the principle of "developing a healthy self-image" mirrors the mind (our mental state of well-being). The "regain balance" principle symbolizes our spiritual well-being (the extent we maintain our peace and inner equilibrium), and the "develop emotional intelligence" principle reflects the state of our emotional well-being (how we manage our emotions). Certainly, these are dimensions of our health that should not be overlooked. The third tier, *Motivation*, reveals our God-given ability to catch a glimpse of our highest self. By seeing ourselves the way God intended, we become inspired; "setting our vision" therefore, symbolizes our mission. The desire to pursue our goals and fulfill this mission leads us to the fourth tier, *Program Design.* Here, our physiological response to a nutrition and exercise program represents our physical body. The fifth tier, the apex of the pyramid, *Discipline*, reflects an alignment between the value we place on our health and a myriad of our thoughts and actions. Being persistent symbolizes our commitment. Even as the top of a pyramid is aligned with the sun, so too can we align ourselves with optimal health.

PHS Principles   Symbolizes

PHS Principles	Symbolizes
Be Proactive:	*free will—God's gift to you*
Take Responsibility:	*accountability—your gift to God*
Develop Healthy Self-Image:	*mind*
Regain Balance:	*spirit*
Develop Emotional Intelligence:	*emotions*
Set Your Vision:	*mission*
Nutrition and Exercise:	*physical body*
Be Persistent:	*commitment*

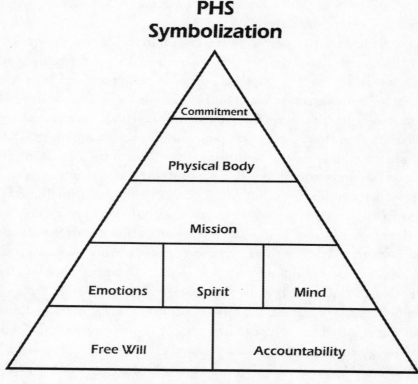

PHS Symbolization

Figure 3: PHS Symbolization

So you can see that following a nutrition and exercise program is only part of the PHS. To be proactive with your health, you must to be willing to dig deep into your subconscious. Many answers lie within. Whenever you resolve personal issues, you release blocked energy and improve your entire well-being. You gain personal power from living a principle-centered life. As you begin to align your life and behaviors with the PHS principles, this will promote your well-being while it simultaneously allows you to work on the five components.

The PHS helps to keep you focused in the right direction. As a pyramid, you can view it from the bottom as a journey going upward, with discipline being your top destination. Or perhaps you'd like to envision a star, which symbolizes guidance and hope. The five points are the components and twinkling within are the principles. The principles reflect the cuts that are made within you to create a greater brilliance—to bring out the best in you and make you shine with optimal health.

Health experts, life coaches, and behavior psychologists will be quick to point out the many implications associated with each component, from lifestyle management to discipline—and rightly so, as there are numerous considerations. The PHS, however, is simplified; it relies upon principles to convey what matters the most in terms of empowering individuals. This helps to reinforce the obvious and makes it practical to apply in daily life. We can turn to these principles for guidance every day, no matter where life takes us. Consider Kyle, in our initial consultation, he told me that he used to exercise avidly for at least one year. Then he moved to Europe for a few months, indulged in delicious French pastries, and didn't exercise at all. He said that going to Europe interfered with his exercise program because the gyms were too expensive for his budget. Coming back to the United States, he never bothered to start exercising again, and two years later, he came to see me, completely de-conditioned and eighty-five pounds overweight.

When I shared the two principles of the lifestyle management component—to be proactive and take responsibility—Kyle realized that exercise and portion control needed to be part of his lifestyle, regardless of where he was. Though this may be common knowledge, it wasn't until Kyle made a conscious decision to apply the principles that he was able to manage his lifestyle in this way. After taking these principles to heart, Kyle gained control over his sweet tooth and today, he looks like a new person! So far, he has lost over sixty pounds and continues to exercise even when he travels by taking very long walks and climbing high staircases.

Living a principle-based life calls for your concerted effort. It requires an open heart and mind; a willingness to face up to the good, the bad, and the ugly. Transformation won't happen overnight, but as long as you're willing to learn, change, and grow on different levels, you can rid yourself of harmful behaviors and become healthier in the mind, body, and spirit. As you start applying the PHS principles in your daily life, you will begin to notice improvements in your lifestyle and health. This shift occurs naturally, as you create the healthy behaviors that allow you to live in harmony with the principles. Perhaps you will manage your time better, or your outlook becomes more positive, or you gain a deep inner peace, or you stop at one cookie instead of eating the entire carton. Every positive change that unfolds has a ripple effect and can make a profound impact upon your health and well-being. Before you know it, the PHS will go to work for you. Better lifestyle management leads to healthy self-management, which makes healthier outcomes sure to follow. The flow chart below presents a common path toward this destination.

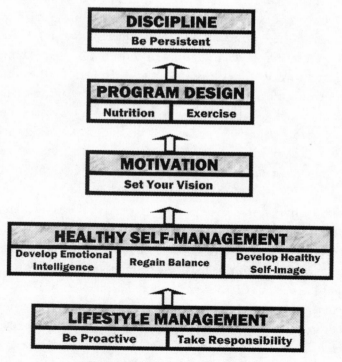

Figure 4: The PHS Flow Chart

42

As you follow the basic course, you'll discover which areas on the PHS flow chart need the most work. It's not uncommon for several obstacles to block one or more of the components, preventing you from moving forward. Like a road congested with traffic, you can't make any headway until the path is clear. For instance, if you lack motivation and have no desire to better yourself or set any goals, ask yourself why? What's blocking this PHS component? Your motivation may be trapped underneath a layer—or perhaps many layers—of unresolved past issues.

For example, Michelle, one of my clinically obese clients, who weighed nearly five hundred pounds, had been sexually abused while growing up. This unresolved issue from her past posed a great fear of being attractive to the opposite sex. Instead of being motivated to take care of her health, she sabotaged it. Her motivation was blocked by a huge boulder of fear, which created an eating disorder. She needed healing deep in her soul and spirit. This meant spending more time in the second tier of the pyramid—healthy self-management—before she could move forward.

As Michelle sought God and began to apply the PHS principles, she chose to meet regularly with a clinical psychologist. In time, she was able to put the issue to rest. Conquering this fear put a stop to her eating disorder and gave her new motivation. When food was no longer a coping mechanism, her path was clear to set and pursue some realistic fitness goals. She began to exercise regularly, eat healthier, and control her portion size. It was a long process, but she finally lost weight and quit smoking.

The type of self-exposure that Michelle faced was intimidating and uncomfortable. It required her courage along with some time and effort. Yet what's the alternative? If we don't confront our hidden demons, they will rear their ugly head in other ways. The gamut runs wide for developing all sorts of dysfunctional, unhealthy coping mechanisms. Fortunately, the PHS will help you get to work on resolving deep-rooted personal issues, but you only need to take action when you're ready. Some steps need to be bold, others can be slow and steady; it's all part of the same process. Use whatever resources you need and trust the universe to support you along the way.

So, where do you start? If you're new to this health journey, it's best to start from the bottom of the pyramid and climb upward. This gives you the clarity to move forward. Children, in particular, can learn to develop healthy habits this way, from the ground up. However, if there's an area on the pyramid you feel drawn to, then start with whatever resonates the most to you. Afterward retrace your steps downward to ensure you didn't miss anything along the way. For example, if you've struggled with yo-yo diets or binge eating, you can go to the fourth tier of the pyramid, program design, and review the section on nutrition. However, if the reason you struggle isn't because you lack knowledge, but it's because you're a compulsive emotional eater, then you need to go down to the second tier of the pyramid and work on developing emotional intelligence and becoming a healthier self-manager.

Whether you move directly up the pyramid or start from the top and go down, every principle you apply can take you to a higher place. That's because principles or laws can't be defied. There are natural consequences, whether we choose to live in accordance with them or not. For instance, not too many people think about the law of gravity, yet they still abide by it. What would happen if you tried to defy it? Would you be crazy enough to walk off the roof of a high-rise building? Likewise, if you try to defy any principle of health, whether this is failing to take responsibility, neglecting to exercise and so on, there will be consequences. It's just that simple. To make a healthy lifestyle transformation, you need to be aligned with the right principles. Some highlights of the PHS components and principles are listed below.

Highlights: The PHS Components and Principles

Resting at the base of the PHS Pyramid is **Lifestyle Management**; it's the foundation that supports every part of your life—health, career, marriage, family and so on. This initial component teaches you to *be proactive* and *take responsibility* for managing all areas of your life, particularly as this relates to your health. To manage your life, you need to get your priorities straight and line up these values with actions. Life is often the best teacher for many lessons we need to learn. Trials and tribulations test your character; how you respond is uniquely up to you. Do you willingly take responsibility for your life and health, or are you filled with a bunch of excuses? Do you trust in a higher source of power?

A positive response to life reflects a proactive mind-set. Consider Ivan;

when we first met, he was going to school full time and working two part-time jobs, just to make ends meet. Still, he proactively chose to make his health a priority, regardless of his limited time and tight budget. His motto was "Don't feel sorry for me. I'm a man; I can take it like a man." Okay—enough said. In spite of life's challenges, Ivan stood by his core values with a "bring it on" mentality. We should all learn to accept the ebb and flow of life in the same way. Managing your lifestyle effectively, in part, means learning to recognize the things in life you *can* and *can't* control. Taking responsibility for your health is your choice. When it comes to life and how you deal with it, take a quick lesson from Ivan. Man or a woman; we can all learn to take it like a man!

The extension of Lifestyle Management is **Healthy Self-Management**. It's a bridge between your psychological and spiritual well-being. This second tier of the pyramid requires you to do homework on your inner-self. Here, three principles will guide you to: *develop a healthy self-image*, *develop emotional intelligence* and *regain balance.* Working on these three dimensions of your well-being will bring more synergy between your mind, emotions, and spirit. Think of yourself as a puzzle composed of many different pieces. Putting these pieces together requires your time and effort. As you take inventory of all the pieces, you'll discover that some pieces need mending. Other pieces may be lost. Your consciousness, however, holds and connects everything.

Anything that has deeply wounded your psyche and spirit can have an effect upon your physical body. Trauma and accumulated toxic emotions that still reside within your body need to be released in order to experience healing and restoration. How can this be done? If you're willing to seek God wherever you are powerless, the torn or missing pieces will come together. *God is God for a reason.* He alone can do miracles. God doesn't lose hope like a mere mortal. He can heal and restore you in ways you can't yourself. Nobody understands the depth of your pain like God. He is the ultimate healer because he knows exactly what needs to be healed, and he alone can do it. After all, he's God. He can do anything. If you seek him, he can make you whole by bringing soundness back to your mind, spirit, and emotions. We've each been created in God's image as an artistic form of expression. So ask yourself, what piece of work will you represent?

After working on your inner-self and becoming a healthier self-manager, you will gain intrinsic motivation. This is conducive to setting health and fitness goals, because then you'll be more likely to achieve them. Arriving at this third tier of the pyramid, **Motivation,** means it's time to *set your vision* on your mission. Here you will consider what you want to achieve and use creative visualization to help you focus on your personal goals and optimal health. At this stage, you will also need to self-assess your progress. If you find yourself slipping into old behaviors, you may be stuck somewhere in the first or second tier of the pyramid. For example, if you still resort to emotional eating every time you get upset, this is an issue that falls in the second tier of the pyramid. However, as you continue to apply the PHS principles, you won't relapse as often. You'll find better options to deal with your emotions and interpersonal struggles. Learn to treat all your setbacks as opportunities for self-discovery and keep pressing forward.

The fourth tier of the pyramid is **Program Design.** When you reach this component, it's time to get your fitness plan in place and start doing what you need to do. To help you transform your body and achieve your health and fitness goals, you must follow a proper *nutrition and exercise* program. In this phase, you will find valuable information to help you eat right, lose weight, burn fat, build muscle, develop aerobic endurance, improve core strength, increase flexibility, correct nutritional imbalances, and so much more. Not everyone has the same goals however, so consider working with a variety of health and fitness experts as needed.

The fifth tier of the pyramid is **Discipline**—this is your highest destination. When you're disciplined, taking care of your health becomes second nature; it's an extension of who you are. It's through the principle of *persistence* that you develop this skill of maintaining healthy behaviors.

Now, let's briefly consider several widespread obstacles that lurk behind the PHS components. Is every minute of your day scheduled? How do you find time to manage your life and health? Are you completely overwhelmed by the responsibility of being a parent or bogged down by a demanding career? Does the thought of taking care of your health never cross your mind? Are you so depressed that you can't get off the couch? Do you resort to food, alcohol, or drugs to self-medicate? Do you have any inner peace or balance in your life? Do you neglect your spiritual well-being because you don't believe in God? Do you have a negative mind-set and poor self-image? Do you yo-yo diet? Do you believe that you're just not the "exercise type"? Are you going to a gym but not getting any results? If any of these points resonate with you, you're not alone. These are common problems many people face. Globally, we've witnessed the effects of stress and obesity in record numbers.

According to the Philips Index, health and well-being scores of developed nations are among the lowest, whereas emerging economies achieve the highest. "A report from Amsterdam, the Netherlands, in November 2010 revealed that people in India, the United Arab Emirates (UAE), the Kingdom of Saudi Arabia (KSA), and Singapore feel significantly more positive about their state of health and well-being when asked than those in some of the most developed economies of the world, such as Japan, much of Europe, and the Americas. These results reflect the differing importance and satisfaction that people place on issues relating to health, jobs, and personal relationships, which the report identifies as the fundamental drivers to health and well-being. Philips is a people-focused company, and the Philips Index has been created to explore what it is that drives our sense of health and well-being, so that we can respond to the needs of an increasingly urban and aging population, Katy Hartley, director of the Philips Center for Health and Well-Being, commented. Philips will continue to build on these trends to expand leadership in our key businesses. The report, which examines global mega-trends in health and well-being, marks the culmination of a massive global consumer research initiative in which the Philips Center for Health and Well-Being surveyed over thirty-one thousand people across twenty-three countries."[1]

It's clear that the modern lifestyle has left a multitude of people disconnected and hankering for something more meaningful. We've missed the mark in addressing these deeper, personal matters, and this has led many to rely upon unhealthy coping mechanisms. One unresolved issue leads to another and this takes its toll on our health and well-being. It's time to take an integrated approach to health by teaching people to develop a better-quality lifestyle. A doctor who recognized this holistic course was Dr. Edward Bach (1886-1936). He was a physician well ahead of his time. In his short career, he moved from orthodox medicine into developing a natural form of medicine to treat emotional and spiritual health.

He believed, as many doctors do today, that the attitude of our mind plays a vital role in maintaining health and recovering from illness. When he died in 1936 he had developed a complete system of 38 flower essences; each prepared from the flowers of wild plants, tree or bushes. They work by treating the individual rather than the disease or its symptoms. He did most of his research at the Bach Centre at Mount Vernon in Oxfordshire, England and received thousands of testimonials from both patients and practitioners. Today, these safe and gentle essences are used worldwide by private individuals, medical and complementary health practitioners, psychotherapists, counselors, dentists, vets and healers across the world. They support the patients fight against illness by addressing the emotional factors like depression; anxiety and trauma that are thought to impede physical healing. These essences can also be used preventively, at times of anxiety and stress, and are particularly helpful for the many people who feel generally tired and unwell without a specific medical diagnosis.[2]

. . . .
Health depends on being in harmony
with our souls. —Dr. Edward Bach
. . . .

In the following chapters, you'll find a multifaceted approach to help you incorporate each PHS principle. You will personalize your plan for progress and decide how you want to proceed. This is a tremendous advantage since we all have different agendas, life experiences and we each come with a unique set of strengths and weaknesses. It's not uncommon to fluctuate between several sections of the pyramid. That's okay. Remember, the PHS is a mission of personal empowerment, so do what works for you. Whether it's one component, one principle, or one step at a time, you'll discover for yourself, how to bring the fragmented pieces of your life and health back together.

Don't worry if you don't see results immediately. Focus on the actions you've taken, not on the immediate outcomes. In essence, you will rebuild a house—the temple of your body. What's on the inside is just as important as what is on the outside. You may need to tear down some junky old material and clean up a lot of debris. Don't short-change yourself, or your best intentions might backfire. You don't want to build haphazardly, cut corners, and get stuck living in a shabby house. Work diligently but have patience. You wouldn't tear down a house and rebuild it in one day. The house of your body is no different. Consider it a temple, a storehouse for your mind and spirit. It's worth the extra effort to get the construction right the first time. Death is a cycle of life. Your physical body will pass, but in the interim, you can choose to be your best.

CHAPTER 5

Lifestyle Management—
PHS Principle: Be Proactive

A great mind once said there are
three kinds of people:
Those who make things happen,
Those who watch things happen, and
Those who wonder what happened.

The guiding principle within the PHS methodology is to *be proactive*. It's the star that shines throughout the transformation process by empowering you every step of the way through your choices and responses. Though positioned at the base of the PHS Pyramid as part of *lifestyle management*, this principle can illuminate at any point of your health journey. When you're proactive, you own your power in every sense of the word; you're free to think, initiate, and partake in whatever you want and to choose your own response. Being proactive with your health serves as preventive maintenance, and this begins with a lifestyle-management choice. You must choose health as part of your life paradigm. Within the PHS format, this means you start by making this important lifestyle decision before progressing to the next component on the pyramid. When you work on managing your life first, it becomes much easier to manage and coordinate the ideals of your health. This powerful principle can serve as a catalyst for behavior modification on several fronts of your life, and ultimately, it's what prompts you into healthy self-management.

Being proactive holds a powerful connotation, both individually and collectively. The term "proactive" was coined in 1933, yet it wasn't readily found in most dictionaries until the turn of the twentieth century. It became an expression popularized in the business press in 1989 after the release of Stephen R. Covey's book "The 7 Habits of Highly Effective People."[1] Since then, companies worldwide have taken advantage of the competitive opportunities that result from being proactive. Researchers have identified that proactive behavior is an increasingly important factor of managerial success in dynamic and uncertain economic environments. Corporate organizational structures have improved their efficiency and resiliency through various proactive business models. There's been considerable growth in proactive concepts, but we don't need to work for a cutting-edge company in order to be proactive in our personal life. Within the framework of the PHS, we succeed in this area of *lifestyle management* whenever we benefit from being proactive. First, let's gain a better understanding of what this proactive concept really means.

Webster's defines proactive as: "1) relating to, caused by, or being interference between previous learning and the recall or performance of later learning; 2) acting in anticipation of future problems, needs, or changes."[2]

The first part of this definition explains that being proactive is associated with a change in the way we think. There's been interference between what we've known and what we now know. At some point, our understanding was altered; we're not locked into our old mind-set. We have a different response to the same stimuli by choosing to think in another way; our thought paradigm has changed. Consequently, thinking proactively allows us to gain new and better insights into decision making. The second part means taking action based on the future by anticipating potential problems, needs, or changes. When we behave proactively, we act ahead by taking the responsibility that is tied to our choices. This will allow us to avoid more work down the road, avert disasters, and plan well for the future by instituting systems at work, at home, and in any aspect of our life.

PHS—Lifestyle Management 101

When most people think about being proactive, they usually interpret this to mean that someone is taking initiative or some kind of action in order to prevent a potential problem. While this is true, it's not the whole picture. We must consider other important features of proactive behavior.

We Have the Freedom to Choose our Own Response

Believe it or not, even in the midst of an excruciating situation, we still have a choice. We can respond resourcefully, or we can react impulsively. Stephen Covey points out that we can exercise the freedom of choice through our unique human endowments of self-awareness, independent will, conscience, or imagination. We can choose our own response based upon our priorities and value system. There's a world of difference between proactive and reactive behavior. Reactive people don't behave according to personal choices or established values; instead, they *react* to feelings, conditions, circumstances, and their environment. If they're treated well, they feel well, but when treated poorly, they react poorly. Stephen Covey provides an outstanding illustration of this distinction. People who are reactive will feel bad if the weather is bad, but "proactive people carry their own weather with them."[3] It makes no difference to them whether it rains or shines. They're value-driven and can still feel great if the weather outside is raining cats and dogs. Likewise, if they value their health, they will do so, regardless of any extenuating circumstance.

. . . .

"Proactive people are still influenced by external stimuli, whether physical, social, or psychological. But their response to the stimuli conscious or unconscious is a valued-based choice or response."[4] —Stephen Covey

. . . .

The epitome of proactive behavior was exhibited by Jesus Christ. Even if you're not a Christian, you can still learn something from the way Jesus exercised proactive thinking and behavior. Jesus had a purpose; he had set his sight on a decision to do the will of the Father. Did he look forward to being tortured, humiliated, and hung on a cross? Not at all! In fact, his soul was filled with sorrow as he prayed to the Father. "My Father, if it is possible, may this cup be taken from me. Yet not as I will, but as you will."[5] Jesus experienced all the emotions common to humanity—he wept and bled like everyone else. Yet he still submitted *his will* to do the will of the Father through the power of a proactive choice.

His desire to do the will of the Father was more valuable to him than anything else. However, at any point he could've allowed his hurt feelings and the enormous physical suffering to take control and thwart his purpose. When they mocked and spit on him, he could've reacted by yelling out obscenities. He could've complained to the Father that it wasn't fair and that he didn't deserve to suffer. Instead, he made a proactive choice to focus on the end result and not to *react* to the inequity and excruciating pain. In spite of the all mockery, injustice, and unfathomable physical suffering, he maintained his peace and kept his word to the Father.

"Let us fix our eyes on Jesus, the author and perfecter of our faith, who for the joy set before him endured the cross, scorning its shame, and sat down at the right hand of the throne of God. Consider him who endured such opposition from sinful men, so that you will not grow weary and lose heart. In your struggle against sin, you have not resisted to the point of shedding your blood."[6]

Jesus responded by receiving the cup set forth, because he knew there was a higher purpose for it. By making a *proactive choice*, he anticipated the future. He endured the short-term persecution for the eternal joy set before him. After Jesus was crucified, he prayed: *"Father, forgive them, for they do not know what they are doing."*[7] Talk about proactive thinking! His response alone should put everything in perspective! Jesus Christ set the highest standard and example of proactive behavior. In this same way, whenever we're personally faced with an absolutely awful situation, we also have a choice about how we'll respond. We can choose to look beyond our present circumstance and recognize that our hardship serves a higher purpose. We might not know what the purpose is, but there's a reason for it. God's word tells us to endure hardship as discipline. It's true we're only human, we all experience physical pain, suffering, and sorrow, but our basic identity doesn't need to be affected at all.

"Endure hardship as discipline; God is treating you as sons. For what son is not disciplined by his father?"[8] "No discipline seems pleasant at the time, but painful. Later on however, it produces a harvest of righteousness and peace for those who have been trained by it."[9]

We're each endowed with the ability to make powerful choices. We literally can reshape our life experience through our choices. Nobody can take this power away from us. We can still choose our own private response *even* in the midst of suffering. Eleanor Roosevelt said, "No one can hurt you without your consent." Gandhi said, "They cannot take away our self-respect if we do not give it to them."[10]

Be Proactive: If You Fail to Plan, You Plan to Fail.

PHS—Lifestyle Management:
Be Proactive and Take Responsibility
Plan Your Day and Follow Your Plan

Successful people do things they don't like to do. They focus on the result, not the task.

Within the PHS methodology *being proactive* is teamed up with *taking responsibility*. These two principles merge into the component of *lifestyle management*. In order to be successful in managing your life, it's critical to recognize how these principles work together. You can be responsible without being proactive, but you can't always benefit from being proactive unless you're responsible. This is why many people start a health program but don't succeed; they weren't responsible enough to stay with it. Sure, they may have exhibited proactive behavior by initiating the process, but they didn't have enough gas in their tank to keep going. They got in the car claiming they wanted to reach a destination, but they never bothered to check the gas gauge. Soon enough, their car conked out. Go figure. Being responsible is the fuel you need to keep your engine running. If you want to be proactive with your health, then you need to fuel up with responsibility on a consistent basis; it needs to be pumped into you regularly over the course of a lifetime. If you attempt to be proactive, but fail to take adequate *responsibility* then just like a puttering car, you'll also conk out. Of course, you may experience setbacks from time to time, but when you're committed to accepting this responsibility, you're not going to quit. You'll find a way to pass through the rough terrain and you'll be sure to fuel up before driving off.

When you *think* proactively, you exercise the power to establish choices and responses based upon your personal values. You *behave* proactively when you take the responsibility that is tied to those choices. Managing your lifestyle effectively requires you to be responsible, to make an effort or respond in a way that's aligned with your core values and choices. A natural order of human reality is that actions speak louder than words. This is why you need to evaluate your priorities and be honest about the choices you make and whether you truly choose to be healthy.

Consider Ashley, one of my clients, she had been smoking a pack of cigarettes every day for many years. The week before she was scheduled to train with me, we had a consultation. She told me that she really wanted to lose weight and get in better shape before her wedding. We discussed the changes she needed to make in her eating and lifestyle habits, which included quitting smoking. Before she left, I gave her a copy of the PHS flow chart. She went home and posted it on her refrigerator. Later in the week, she called to tell me that the PHS hadn't just helped her break bad habits, but it completely transformed her life! She explained that every time she wanted to light up, she paused for a moment and thought about being proactive and taking responsibility for her health. She reminded herself that being healthy is what she really wanted, not that darn cigarette. Instead of smoking, she made a conscious choice to do something else. Within one week, she was down to four cigarettes a day and cut out all the soda pop from her diet as well. The following week, she had quit smoking entirely. She changed her lifestyle behaviors and started feeling better every day, simply by the power of her choices.

Getting healthy isn't about going through the motions. It's about making healthy choices and behaviors a way of life. How will you manage your lifestyle? If you value your health, then it will be a part of your life paradigm and reflected in your day-to-day living. However, if health is not part of your life paradigm then that will become apparent as well. Keep in mind, though, that acting proactively while neglecting this notion of responsibility will result in poor lifestyle management. In order to manage your life well, both principles must function synergistically. Within the PHS format, this means applying each of these principles to your life in the right measures. Though these principles are similar, consider the fictional example below to see how they differ.

Proactivity — Responsibility = Poor Lifestyle Management

Donald Dingdong decided to start a small business, a donut shop in the hub of a city. Nobody told him to do it; this was his own brilliant idea. He was proactive in creating scrumptious donuts in a variety of mouthwatering flavors. He designed a business plan, handled the marketing, and set up a shop for his new enterprise. On opening day, however, when people lined up to enter, the front door was locked. The lights were on, but nobody was home. Patrons left, some disillusioned and some infuriated. There had been so much hype about this new donut shop—fliers in the mail, discount on a dozen, unique flavors—but now, no donuts were being served. Every week, people cruised by, anticipating those tasty treats, but still, nothing! Donald failed to take adequate *responsibility* for this new venture by not providing any service. He didn't follow through, delegate responsibility, or provide any sort of backup plan. Donald's Donuts should have been called "Daydream Donuts." Keep dreaming because those donuts . . . well, they just don't exist. They have the biggest zero-shaped donut holes anyone could expect to find! What in the world was the purpose of his plan?

Rumor has it that Mr. Dingdong actually skipped town with Miss Hostess Cupcake. As he drove away, he also drove his business into the ground. What a buffoon!

Although most people would never admit to being as foolish as Donald Dingdong, sometimes they certainly can be. Over the years, I've seen plenty of people sign up and pay big bucks to get in a training program, but never bother to call or show up for their scheduled sessions. Of course, emergencies arise from time to time, but that should be the exception, not the norm. Some personal trainers waste their time trying to chase down these types of clients, but they never get paid to babysit. How we manage our lifestyle is up to us. We can initiate many plans to get healthy by being proactive, but without taking the adequate responsibility to follow through, we won't succeed in managing our lives.

Responsibility Seals the Deal on Proactive Thinking

What happens when we only *think* proactively? We know that proactive thinking is wonderful—it opens our minds to new insights and choices. Part of this means we have the freedom to use our imagination, the creative ability in our mind to envision something beyond our present reality. This is certainly helpful when we're stuck in a tough circumstance; it gives us the hope to stay positive. Sometimes, however, thinking proactively could have limitations—unless it's also sealed with responsibility.

Consider Frankie Flighty. From the time he was a kid, he always fantasized about flying a plane. Well, that's just fine; nobody could stop Frankie from using his imagination. He was exercising his ability to think proactively. Today, he still imagines the exhilaration of takeoff, flying over the clouds, and passing through turbulence, followed by a safe landing. Frankie sincerely believes that one day, he'll become a pilot, but he has not taken any steps whatsoever to pursue this ambition. Each passing year rolls by, but still he makes no plans. Now, Frankie is eighty years old, yet he continues to believe and talk about his dream. Someone finally broke the news to him: "Sorry, Frankie, it's just not happening!" Unfortunately, his only "flight destination" was departing to nowhere.

"As the body without the spirit is dead, so faith without deeds is dead."[11]

It doesn't matter how many good intentions you have in life; you need a plan of action to back them up. When you're proactive, you create the plan; when you're responsible, you follow it. This is what managing your life is, all about. The problem is that unless you've established "health" as part of your life paradigm, it's just lip service. Start by asking yourself how valuable your health is. Is it important enough to be part of your life paradigm? This proactive principle means *you choose* what you want out of life. To pursue any goals in life, you need a proactive plan, followed by responsible action steps. Unfortunately, some people can be just like Frankie. They only talk about their dream of getting healthy. Their eyes light up as they try to keep up with the latest diet trend. Thinking that new diet will finally solve their weight loss problem, they ramble on and on about it—yada, yada, yada. There comes a point to just "zip it", but years later, they're still talking about it!

If you truly want to transform your health, you should learn how to manage your lifestyle *first*. To assist you in this process, you'll find a multifaceted approach to help you apply this <u>Be Proactive</u> principle to your own life. Remember, part of the PHS lifestyle management component includes *taking responsibility*. (That principle will be covered in more detail in the next chapter.)

Proactively Evaluate Your Priorities

Do you sincerely believe that your health should be a priority? Think about it—should this even be a question? As a responsible adult, you ought to recognize the value of making that choice for yourself, but it's your life, and there's no health police. When it comes to managing the many facets of your life, you alone need to evaluate your priorities. Hopefully, the decision to be healthy is one of them. Unfortunately, many people backpedal toward this realization—they only recognize this later, after suffering the dire ramifications of being unhealthy.

Given the option, however, most everyone will choose good health over poor health any day. We all seem to acknowledge this preference, yet many people still neglect doing anything about it. Whether this is done consciously or unconsciously, it often turns out to be a way of life. Numerous individuals believe that as we get older, it's just natural to gain weight, get flabby, lack energy, get shortness of breath, develop postural distortions, lose flexibility, and develop diseases. Our nation, along with many countries worldwide, has become disillusioned with misconceptions. Poor health gets blamed on the aging process. While it's true some changes will naturally occur as we get older, becoming unhealthy has little or nothing to do with the aging process. Plenty of younger people have a biological body age that is much higher than their chronological age. The opposite holds true as well.

Yes, there are some aspects of health we inherit genetically, but that doesn't give us a license to be neglectful. The reality is that people everywhere become unhealthy simply because they fail to be *proactive*. First, they remain *passive* and then, after enough neglect or abuse, they become *reactive*. Desperate to lose weight, they will attempt to find the answers through a fad diet; liposuction, or bariatric surgery. Others will end up on all types of medications. One health issue leads to another until all sorts of problems spiral out of control—morbid obesity, high blood pressure, high cholesterol, chronic fatigue, heart disease, diabetes, cancer.

When it comes to managing our health, if we're not *proactive*, what's the alternative? Is it neglect, overindulgence, senseless behavior, a sedentary lifestyle, or unhealthy coping mechanisms? If we're proactive, we can prevent numerous health issues that typically are written off as the "natural aging process." Certainly, we could be predisposed to certain diseases, or we may develop a peculiar, sudden symptom that baffles the medical and health community. Yet even still, a vast majority of our health problems can be averted. It is sheer nonsense to assume that obesity and the health complications that follow can't be prevented when it's predominately, the direct result of irresponsible behavior. Obese children are excluded from this implication since they're not the ones buying the groceries and planning the meals. Obesity may trigger a slew of health issues, but by itself, it's not a natural part of the life cycle. When we take responsibility for managing our own lifestyle and health, then we can maintain a healthy weight *naturally*.

This translates into a huge cost savings of medical expenses and prevents a whole slew of insurance reimbursement hassles. The benefits of health are all-encompassing; the advantages take place on many levels—personally, socially, and economically. When we feel better, we function better. This becomes obvious in every sense. It helps our families, pocketbooks, economy, and society as a whole. We need to turn inward and ask if we have forfeited this personal life choice and responsibility.

The truth is that you don't need to compromise your health or the quality of your life anymore. It's your God-given privilege and personal responsibility to take care of your health. Of course, your family, kids, and job are important, but without your health, you can't effectively support these priorities. For example, a client I'll call Tiffany has a couple of kids who really wanted to go swimming, but they couldn't go without written consent and the presence of a parent. As much as Tiffany truly wanted to swim with her kids, she wouldn't dare to be seen in a bathing suit *anywhere* until she lost weight. Tiffany finally realized that unless she took care of herself, she'd lack the self-esteem to set a good example for her children. Indeed, weight management and self-esteem are part of being healthy.

Being unhealthy and out of shape can put a damper on everything. But if you're healthy and fit, this makes everything in your life much easier. You become a better spouse, parent, and employee. Do any of us really need to be coerced into a decision that will enrich the quality of our life? The choice should be obvious.

"Do not forsake wisdom, and she will protect you; love her and she will watch over you. Wisdom is supreme, therefore get wisdom."[12]

Use Wisdom for Major Decisions by Seeking Your Higher Source of Power

Are you *proactive* in your thinking and decision making? Do you seek a higher source of power to help you make wise decisions for your life?

Granted, God may not have an audible voice, and unless you're Moses incarnate, chances are you never got close up to see him. Nonetheless, God still communicates. You've probably sensed his presence if you ever sought him regarding major decisions for your life. What's a major decision? Basically, it's any decision that has a major consequence. These are big chunks of your life that have a profound influence—health, marriage, family, career, relocation, a specific calling.

Health is an area that needs major attention, because it can have a major impact on the quality of your life—for better or worse. Nobody needs the extra hassle that comes from health issues, but when you're healthy, the benefits are exponential. So ask yourself what's preventing you from taking care of your health. Are parts of your life out of control? Do you have addictions to food or alcohol that you haven't faced or can't seem to overcome? If there's an area of your life that's posing a major problem, turn it over to your higher source of power. Whatever name you prefer to use for God, he can help you. God is an infinite source of wisdom, inspiration, guidance, justice, miracles, and love. Seek him for wisdom when making major decisions for your life. He can help you to break bad habits. God works in mysterious ways, but learn to listen for that still voice that brings clarification and peace. When you experience a deep inner peace, you'll intuitively sense that God has spoken.

· ·

The Serenity Prayer: God grant me the serenity to accept the things I cannot change, courage to change the things I can, and the wisdom to know the difference.

· ·

Health is a Major Decision

You can make a conscious choice to pursue your health—or to not pursue it. Even if you default on making this major decision, that's still a decision. Either way, the consequences can be major. Below is a brief list of outcomes associated with particular lifestyle choices and behaviors. While these are not always black and white, they are fairly common.

Common Outcomes of Healthy vs. Unhealthy Lifestyle Choices and Behaviors

Healthy Outcomes	Unhealthy Outcomes
Healthy weight and body fat	Overweight / obese / high body fat
Better mood, mindset and outlook	Depression, anxiety, negativity
High energy	Lethargic, lots of aches and pains
Stress management	Tension, misdirected stress
Healthy self-esteem / confident	Low self-esteem / poor body image
Reduced risk of developing disease	Increased risk to develop disease
Low medical expense / insurance	Higher medical expense / insurance
Improved flexibility	Limited range of motion
Good strength / muscle tone	Weak /muscle atrophy / flabby
Better relationships	Strain on relationships
Positive influence on family	Spouse and children overweight /unhealthy
Good cardiovascular condition	Poor cardiovascular condition
Good night sleep	Sleep deprivation
Strong immune system	Weak immune system
Younger biological age	Older biological age
Good posture	Postural distortions
Clothes fit well	Clothes too tight

"Blessed is the man who finds wisdom, the man who gains understanding, for she is more profitable than silver and yields better returns than gold. She is more precious than rubies, nothing you desire can compare with her."[13]

Healthy lifestyle choices and behaviors yield obvious benefits. Making the choice to live a healthy life is liberating. It can prevent or reduce the risks associated with disease. To a startling degree, much of what is attributed to aging and the deterioration of health can be controlled through diet and exercise. Exercising one hour a day has recently been touted to add two hours to your life. It's no wonder—exercise strengthens the bones, heart, and lungs; tones muscles; improves vitality; relieves depression; and helps you sleep better. Regular physical activity substantially reduces the risk of coronary heart disease, which is the nation's leading cause of death. It decreases the risk for stroke, colon cancer, diabetes, and high blood pressure. It helps with weight loss or simply controlling weight. It relieves the pain of arthritis and reduces symptoms of anxiety. In short, exercise gives you more energy and makes you feel better all the way around.

Likewise, many chronic diseases and health issues can be prevented by eating the right foods and adding the proper supplementation. This is why there has been an explosive push toward the use of antioxidants over the past couple decades. Antioxidants contain a single underlying mechanism that go to work on stifling the damaging effects caused by free radicals within your cells. This can help to slow down the aging process, ward off cancer, prevent heart disease, arthritis, and many neurological disorders. There are hundreds of antioxidants, (the most familiar are vitamin C, vitamin E and beta-carotene) but luckily, you don't have to spend a fortune on vitamins and supplements. Abundant evidence suggests that obtaining these powerful antioxidants naturally, through a variety of food sources provides the best protection against the ravages of aging. So if you've been searching for the fountain of youth, be sure to take a trip to the produce section in your grocery store—fruits and vegetables are the antioxidant leaders. However, whole grains, herbs, spices, tea and even dark chocolate contain antioxidant substances, called phytochemicals, or polyphenols. All these compounds can protect your cells from oxidative stress and bring healthful benefits to a diseased body.

In addition, you should make it a point to get an adequate amount of omega-3 fatty acids in your diet, because these nutrients are needed for numerous normal body functions. "Omega-3 fatty acids are also associated with many health benefits, including protection against heart disease and possibly stroke. New studies are identifying potential benefits for a wide range of conditions including cancer, inflammatory bowel disease, and other autoimmune diseases such as lupus and rheumatoid arthritis."[14] Good food sources include fish, walnuts, ground flaxseed, brussel sprouts, kale, spinach, and salad greens. However, if you don't eat fish or foods rich in these nutrients, you should consider taking an omega-3 supplement.

By making the right food choices and adding supplementation if needed, you can fuel your body with all the essential nutrients it needs to function at its best. There is so much you can do to take care of your health, and it doesn't need to be complicated. For instance, taking a twenty-minute nature walk helps to circulate blood flow, clear the mind, and nurture your spirit. Portion control can help you reach and maintain a healthy body weight.

On the other hand, poor choices, neglect, and bad habits give rise to plenty of complex health challenges. Being overweight or obese increases the risk of developing heart disease, diabetes, and several types of cancers. It puts more wear and tear on the joints and greater pressure on the heart; it causes more sick days and lost productivity and results in exorbitant medical expenses. If we're careless in our eating habits and consume too much saturated fat, our LDL cholesterol may rise. Elevated LDL cholesterol, a condition known as atherosclerosis, can lead to heart disease. Consuming too much salt and neglecting exercise can raise blood pressure. High blood pressure increases the risk for a heart attack or stroke. Smoking cigarettes lowers oxygen consumption and is commonly associated with a wide variety of diseases—it increases the risk of lung, head, and neck cancer. Furthermore, tobacco users pay twice as much for life insurance and will die an average of over twelve years sooner than non-smokers. In fact, depending on where you live in the United States, a habit of a pack a day can cost, on average, $1,800 a year. The annual cost of tobacco use is more than $50 billion in direct medical costs, for a total of $97 billion in health care costs and lost productivity.[15]

"You could have had an estimated $1,000,000 if you invested the money it costs to smoke two packs a day for fifty years in a major tobacco company."[16]

While an occasional glass of red wine is healthy, heavy drinking is the second leading cause of all premature deaths (smoking is the first). Excess alcohol consumption can lead to headaches, dizziness, slurred speech, anxiety, hallucinations, convulsions, aggressive acts of domestic violence and child abuse. Studies done through the Imperial Cancer Research Fund at Oxford University discovered that people who have more than six drinks a day are more apt to have cirrhosis, liver cancer, mouth and throat cancer, bronchitis and pneumonia.

If people don't eat the proper diet and digest too much sugar, this can spike blood glucose levels and cause hyperglycemia. Unstable glucose levels and chronically high blood sugar can cause progressive damage to body organs, such as kidneys, eyes, heart, and pancreas. Chronic hypoglycemia can lead to brain and nerve damage, and when glucose levels in the bloodstream aren't regulated, this can lead to diabetes. A diet that's full of sugar, saturated fat, and alcohol can elevate triglycerides. Excess triglycerides may contribute to fatty plaque deposits on the artery walls, and the buildup of plaque may result in heart attack or stroke. Unmanaged stress can speed heart rate, produce hormonal imbalances, slow digestion, set off migraine headaches, contribute to stomach problems, cause sleep disturbance, and disrupt relationships. Not getting enough sleep does not allow the body to detoxify and rejuvenate. The issues associated with unhealthy behaviors are extensive and alarming.

Proactive Lifestyle Modifications for Optimal Health

The medical profession is there to help us, but there's so much we can do to become healthy by being *proactive*. We can choose to exercise, eat right, add supplementation where needed, manage stress, stop smoking, limit alcohol, sleep enough, drink adequate water, nurture our spirit, deal constructively with emotions, develop a healthy self-image, set fitness goals to keep us motivated, manage our weight and body fat, and become disciplined. Now you can see that getting healthy is not just about eating your spinach. The PHS provides a method to help you do all these things and more. Right now, you're working on the first component of the PHS Pyramid; *lifestyle management*. By proactively considering ways to modify and manage your life, you're setting the proper foundation. This will lead into the next component, *healthy self-management* and that keeps you progressing up the PHS Pyramid.

. . . .
Use wisely your power of choice.
—Og Mandino
. . . .

Clearly, your health and well-being can influence every area of your life, from those seemingly ordinary tasks to all those special events, even your relationships. I recently spoke with Todd, who told me about his "defining moment." Todd was always running late for work every day and getting harassed about it. He was so overweight, it was a major struggle for him to just bend down and tie his shoes in the morning. Being flexible enough to tie your shoes is something most people take for granted, but for Todd, it became his big decision to change.

We must also keep in mind that our psychological well-being is part of being healthy. Consider Luke, a middle-aged man who got severely depressed when he lost his job after twenty-five years with the same company. He stopped communicating with his family and friends for several months. During that time, his girlfriend, Rachel, who adored and loved him very much, didn't even know what was going on. She was extremely hurt that he wouldn't return any of her calls, e-mails, or text messages. In the meantime, another man was pursuing Rachel, who was emotionally stable and very attentive to her needs. When Luke finally came around to communicating with Rachel again (six months later) it was too late; she was happily engaged to the other man.

Your psychological health is no joke. God has given you stewardship over all aspects of your health—your mind, body, and spirit. So if you want to make your health a priority, then take the responsibility that's aligned to that choice—that's effective PHS lifestyle management at its roots. However, just like a tree doesn't grow overnight, developing healthy behaviors doesn't either. We must each make conscious decisions daily, based upon on our values. We're responsible for uprooting our bad habits, plowing the soil, sowing good seed, and nurturing the area.

Here's an example. Jarvis told me that he promised his wife he would start exercising, lose weight, and set an example of health for their kids. He wanted to be fit enough to take them on a family ski trip in the upcoming winter. In that same week, however, a few friends invited him to meet up for several beers before Monday night football. Jarvis described how he thought this through. He realized that if he agreed to meet his buddies before the game, he would be tempted to drink his typical six beers—approximately 1,080 calories; hardly a way to start getting healthy! Instead, Jarvis decided he would still go to watch the game, but he refused to go earlier to drink. His decision was win/win. He was able to stay true to his word, spend time with his friends, and improve his health.

We are made wise not by the recollection of our past but by the responsibility for our future.—George Bernard Shaw

---

Stress Management

We all get our fair share of stress. Many people can't manage their lives because they're stressed, and they're stressed because they can't manage their lives. The good news is that whenever we manage our stress, we become better managers of our lives, and vice versa. So whichever way we decide to go about it, it's all good! Before the end of every day, we should each take some time out to de-stress. This is an important part of lifestyle management, as well as healthy self-management.

What is stress anyway? We usually associate it with anything that causes us psychological strain, but some stress can be good. Stress falls into the following four categories:

- **Eustress**—keeps us vital, this stress is fun and exciting.

- **Acute stress**—short term, usually occurs day-to-day and can be positive or distressing.

- **Episodic acute stress**—runs rampant and creates a life of relative chaos.

- **Chronic stress**—seems never-ending and inescapable (like a bad marriage).

There are numerous reasons for our stress—tight schedules, a troubled marriage, unemployment, poor-quality living conditions, demanding jobs and bosses, out-of-control kids, annoying in-laws, divorce, traffic jams, senseless crimes, a faltering economy, disease, unresolved psychological issues and so on. The complexity and enormity of these challenges seem relentless. Our inability to cope with these life challenges causes us stress, yet oddly enough, this stress is self-induced. Nobody wants to hear this, but if we can choose our own response in any situation by being *proactive*, then stress is created by our own *reaction*. This means we actually have the power to proactively manage our stress—now, that's some truly good news!

Stress isn't solely the result of our disappointments or difficult circumstances. While it's true that there are consequences to such events as natural disasters, financial hardship, accidents and injuries, wars, and numerous grave injustices, *our options and choices are always freely available*. It's through our own impaired interpretations and perceptions that we give power away to other people, problems, or situations. In essence, this is what creates stress. At our core, we're still the same person, whether we live under a rock or in a glorious mansion. This is why two people who experience the exact set of seemingly painful circumstances can respond in opposite ways. One person may soar far above the situation and create something wonderful and exceptional from it, while another might use it as an excuse for every shortfall.

Common Stress Triggers: Marriage and Kids

Has family life taken a toll on your health? For many people, as soon they get married and/or have kids, something seems to go haywire— they get stressed, gain weight, and neglect exercise. Basically, their health goes south. Within a couple years of marriage, it's not uncommon to see that each spouse has gained twenty or thirty pounds—some balloon-out, packing on a great deal more. Much of this weight gain is directly attributed to having kids, although sometimes it's blamed entirely on the spouse. At some point, we must question; who are we really kidding? In reality, this is nothing but an excuse mentality and it is very disconcerting, since the development of healthy habits should start within the home. If spouses and parents established this core value of health within their families, they could begin to lead by example. Instead, many children today enter kindergarten overweight or obese.

I've listened to numerous parents complain that their kids take up so much time, and this is why they're unhealthy and out of shape. It's the same story over and over, but it makes me wonder, who's in control—the parents or the kids? It appears that the current mind-set of many parents has become *reactive*, rather than *proactive*. As a society, we haven't been moving forward toward the progression of healthy lifestyle habits; rather, we've been moving backward. Why? Responsibility has been thwarted on many levels—people have lost their ability to uphold this core value of health. Instead of recognizing their personal role in the matter, many seek justification of this neglect through the family system. How is this faulty notion propagated in society? Apparently, there is a societal bias in this area wherein many parents enter into a league of entitlement. Some believe they should receive special treatment when compared to other individuals in society. The underlying presumption condoned by a great majority is that when people have kids, (whether they're married or not) they earn a license to stockpile their stress and neglect their health. Yet this notion is pretty ridiculous, and it's high time to remove the blinders.

Do you really think you become an exception, experience more stress, are busier, and have fewer than twenty-four hours in a day, just because you're a parent? If you think that others can't relate to the same hassle of time constraints and stress, just because they don't have any kids, then you'd better think again. Some people work sixteen hours days, seven days a week. Some go to school full-time while working full-time. Others are juggling two or even three part-time jobs. Nobody is excluded from stress; it touches all ages and spans every culture. Consider the two-year-old girl diagnosed with cancer, or the soldier who lost his leg in battle, or the boy sexually abused by a priest, or the couple longing for a child, only to experience several miscarriages or a stillborn—they all experience stress. Whether your job is to raise a family inside the home, work outside or both, the level of stress you experience is not a competition. All stress is relative, it can affect everyone of any age—single, married, divorced, widowed, those with kids or those without.

This is not to discount the enormity of bringing a new life into the world. Becoming a parent is truly an overwhelming and life-transforming experience. It changes a person's disposition on many levels, and nobody claimed it would be easy. And of course, parents with special-needs children face an even greater challenge. Yet contrary to what many parents may believe, it *is* possible for people without kids to recognize the stress associated with child-rearing. It's life changing, challenging, and time consuming—people get it. Even when teenagers find out that a peer got pregnant, they understand that such a huge obligation means missing out on a lot of fun to care for the baby. A pregnant teen would never consider giving her baby up for adoption if she underestimated the magnitude of child-rearing. In fact, if people were really that clueless, there would be no adoption agencies. But this is not the case; most people understand that raising a child can be a daunting responsibility.

So then, what does this signify? As a society, are we predisposed to the belief that if we have children this ought to justify our own self-neglect? Have we become so disillusioned and self-absorbed with this mind-set that we can no longer see any other point of view? Does being a parent automatically equate to loss of self-care? Does it drive you to mindlessly overeat and succumb to an unhealthy lifestyle? If you're a parent, must you forego good habits such as exercise? Do right-minded parents condone this irrationality under the presumption that taking care of their health is selfish, or that there's not enough time in the day? Before parents can uphold healthy behaviors and set an example for their children, perhaps a change of perspective is necessary.

Let's reevaluate the life of a single person who has no kids. Singles are responsible for every single task, big and small. Not only are single people responsible for everything from the mortgage payment or rent to handling all the chores, many experience deep heartbreak, severe loneliness, and relentless societal pressure to marry. Some singles are shunned in society and treated like second-class citizens, especially if they have no kids. Talk about stress! The single life is not the smooth sailing you may think it is. All of humanity undergoes stress. If we presume to be a responsible adult; then we should behave like one. This means whether we're a parent or not, we can find a way to manage our health.

For starters, if you have a child, you must recognize that this is truly a gift and blessing from God. What's your perspective? Do you see your children as blessings, or do you use them as scapegoats for everything? What about your spouse? Do you cherish one another, or take each other for granted? Keeping a family intact isn't always easy, but when you think proactively, the response is up to you. Regardless, marriage and kids are not an alibi to neglect your health.

> If you're stressed out and unhealthy;
> this is not your kids' fault. Kids give you
> "bragging rights," not "blaming rights."

Anyone who has developed healthy habits knows that these skills can be used throughout a lifetime. This holds true whether or not you have kids and whether or not you're married. It's just like driving a car. If you learned how to drive a car, would you lose that skill after getting married and having kids? On the other hand, if you never learned how to drive a car, would you blame it on your kids or your spouse? That logic just doesn't add up. If you're unhealthy, much of this is due to the decisions *you* made, whether those were done consciously or not. Learn to recognize your responsibility and choice in the matter. It's simple, you either acquired these lifestyle and healthy self-management skills, or you didn't. You either use them, or you don't. It might finally be time to manage your life and make your health a priority—but accept this responsibility without blaming your spouse or kids.

While it's true that your newborn might keep you up all night making you sleep-deprived, you should realize that is only a phase. We must accept that there are phases in life for everything. The commitment of marriage comes with a transitional phase; it also has cycles of highs and lows. Most people recognize this when they take their vows for better or for worse. When you experience those lows, surely this can take its toll in several distressing ways. However, if you uphold this core value of health, you'll be able to keep your sanity during those tough times. When you maintain healthy behaviors, this significantly reduces your stress levels. It will help keep you calm and grounded. Be true to yourself always. Being married and raising a family certainly has some unique and challenging moments—it's just part of the package. Learn to accept it all with gratitude.

Just because you love and care for others doesn't mean you should lose your mind and stop taking care of yourself. Realistically, there are ways to do both. For instance, when it comes to exercise, do you think there's no time in the day for it, just because you're married? It is your spouse's fault that you can't find twenty minutes to take a brisk walk outside? If you have a baby, couldn't you put him or her in a stroller and do the same thing? Is this your baby's fault? Take a moment to ponder these questions. Why not make time and take a walk together? Schedules may not always coincide, but you're still entitled to be proactive and take responsibility for your own health.

Starting right now, you can be the one to set the tone for healthy habits within your family. You can lead by example. The blame game states that anything above the bar is taking responsibility; anything below the bar means not taking responsibility. Stay above the bar, and you will keep your sanity and composure. If you blame your inabilities on your spouse or child, you're probably the same kind of person who says there's no time for breakfast in the morning. Guess what? There's time. Many people have this same issue of longing to sleep-in or feeling rushed in the morning, yet somehow they manage.

We're all granted only twenty-four hours in the day. It's simple; get up five minutes earlier each day. It takes approximately two and a half minutes to prepare breakfast and two and a half minutes to eat it. You can drink a refreshing glass of juice or grab a piece of fruit, and/or nuke an egg or two (or several egg whites, if you're watching fat). Simply, grab an egg, crack it in a bowl, whisk briefly, and pop it in the microwave for one minute. Then put a piece of whole-grain bread in the toaster or have a bagel. Now you can have an egg and toast or a bagel, or forget the egg and use cream cheese or peanut butter—whatever you prefer. *Voila*—there's your breakfast. If necessary, take it in the car, or just grab a ready-made breakfast bar with a piece of fruit. You also could try ready-made fast-fuel shakes loaded with vitamins and minerals or instant oatmeal, which only takes a couple of minutes as well. The point here is that you have plenty of options.

· ·
It's not your spouse's fault if you
neglect your health and gain weight.
· ·

Of course, marriage and kids could pose some enormous challenges, but get rid of the notion that these are reasons for weight gain, health issues, and unhealthy lifestyles. Any responsible adult wouldn't tolerate this excuse type of mentality. The power is within you. As a parent, you're on the front lines of a new era—you have the opportunity to make a significant and positive impact on society by embracing healthy behaviors and teaching your children to do the same. Health education should start at home, and that's where true economic progress begins.

You don't need to get approval from anyone to think proactively. Nobody can put you in a cage but you. Those limitations you may be experiencing are self-induced. If you feel like you're stuck in a proverbial cage, recognize that it's your personal responsibility to bust out. If you're married, this doesn't mean you should head for divorce court, dodge all your responsibilities, or jump into an affair to escape from the mundane. This isn't about neglecting your family and losing your senses. It's about losing the fear and finding your inner freedom, so that you can do what's important to you. Then hold on to it, and cherish it. When you're proactive, you can find a way to manage your own life. Begin by listing your priorities (health being one of them!), set some clear boundaries, get organized, jot down actions steps, and start making time for yourself. Don't let anything or anyone cloud your judgment.

Being *proactive* means you can make your health a priority, regardless of your circumstance. For instance, in some countries women aren't even allowed to walk outside unescorted, let alone given access to a gym to exercise. Still, arrangements can be made in advance and alternatives are possible. Marching in place or dancing is great physical exercise and so is climbing a staircase. Jumping jacks, push-ups, line jumps, sit-ups, a plank hold, all-four stabilization, stationary lunges, repetitive squats, and wall sits are all exercises that can be done in close quarters. (Some of these activities are covered in the *Program Design*—exercise section.) Also yoga—performed by holding certain poses and stretching correctly; improves flexibility, reduces tension in the body, and helps to ease the mind. Whenever and wherever people exercise, they remove accumulated tension and stress from the body. So recognize that no matter where you live, you can exercise. Physical movement is necessary for the human body and where there's a will, there's a way. How you manage your lifestyle is essentially up to you. Being proactive allows you to find this power from within—indeed; this is your ultimate health solution.

> The law of attraction states that whatever you desire is already attracted to you.

Whenever we reduce our stress levels and become healthier, this brings more harmony into the world. An infinite number of choices await you. You can create your own game plan for managing your lifestyle and health. You don't need to dishonor your body and neglect your health just because you got married or became a parent. In reality, that sounds quite absurd—don't go there. Being proactive allows you to uphold this core value of health. It helps you to help yourself *and* your family.

> If you neglect your health, this is your choice.

As part of lifestyle management, you must make some time to de-stress. Exercise is definitely a top-of-the-line stress buster, but there are other ways to de-stress as well. You might want to meditate or pray, spend time outdoors, curl up with a good book, get a massage, take a hot bubble bath, get pampered at a spa, or just dance unabashedly to your favorite song. Most people would agree that finding healthy outlets to nurture our mind, body, and spirit is not the problem; making this part of our daily life is the *real* problem. The world we live in today is fast-paced, and times are challenging. Consequently, allotting time to de-stress becomes all the more crucial. Everyone needs some time alone to de-stress, including parents, or should I say, *especially parents!*

Parents set the pace and lead their children by example. If they remain careless, stressed-out and unhealthy, this represents a tremendous loss of power to all. It affects everyone in a dire way and leaves a huge footprint in society—the health of families and our entire nation will suffer. What can be done? Perhaps a National Parent Health Day should be instituted that would require a parent to take time off work to de-stress in order to demonstrate the value of health. Parents can set an example for children by doing something healthy on that day—get a massage, go for a jog, swim, work with a personal trainer, take a team class, prepare a healthy homemade meal. Whatever promotes a healthy lifestyle and helps parents to de-stress can simultaneously be conveyed to teach and inspire their children.

In 2010, the first Monday of October was declared as National Child Health Day, thanks to the task force on childhood obesity and the "Let's Move" initiative led by First Lady Michelle Obama.[17] This day was instituted, as a response to the health care crisis, for parents to collaborate with health educators and professionals to teach children the benefits and habits of living a healthy lifestyle. This is an absolutely awesome step in the right direction. Still, we can do more. Parents should practice what they preach and become health-conscious role models to their children. When parents become healthy, their influence touches more people, whether they have one kid or one dozen.

It's time for parents to step up to the plate. They must be proactive and focus on recapturing this lost value of health for themselves. This will not only teach children, but more impressively, it will *inspire* them. Unfortunately, some children are embarrassed by their parents for being overweight; they don't even want to be seen with them in public. Ironically, the beauty of children is their innocence. They don't sugarcoat the truth; they call it like they see it. Clearly, parents will do more to help their children by focusing on improving their own health.

Parents need to schedule time alone, weekly, for their own sanity and well-being. A few hours per week, at a minimum, are needed. Still, parents may balk and complain that they can't find any time. Round and round they go in a vicious cycle. It doesn't change the facts; it's simply a part of lifestyle management. If parents sincerely value their health and want to set a good example for their children, they will have to find a way to make this happen. When parents take better care of themselves, everybody wins. This time alone is necessary in order to clarify their perspective. There are tremendous psychological benefits to taking a "personal time out." Even taking five-to ten-minute intervals to break away, breathe deeply, or meditate can help us to re-energize, regroup and de-stress. Setting the foundation for a healthy lifestyle begins in the home, and parents need to get on board.

Consider this practical analogy: when flying on an airplane, it's always recommended that the parent put the oxygen mask on *first*, before putting it on the child. There's a reason for this; parents need to be well enough to take care of their child. In everyday life, one of the best things parents can do for their children is to set an example of good health. Sometimes it's completely natural to get carried away with your children, to be doting on their every whim or desire. While there may be times its okay to put the child first, take caution. If parents can't set boundaries with their children, or if they begin to feel like victims, that's a red flag that their psychological equilibrium is already at stake. Ever wonder why some parents say and do crazy things? They've lost their perspective. So while many activities should be centered on the children, parents should not *always* put their kids first, no matter how much they love them.

If parents never make time for themselves, they'll get stressed out and blame it on their kids. If enough frustration builds, domestic and verbal abuse may be the result. You can prevent this from happening by taking regular personal *time-outs*. Remember, your unmanaged stress is not your child's fault. Kids will always be kids. It's your responsibility to make the time and find constructive ways to de-stress. Don't be reactive. Be proactive. Make it a point to take care of you. If needed, don't hesitate to enlist in some help. Call a friend or hire a nanny!

Lives are impacted all over the world by the birth of one child, and the overall impact is good—children are wonderful, dearly precious gifts from God. Without them, this world would be a gloomy place, and people would still be out of shape and unhealthy. Don't use your kids as a scapegoat for all your stress and health issues. Instead, appreciate them, love them, and be proud of them!

"Sons are a heritage from the Lord, children a reward from him. Like arrows in the hands of a warrior are sons born in one's youth."[18]

. . . .
It's our inability to hold our own power that causes stress.
. . . .

Our boss, spouse, kids—no one can force us to do anything outside of our freewill. We imprison ourselves; stress is not our prisoner. We must to learn how to free ourselves from the inside; that's how we manage our so-called stress. It's our power within that needs to be activated. We were born with a purpose—to take this power out into the world and experience it as a wonderful life-changing force that can bring great joy to many. Whenever we create limitations upon this power, we experience stress. But when we release fears, doubts, defenses, and any sense of unworthiness, we will fan the flame of our divine light. As we learn to stand in our own power, it becomes much easier to manage our life and health.

Time Management

When it comes to time management, we ought to be proactive in our thinking as well. This means sometimes we need to think about the big picture. On a day-to-day basis, it's often hard to think this way, but we can equate this big-picture mentality to making a purchase. Let's say you want to buy a new pair of jeans. Should you buy the kind that's good quality, fits well, and has style for years to come? Or should you buy the bargain brand? Go for the good quality, because it's going to last for quite a while. Though it may cost a bit more, in the long run, it's the better choice. If you don't think about the big picture, you'll end up cutting corners—you won't make the right purchase decision that can yield the greatest benefits. Think of your time in the same way—as money that you invest well.

When you invest time into your health, it will last long and pay dividends year after year. Just like a good-quality purchase, it's a decision you won't regret. So don't just look at what's in front of you, think big and focus on making the most of what you have now. By thinking proactively, you can keep this big picture in mind and become resourceful. Start taking baby steps, by focusing on *quality*, not *quantity*. For instance, even a ten-minute walk may seem like a tall order when time is tight, but do it anyway. Before you know it, those ten-minute intervals here and there will pay off in the long run. Do what you can in the time you have, and you'll be investing in the big picture of optimal health.

Murphy's Law Versus the Reliability Factor
Would Have, Could Have, Should Have

How many times have you kicked yourself, saying, "I just knew I should've done that"? Or perhaps someone blocked an opportunity for you to do something because you were caught off-guard. Every single person you allow in your life can have a profound impact on your time. "Murphy's Law" states that if there's a chance that something can go wrong, it usually will. Focusing on what's negative is not very encouraging, but we must consider this law when it comes to time management. Most people have good intentions, they want to manage their time effectively, but then all kinds of things come up and seem to get in the way. Since Murphy's Law has a negative connotation, let's focus on the opposite—Yhprum's Law. Yhprum's Law is Murphy's Law spelled backwards, and it appeals to the probability that everything that can work, *will* work. It supports the notion that sometimes systems that should not work, do work nonetheless. But Yhprum's Law is cumbersome to pronounce, so I coined another term, "Reliability Factor" (RF).

When we think of something *reliable,* we think of something we can count on or trust. So instead of looking at the possibility of what can go wrong, we focus on the possibility of what can go right. This new perspective is golden, because when it comes to time management, we can schedule a time to take care of ourselves within this reliable window of opportunity. You may have heard the slogan that life is what happens to you while you're busy making other plans. That's because life is fluid and unpredictable. Sometimes, we just have to roll with the punches. Maybe life doesn't even punch that hard, but it can cause several unexpected twists and turns within a short time span. Life doesn't check with us first, to make sure those changes will adjust and fit into our schedule. We might set up our agendas with certain expectations, and then life comes along and turns everything upside down.

We should remain flexible, but not to the point where we can no longer uphold our values or keep a commitment to ourselves. When you're proactive, you will discover that not everything in life is left up to chance or circumstances. We don't need to lose our focus or feel so helpless just because something didn't turn out the way we expected. In any situation, we always have a choice about how to respond, this is part of being proactive. Although the route we take may not be the one we intended on; it's part of our journey. Those unexpected twists and turns will test our ability to defend our values—what we truly want in life. On the other hand, if we have no idea where we're going, then any road can take us there.

When it comes to life, we need to go with the flow. When it comes to our time, we need to manage our dough. Dough is not necessarily money; it's whatever we value in life. Once we learn to manage the important areas of our life, the rest will fall right into place. People often say that time is money because when we make a good investment in our time; we make a good investment in our life.

· ·

Go with the flow, and manage your dough.

· ·

Since you can't control life, circumstances, or some individuals from affecting your time, then include the "Reliability Factor" when scheduling your priorities. Here's an example: Claire has a day off that's not crammed with activities. Aside from one appointment later in the evening, most of her day is unstructured. She knows she has time before her evening appointment to exercise. She relishes the fact that today she's not on a rigid schedule and will go whenever she feels like it. In the meantime, she's preoccupied doing something else. A couple hours before her appointment, she finds herself in the mood to go work out.

Claire looks at the clock and begins calculating the time by considering everything she needs to do—drive to the gym, work out, drive back, shower, eat and drive to her appointment. She discovers that she's actually hard-pressed for time. How can this be, she thought, when she had the whole day off? Now she's really in the mood to work out, but she doesn't want to rush or worry about getting stuck in traffic and being late. Instead of trying to cram the workout in a tight spot, she decides to forego it.

Instead she hops in the shower to get ready. After stepping out of the shower, she gets a call that tells her that her appointment is canceled. Darn! With hair dripping wet, she says to herself, "I **would've** worked out if I'd known in advance she was going to cancel. Now I can't work out because I've already showered. I **could've** worked out like I wanted to. Darn, I **should've** worked out earlier!"

Claire could have avoided all of this **would've, could've, should've** if she implemented the RF. The RF doesn't leave things to chance. If she proactively took the RF into account, she wouldn't have scheduled the workout so close to her appointment. The second point to consider is that of "being in the mood" for the workout. It's true that she was more in the mood to work out later, but to wait until the 'moment feels right' is not feasible—we're talking about time-management here, not a romantic rendezvous! You can't rely on your moods to get things done because in the real world, you have to be a responsible adult.

Successful and proactive people do things they don't always like to do; they focus on the end result, not on the task. They don't schedule priorities based on their moods. They bank on what's reliable—a good habit. This is not to say we shouldn't pay attention to our feelings or moods, but there's only twenty-four hours in a day. We need to focus on what's reliable and what works. We must evaluate potential problems in our daily-life equation, plug this into our scheduled timetable, and find what works. That is proactive thinking.

You can learn to develop good habits by being *consistent* in your efforts, and including the RF. This makes it much easier to build a good habit. Sticking to a consistent time spot can help initially, because many of us tend to be creatures of habit, but this doesn't mean that a particular time will always be open in our schedule. The reality is that we need to work with whatever time we have. Eventually, with a *consistent effort*, finding the best time to exercise will become a non-issue. We should be more concerned with developing this *consistency*, not making sure we always have the same day and time slot open—nothing in life is that certain. Once the consistency has been developed, then it can become part of our everyday routine. Hard-working, busy people can't afford to waste precious time. If you want to develop healthy habits, then plan on maximizing your time. As an analogy, think of the Drama Queen who always turns to people for advice—others may comment, "I wouldn't have put myself in that situation in the first place." Time management is no different; don't put yourself in a tight spot. When planning an exercise schedule, think proactively and consider potential problems that may arise. Here is a checklist of several common time-management considerations.

What's the likelihood this time slot won't work due to:

- Family obligations?

- My personal appointments?

- A change of work schedule or overtime?

- Prior engagements and social commitments?

- Circumstances outside my control (such as traffic or the weather)?

- Sleep deprivation or sheer exhaustion?

When you plan your day, these are important considerations. Weigh your options, and ask yourself, "What's the best time for me to exercise or do something good for my health?" "There is no time" is not a viable answer! Before you can effectively manage your time, you must have your priorities straight. If your entire day is scheduled except for a few hours to sleep or eat, then you're headed for major burnout. And you probably already know this, but some changes are definitely in order. Living day-to-day in constant stress is a surefire way to ruin your health.

CHAPTER 6

Lifestyle Management—
PHS Principle: Take Responsibility

Our life has been given to us as a gift. Taking responsibility for it is a fundamental principle we must learn. God has given us stewardship over our mind, body, and spirit. Each of us will be held accountable for our time, talents, resources, everything we say and do, and all our choices— right or wrong, good or bad. When we are *proactive* and *take responsibility* for managing our life, it becomes much easier to manage our health. As indicated earlier, these two principles are partnered up to support the base of the PHS Pyramid: Lifestyle Management. Our choices and behaviors will be reflected by how we manage our lifestyle.

Webster's definition of **responsible**: Trustworthy, in charge, having authority, being answerable for one's actions or the actions of others.[1]

• •
Being proactive reflects your choices;
taking responsibility reflects your actions.
• •

When we're children, parents have authority over us. As we mature into adulthood, we should learn that it's our responsibility to manage our life. Apparently, however, some adults have been convinced otherwise. It appears that someone or something else has usurped their God-given responsibility. These individuals have blocked out their consciousness. At some point, they involuntarily chose to give this power away to a family member, spouse, boss, or social order. Consequently, this creates a huge schism—a conflict of interest when attempting to get healthy. It's as if they have split personalities. On one hand, they want to pursue their health and fitness goals; on the other, they believe it's their duty to appease everyone else first. A self-imposed system of martyrdom seems to be getting in their way.

As mentioned, much of this difficulty stems from parenting. Women in particular, have a tendency to drop everything for the sake of their children. On some level, this is entirely intuitive—a mother's natural instinct kicks in. However, continually putting others first is not healthy. As a parent, you're no exception to this rule. If you fail to set appropriate boundaries with your children and fall into unhealthy behavior patterns, you must realize that this issue is your responsibility. Taking time for oneself is a skill that *everybody* needs to learn. Anyone can claim that there's not enough time in the day—there always going to be someone or something vying for our time. However, when you take responsibility for your life, this means that healthy behaviors can *become part of your life,* not something that interferes with it.

We must get to the root of these common misconceptions. Often these moments of self-neglect occur right within the home and family unit itself. Consider Loretta; she's always complaining about her obese husband, Ralph, who likes to eat out frequently and sees nothing wrong with fast food. Loretta, on the other hand, prefers to prepare healthy meals and eat dinner at home. The problem is that Loretta works late, and Ralph gets too hungry to wait for her to make dinner. When she's unavailable but knows that her kids are hungry, she drops the ball back in Ralph's court. Ralph doesn't know how to cook, so he often heads off to the Greasy Spoon to order some takeout food for the family. While he awaits the processed, deep-fried chicken nuggets, he inhales a couple of pizza slices and washes it down with a cold brew. By the time Loretta gets home, Ralph has conveniently distributed bags of greasy food to the kids. Loretta always has good intentions of making a nutritious homemade meal, but at the end of the day, she's exhausted and doesn't bother. It's become a vicious cycle.

Granted, Ralph seems clueless about cooking or eating healthy, but he is right about one thing. He doesn't like waiting long to eat when he's hungry—and that's actually smart. Eating frequently throughout the day prevents the body from storing fat and slowing down metabolism. On the other hand, Ralph consumes too many fat calories and doesn't make healthy food choices for himself or his family. Meanwhile, Loretta's wishful thinking and good intentions don't count. Instead of complaining, she needs to take some responsibility in the matter. She can come up with a game plan for her family—cooking the night before, having wholesome snacks available before dinner, using a crock-pot to slow cook during the day or helping Ralph learn to prepare easy meals and make better choices. She can also compromise or put a limit on how often they eat take-out.

Another option which can be extremely helpful is to cook in the morning before going to work. Shortly after I got married, I told my husband that every Monday and Thursday evening, I'd be working late. On these evenings, we decided to take turns on cooking dinner, I'd get Mondays and he got Thursdays. So while getting ready for work in the morning, I'd prepare 'Monday Mjadra'—a healthy and delicious Arabic dish of brown rice and lentils. (The original version is made with white rice and it can be topped with sautéed onions and/or a small salad). I put the main ingredients together in less than three minutes on the stove-top. After the water boiled, I let it simmer for approximately a half-hr. I didn't have to do anything else except turn the heat off. At the end of the day, my new husband and I sat down for a wonderful meal, virtually ready-made when I walked in the door! Everyone has the opportunity to set the ground rules within his or her own family. Unfortunately, Loretta short-changed herself by neglecting to follow through. If you don't take responsibility for managing your own life, you can hardly be expected to set a good example for your family.

Consequently, this failure to teach self-responsibility will trickle down throughout various ranks of our social system. For instance, Mark, a high-school teenager, recognizes that smoking is unhealthy but he does it anyway to be "cool." While experimentation among teens is quite common, eventually he could reach the point where he always has to check in with his "posse" to make a decision. Mark becomes a follower, not a leader. Before you know it, he's hooked on smoking a pack a day, even before graduating high school. If Mark learned this principle of taking responsibility for his own life, he could turn down the cigarettes and develop healthy behaviors instead. He could set a new precedent for being cool.

Whenever you cease to think for yourself and fail to take responsibility for your life, you forfeit your power on many levels. If you're struggling to develop a healthy lifestyle, chances are you're having more difficulty managing your life, rather than managing your health. In other words, unless you're faced with a health crisis, you're not so focused on your health that you neglect other parts of your life. Typically, the difficulty starts the other way around; people who have a hard time managing their life often neglect their health. Although both of these components are intertwined, healthy self-management is actually, an extension of lifestyle management. That's why it's easier to start taking responsibility for managing our lives *first*.

If this lifestyle principle was taught in our formative years, society wouldn't be faced with the great health care crisis of this era, but we've been left chasing our tail. When insurance companies hold people's lives in their hands, this does not signify progress in health care reform. This is backpedaling on the route to health. People have suffered and died waiting to get approved for health insurance. The good news is that transformation toward a healthier society is still possible. When individuals learn to take responsibility for managing their lifestyle, they'll be more apt to develop healthy behaviors. Furthermore, if all insurance companies complied with a standard to monitor these healthy behaviors, they would not be able to deny people coverage so readily, that is, for superfluous reasons. In the future, only the insurance companies that implement such a policy will remain competitive and thrive. Why? When they have an agenda to evaluate healthy behaviors, and offer incentives for those who practice them, it becomes a win-win situation.

Sanctioning a means to promote these preventive measures will lead to health care advancements as well as economic recovery. This type of reform won't happen overnight. Some psychological overhaul in society and within our educational system is necessary. School boards, along with educational legislators, need to incorporate a health program to teach children the lifestyle principles associated with healthy behaviors. In time, these learned behaviors will become part of the mainstream.

To educate individuals toward self-responsibility doesn't mean we must teach them to function independently of each other. We're all interconnected in one way or another. In fact, the realization of our potential mostly takes place within society. In the work place of an organization, the ability to function effectively as a member of the team is usually imperative to success. Most of us don't seek a life of isolation; we share our lives with companions or choose to marry. We are social beings, and the desire to experience some sense of community seems universal. However, our relationships shouldn't stop us from *thinking* for ourselves.

Being self-responsible requires us to think independently. The practice of thinking independently means to reflect critically on the values and beliefs offered by others but to decide what's right for oneself. The essence of self-responsibility is that we make an effort to bring about the effects of what we want, as contrasted with hoping, demanding, or expecting that someone else do something while we suffer in silence. Being able to think independently and take responsibility for our life empowers us, and it's vital to our psychological well-being. Nathaniel Branden, PhD, has said, "The abandonment of personal accountability makes self-esteem, as well as decent and benevolent social relationships, impossible. In its worst manifestation, it becomes a license to kill. If we are to have a world that works, we need a culture of accountability."[2]

Even the most passive and dependent people initiate some actions on their own. No one is rendered powerless unless that he or she decides it is so. Some adults however, have inadvertently made choices with which they're not happy, and they'd prefer to ignore their role in the matter. Instead of taking responsibility for their bad choice, they divert attention by complaining about their so-called "powerless" situation. If we're ever going to be a nation of responsible adults, then we must each be able to stand in our own truth. We're each a single point of consciousness, unique and private. We each make choices in our life and whether those choices are right or wrong, we're responsible for them. Self-responsibility is a matter of independent thought and personal effort. This remainder of this chapter will provide some guidelines to help you apply this principle.

Set Boundaries to Honor What's Important to You

We remain psychologically well by maintaining our intrinsic identity, whether we're in a relationship or not. Relationships are only healthy if they're consistent with our core values, and we're able to maintain our personal integrity and responsibility. That doesn't mean we need to agree all the time. Based upon our human nature, there will always be differences of opinions and conflicts of interests. We can agree to disagree. We must recognize where to draw the line and make the distinction between a life based on our truth and one that evades it. Within our life and all our relationships, we need to be able to set the boundaries that enable us to stand by our core values.

For example, one of my clients, Laura, is married to a fabulous chef, Bill, who cooks delicious yet sometimes very fattening and rich meals. Laura told me that before she married Bill, she wasn't overweight at all. Every year into her marriage, however, the weight crept on. During my initial consultation with Laura, we discussed her eating habits, and she told me that she ate whatever Bill cooked and paid no attention at all to the portion size. Now she was forty pounds overweight and wanted to get rid of that excess weight. Following the PHS, she knew that losing weight and keeping it off required her to take responsibility for her own life and health. This meant she needed to be willing to change her lifestyle. I recommended that she start a food log to track the portion size of those delicious meals. At first, she was worried that it would hurt Bill's feelings to not eat everything he prepared, which included warm bread or appetizers and wine before dinner. But she learned to say no thanks, without fearing any repercussions.

Ironically, as she set the boundaries necessary to gauge her caloric intake, the dynamics of their marriage actually changed for the better. Bill realized her mind-set became more positive which made her more pleasant to be around. Her energy and confidence increased. The somber look on her face was replaced with an inner glow and a soft smile. Now she can keep up with him on hiking trips, and he's overjoyed!

Lose the Excuse Mentality

Let's consider Leroy, a former athlete. Now in middle age, Leroy looked like he was nine months pregnant. Leroy claimed that the reason he had a protruding stomach was due to genetics, but at the same time, he bragged about his former athletic abilities and killer physique. (Clearly, if he used to have a very athletic body, then his protruding stomach wasn't due to genetics.) I told him the only way to get rid of that stomach was to *want to* get rid of it. He admitted this was true—and then shared a story. Leroy's wife had been sick with cancer, and for three years, he had to take care of her. He was out of work at the time and wasn't taking care of himself. In the first few months, he only gained fifteen pounds, but since his wife was not well enough to have sex, he figured that it didn't matter if he gained more weight. Within a year or so, he packed on another seventy-five pounds. A few years after his wife passed away, he'd done nothing to get rid of that protruding stomach. He admitted he'd been careless, but he blamed his wife's illness for the weight gain.

In reality, it was not his wife's fault that he failed to take responsibility for his health. Leroy suffers from an excuse mentality—first the protruding stomach was due to genetics, and then it was due to a marriage gone platonic. People with an excuse mentality just don't accept responsibility for their behaviors. They don't live a healthy lifestyle, because something or someone got in their way. Before you can expect to manage your life effectively, you must lose the excuse mentality. The questions on the following page should help you evaluate where this needs to be done.

Excuse Mentality Self-Evaluation:

- Is your health really a priority?

- Do you set boundaries around your time and within your relationships to honor what's important to you?

- Are most of your daily activities organized? Do you plan ahead?

- Do you use your kids, spouse, or work as a scapegoat for gaining weight?

- Do you always seem to be dealing with some kind of drama in your life?

- Do you use food or alcohol to manage stress, anxiety, or depression?

- Are you a workaholic?

- Have you broken promises to yourself?

- Do you take on too many activities because you can't say no to loved ones?

- Do you recognize the value of physical activity and make time for exercise?

- Do you make time to unwind, de-stress, pray, meditate, spend time in nature, or take a vacation?

As you take inventory of your current lifestyle, keep two questions in mind:

1. **What's good in my life?**
2. **What needs to be done?**

The first question will keep you focused on the positives, while the second will remind you that you're responsible for your life and well-being. It keeps you proactive.[3]

To help you lose the excuse mentality, understand that you're not alone with your problems in this world. You're a collective part of the human consciousness and your issues are all common to man. All the hardship or pain we experience in life is relative to our life journey, but everyone has knocked on misery's door and was welcomed to sit down. Nobody lives a completely charmed life. Loss and heartbreak is inevitable. Our pain can come from many sources—our upbringing and environment, the ill will and evil acts of others, a tragic death or accident, an awful marriage or bitter divorce, financial devastation and so much more. There's always a message or lesson, something we need to learn from our pain. If you've been a victim at some point, you can use that experience to deepen and enrich your life. Whatever the situation, it doesn't need to hold you captive, you can triumph over it.

Don't confuse your life with any life situation. Do some soul searching; this will help you in breaking barriers. Consider whether you're making an excuse by allowing someone or some situation, past or present, to take away your own personal power. Learn to forgive anyone who has harmed you and don't forget to forgive yourself. What lessons have you learned from your pain? Can you accept the good times and the bad? Are you grateful for the growth that comes through different life experiences?

When you become self-responsible, you reclaim your power. The challenge lies not from the gazillion issues you may face; it comes from how you respond to them. Some people give up and make excuses, while others find ways to be resourceful. Caving in under moments of weakness means we're only human—that's okay—but we're bigger than our problems. Instead of making excuses, we can look for solutions. Remember, the Proactive Health Solution is about empowering you, so that you can determine your next best steps. There's a path that's personally right for each of us; we just have to find it. If you're committed to overcoming your personal issues, you'll discover that it's impossible to fail. Also, understand that doing nothing is still doing something. The universe will respond to your efforts, one way or another. If you want to lose the excuse mentality, start taking some action. This will ignite the process and in time, the right answers will present themselves. Be aware however, that whenever you make any progress in life, this will usually involve an element of risk. If you're afraid to take risks, take a moment to consider the following thoughts:

❖ Security is an illusion. Life is either a daring adventure, or it is nothing at all. *—Helen Keller*

❖ If you put off everything until you're sure of it, you'll get nothing done. *—Norman Vincent Peale*

❖ Never let the fear of striking out get in your way. *—Babe Ruth*

"So then, each of us will give an account of himself to God."[14]

Find Your Moment of Truth

Part of accepting responsibility for your life means making peace with your past. You can't move forward and develop a new healthy lifestyle, if you're stuck in a rut with old behavior patterns. If your life isn't going well, then you need to recognize how you may be contributing to this discontent. Be open to that moment of truth—it can come at any time. It might happen as you look at a picture of yourself at a party or on the beach. Many of my clients tell me that's exactly what prompted them toward change; they actually saw how overweight they were in a picture and became mortified by the way they looked. A moment of truth can happen within any area of your life. It could be a dead-end job that you've outgrown or a relationship that needs to end. After you experienced enough backlashes, you get to the point where you say, "Enough is enough." A change must be made—this is your "Aha" moment of truth!

David, a fireman, certainly experienced his moment of truth. Growing up, his parents were overweight and out of shape; they never modeled healthy behaviors. David followed suit; he was overweight from the time he was thirteen. As an adult, he was verbally harassed by coworkers—at five foot nine, he weighed in at 270 pounds. His moment of truth came when his dad suffered a quadruple bypass. David knew that he had to take responsibility for changing his life; otherwise, he would end up just like Dad. He started going to the gym regularly and within three months lost thirty pounds. Then he got in a motorcycle accident and was back on the couch for several months; he regained fifteen pounds. While going through physical therapy and healing, he decided to learn everything he could about nutrition. Finally, he was able to exercise again, and the remaining weight came off in increments of ten pounds every month.

One year later, he weighs 170. He's completely chiseled—in his best shape ever! Nobody harasses him now. Though he works as a fire fighter, he's also become an expert on nutrition. Today David is inspiring and helping many people to lose weight and get healthy. This is only possible because David learned how to take responsibility for his life and health.

Finding your moment of truth can be very painful, but it does set off a positive chain reaction. Your life will get better. Arriving at this moment means you've acknowledged the truth about your situation and you're ready to make a positive change in your life. People often initiate personal change only when the pain of remaining the same exceeds the pain of change. Discomfort creates transformation. During initial consultations, a few potential clients end up in tears. Being overweight and unhealthy can be a bittersweet experience. These individuals are grieved by their own self-neglect, yet at the same time, they're extraordinarily grateful to be guided on the right path. Their moment of truth is setting them free.

Nathaniel Branden, PhD, has said, "Opponents of accountability, professing to be humanitarians, often insist that people are sometimes hit by adversities beyond their control. True enough. But when people are down, they are better helped when they are awakened to the resources they do possess than when they are told they have none. The later approach often masks condescension and contempt as compassion, whether practiced by a university professor, parent, spouse, legislator, or social activist. It is far easier to proclaim a concern for others than to think through what is most likely to be productive."[5]

As you make transitions in your life journey, you'll observe people's true colors. Be on guard. If you have faith in God, particularly as a Christian, the enemy of your soul (the devil) wants you to lose hope. He will attempt to shake your faith by using transition periods and every difficult opportunity to pit people against you. For this reason, transition can be progressive and exciting, but it also carries an element of uncertainty and pain. This is where you must stand strong to battle those personal demons; they're looking to penetrate your weak spots.

Often it's an emotional challenge that causes people to shy away from change. Many individuals prefer to take shelter with a box of cookies rather than to face reality. Yet change in life is inevitable; it's really the only true constant. Everything or everyone we may have relied upon can disappear in the blink of an eye. Relationship transitions can pierce the very fiber of our emotional being. Marriages fall apart, people walk away or pass away, and circumstances change. We can't cling to any situation, however good we perceive it to be. In those moments of our human weakness, however, we can pray in faith. God is great—he can help us overcome fears and carry us through a smooth transition. Inspirational author Alan Cohen has noted, "It takes a lot of courage to release the familiar and seemingly secure to embrace the new. But there is no real security in what is no longer meaningful. There is more security in the adventurous and exciting, for in movement there is life, and in change there is power."[6]

Learn to Gain Self-Control

You know there are different parts of your life for which you need to take responsibility, health being one of them. But just because you have a responsibility, that doesn't mean you're a responsible person. For instance, you may have the responsibility of paying bills, but that doesn't necessarily mean you'll be responsible enough to pay them on time. You might have a job but fail to show up when you're supposed to. You may be a parent but still behave like a child. The question is this: will you be responsible with your responsibilities?

"Take my yoke upon you and learn from me, for I am gentle and humble in heart, and you will find rest for your souls. For my yoke is easy and my burden is light."[7]

Before becoming self-responsible, perhaps you need to gain some control of your life. How do you gain control? Gaining control starts *after* you've learned to make wise decisions that bring more balance into your life. This means discovering what's really important and letting go of what's not in your power. Ultimately, it's your decisions that will reflect how well you manage your lifestyle. As part of lifestyle management, when you think proactively, you can make decisions based upon your values and priorities. Taking responsibility means doing what's in your power to follow through on those decisions. God wants you to be at peace; he doesn't want you stressed out constantly. Are you conditioned to believe that you must accept every request that comes your way? Some obligations that we take on are real; they belong to us. False obligations don't belong to us, but somehow we inherit them. As you begin to restructure your life, you must learn to discern which voices are real and which are false.

False Voices	**Real Voices**
How dare you! You have to	It's my decision
Nobody else will do it	Other's are ready and willing to help
It won't get done right	It can be delegated
It's your obligation	It's my choice
There's no time to exercise	I make time to exercise
You can't be that selfish	Taking care of my health isn't selfish

Remember, who's in charge of your life? *You*! You create more peace and harmony in the world by behaving in ways that promote your well-being. Your happiness will have a positive effect on everyone around you. Never forget that being healthy is in your best interest! Don't get caught up in the false obligation trap. Sure, you may have responsibilities and commitments, but you deserve time for yourself too. Taking care of yourself doesn't mean you're being selfish. It means you're being wise—a wise investor of your time. Some people may lay guilt trips on you to get what they want, but your willingness to give should come from your heart. You can't fool or manipulate the higher powers into your faulty thinking or false obligation trap. God sees your heart.

When we invest in this sacred time for ourselves, we're automatically walking in the path of wisdom. Life is too short to be careless with our time. If we don't consider what's in our best interest, then we're not respecting what God entrusted to us. He gave us the responsibility to take care of ourselves. When we follow through and do what's best for us, this helps everyone. We become happier, and the world is better off when we are happy. It's a win across the board!

"For the word of God is living and active. Sharper than any double-edged sword, it penetrates even to dividing soul and spirit, joints and marrow; it judges the thoughts and attitudes of the heart. Nothing in all creation is hidden from God's sight. Everything is uncovered and laid bare before the eyes of him to whom we must give account."[8]

. . . .

"For if the willingness is there, the gift is acceptable according to what one has, not according to what he does not have."[9]

. . . .

Sometimes we need to take rests from our responsibilities and do this without guilt or condemnation. Jesus made time to break away from the masses and pray to the Father. If we overburden ourselves with too many responsibilities or false obligations, we will jeopardize our well-being and compromise the quality of our life. When our responsibilities don't follow a natural sense of order, it creates an imbalance that will wreak havoc somewhere else in our life.

We are not God. We each have a place to make our mark, but we also have needs and limits that need to be honored. When we make wise decisions that bring about a greater sense of balance to our life, this puts other areas in check. Otherwise, we become internally imbalanced or off-center, and this is what seems to spin our life out of control. We will discuss the PHS principle of regaining balance later, but for now recognize that on some level, we long to reconcile these imbalances. The problem is we haven't learned to do this in a constructive way. Instead, we often become self-destructive by turning to food or alcohol. Yet these imbalances still need our attention, they represent—our blind spots, weaknesses, limitations, and compensations. Consequently, a bigger challenge is created when people try to balance their lifestyle without first reconciling some of these imbalances. It throws them off tangent and nothing gets done.

To draw an analogy, let's say you have two hundred pieces of a jigsaw puzzle, and these represent two hundred parts of your life. Twenty of those pieces represent different parts of your health, but they're all jagged or torn. If you don't try to get those twenty pieces back to their original shape, it's going to be a lot harder to get that "health portion" and the rest of the whole puzzle back together. For instance, let's assume that one of those twenty pieces represents your cardiovascular endurance. Your personal trainer put you through a VO_2max test to determine how efficiently your body can use oxygen. He told you that this number is dangerously low—this doesn't surprise you because you're a chain smoker. In order to improve your VO_2max and refurbish that piece of the puzzle, you must quit chain smoking. By correcting the imbalance of smoking first, you can rebuild your cardiovascular endurance.

We're each meant to live a balanced and wholesome life. However, just like a damaged puzzle; most people don't know how to put the pieces of their life and health back together. We may be missing pieces or working with many broken and disheveled ones. We're each a complex network—an interconnection of mind, body, and spirit. To take responsibility and gain control of our life, we may have to work on correcting some imbalances first. But we don't always know what we need. This is why having a higher source of power on our side can help. By seeking God, we can gain the insight and wisdom necessary to reconcile these potential imbalances. Some people have endured so much pain and hardship that they just assume that's the way life should be. But God is interested in every aspect of your life and wants to use all your experiences, both good and bad, for your benefit.

When something creates a huge imbalance in your life, God's desire is to restore you—to bring you back to your original balanced state. He knows what areas of your life needs the most healing and reconciliation. Untrue thoughts can create strongholds—these are delusions that throw us off balance, grip us psychologically and make us lose our sense of self-responsibility. We need a force that's greater than ourselves to help us break these strongholds. When we accept a higher source of power and seek his direction for our life, we will grow in discernment. By drawing upon divine spiritual truths, we are better able to access the light of strength and wisdom. This helps us to find our center and gain control of our behaviors.

Another way to get some control in your life is to experience the therapeutic power of rest. When you step back and quit trying to do everything in your own strength, you'll get a better grip on life. Most life coaches and spiritual leaders will tell you the same thing; sometimes less is more. Answers to life's perplexing questions often come to us when we're relaxed, not when those problems are on the forefront of our mind. We all go through cycles in life, but we must stay open to intervals of rest. It could be a season, several days off, a couple hours, or even just a few minutes. Resting properly is vital to our long-term health. It's part of the life-cycle. Breathing deeply reconnects us to our center. No matter how busy and hectic our lives may get, if we take approximately ten minutes a day to de-stress, we're investing in our long-term health. As we make time daily to pray, meditate, and breathe deeply, we reclaim control of our lives.

Taking responsibility for our life is a wonderful privilege. It's the foundation we must stand upon to empower us and propel us forward. Nobody could ever be happy or experience a sense of fulfillment without self-responsibility. Our life serves a purpose other than just to exist and take up space on this planet. Yes, we can find joy in just being, but when we cease being responsible, our life will lose meaning. We can only become healthy and fulfill our calling in life if we take responsibility for it.

"She watches over the affairs of her household and does not eat the bread of idleness."[10]

CHAPTER 7

Healthy Self-Management—
PHS Principle: Develop Emotional Intelligence

This PHS principle encompasses a broad spectrum of feelings, behavior patterns, and issues that need your work and attention. For a great majority, this is where most of the psychological baggage resides. In order to develop emotional intelligence, you must be able to make some important connections toward optimal health. Fortunately, since optimal health is a balanced integration of the mind, body, spirit, and emotions, it's fairly easy to make a connection that's aligned to your emotional state. For instance, if you think negative thoughts, this makes you feel depressed—that's a connection, *mind to emotion*. If you nurture your spirit, you'll feel more at peace—that's a connection, *spirit to emotion*. If you're feeling depressed, this affects your chakras and depletes the energy in your spirit—that's a connection, *emotion to spirit*. What if every time you're upset, stressed, sad, lonely, or bored, you turn to food for solace? Emotional eating will affect your physical body—that's another connection, *emotion to body*. There's no doubt that people use food as a drug instead of dealing constructively with their emotions—roughly six million adults are at least one hundred pounds overweight.[1] It should be clear that your psychological condition is aligned with your physical body—everything is connected.

As you connect the dots toward optimal health, you'll recognize that not only does your mind-set affect how you feel, but your emotions can influence your thoughts and decisions. We've all regretted having said or done something rash, in the heat of the moment. Let's face it, when we're in the middle of a heated argument, it's harder to think clearly and control our emotions. With our mind racing, sometimes we might fly off the handle and make matters worse. For instance, I once heard a story of how whenever a wife was angry with her husband, she would throw things at him. The last straw in their marriage was when she threw a toaster at him and he ended up with a black eye. Guys in particular, if you're the type that builds up enough aggression, you might offer to just "take it outside."

In those fuming moments, if we were to step back and cool off, we would realize that our mental and emotional state is intertwined; each derives energy from the other. In order to develop emotional intelligence, we can't afford to lose sight of this basic connection; it's this very type of consciousness that allows us to grow in self-discovery. From a psychological standpoint, we need to gain knowledge about our emotions as this relates to the culmination of our well-being. We should also recognize how our emotions affect those around us. Ultimately, our emotions can impact all of humanity. By developing emotional intelligence, we can be the one in charge of our emotions, instead of allowing our emotions to take control over us. This is part of the PHS—we always have within us the freedom and power of choice. Our lifestyle and the way we manage our self is primarily a reflection of the choices we make.

In certain circumstances, feelings can be our best guide. A mother, for instance, intuitively senses when her child is in trouble and follows her instinct to move him out of harm's way. Some people are experts at reading the expressions and moods of others, while others seem oblivious. Emotions can be just a momentary expression—a person cuts us off in traffic, and we slam the horn as we tactlessly vent our frustration. So many people get confused about their feelings, simply, because they're afraid to accept them. For instance, if a person grew up in an austere environment, where little tolerance was permitted for emotional expression, then he or she learned to deny and stuff feelings inside. Society has its role of influence as well. The male gender has been tragically conditioned to believe that feelings are for wimps. In order to be psychologically well, however, we must let go of such inhibitions. To be sure, our emotions should be clarified and dealt with constructively, yet there's not only one way this can be done. Developing emotional intelligence allows us to get beyond the obvious. Whether we need to deal with a current emotional issue or confront past emotions, there are plenty of ways to start applying this principle.

First of all, if you have strong faith in God, he can help you process and release painful emotions that you've been afraid to face. A divine characteristic of God is that he's always available—you don't need to book an appointment in advance! You can turn to him whenever you need guidance, healing, or help in any way. God is full of compassion and understands each and every painful situation that we've endured emotionally. He's knows exactly where to right the wrongs we experienced in life, and he's keeping the scoreboard upstairs. Don't underestimate the capability and power that *he alone* has to heal and restore you. God's desire is to make you psychologically sound; and with him, miracles are possible—nothing is too difficult. If you've never sought the assistance of a higher power, that doesn't mean you can't do it now. Keep your options open.

"With man this is impossible, but with God all things are possible."[2]

We each have different temperaments, and there are many avenues to express emotions, but consider what works best for you. For instance, a creative person might write a poem or song, turning deep emotional anguish into something truly exquisite. Someone who's introverted might initially be more comfortable venting thoughts and feelings in a journal, while an extrovert prefers talking to get things off his chest. It might be necessary for you to take an anger management class, meet with a professional therapist, or join a 12-step support group. Other times, getting quiet and reflective or reading a self-help book will provide some answers. Maybe you need to release some pent-up physical aggression through a good workout. Or perhaps you need to spend time alone in prayer or meditation.

Also, whenever possible, be sure to make amends with anyone you need to forgive—and this may include yourself. If you're angry with God, then you need to forgive him as well. Research has proven there are remarkable health benefits to forgiveness. It makes you less depressed, increases your energy, and reduces stress. Some people have experienced miraculous healing of physical symptoms through the process of forgiveness. It appears that ailments such as cancer and arthritis are directly related to accumulated anger and resentment.[3] As you forgive others by releasing long-standing burdens of resentment, you'll experience relief in some capacity, be it psychological, physical, or spiritual. Keep in mind that whenever you forgive someone, it's not necessary to speak directly to this person or have a one-on-one meeting. He or she does not need to be present, whatsoever. You can close your eyes and have a little conversation with him or her to dissolve and release constricted energy, or you can write a letter. Again, you don't have to give the letter; remember this is for your benefit. Forgiveness should come from your heart, so no matter which way you decide to do it; you'll reclaim your power. Forgiving someone is a gift you give to yourself; it frees you from bondage. Deep down, you can decide what's right for you.

Bringing about emotional cleansing and renewal requires your conscious effort. For example, if you were so traumatized from something in your past that you buried your feelings and lost touch with part of yourself emotionally, then you need to be willing to tap into and release those emotions. Many emotional issues stem from past wounds that occurred in childhood, so reconnecting with your inner child becomes more than a psychological cliché. The purpose here isn't to rehash old wounds or have a pity party; on the contrary, it's to become aware and let go of whatever emotional chains might be keeping you immobilized in the past. Emotionally, you need to get over it. This isn't to minimize the pain you endured; it's to enable you to experience freedom from any leftover emotional baggage—to help you heal and leave the past behind.

If there's something irking you from the past, be willing to confront that situation; don't gloss it over. The past shouldn't restrict you in any way. You can reclaim your power by cleaning the skeletons from your closet, but you must be willing to face and battle those demons head on. Seek your higher source of power to help, work with a professional therapist, or do both—the choice is yours. How long this transformation will take depends upon your personal situation. It could take several months or several years. The main objective is to rid your inner-self of trapped toxic emotions. Getting those old feelings to the surface and cleansing yourself from their contamination will improve your entire well-being. Healing will follow.

Emotional stress, anxiety, unresolved anger, bitterness, and depression are comparable risk factors to your physical health, as is high cholesterol and high blood pressure. They can definitely wreak havoc on your life, relationships, and health. Depression is a major cause for weight gain, and it has been known to cause fibromyalgia and chronic fatigue. Recent research has determined that severe emotional stress can cause "stress cardiomyopathy," a condition also known as broken-heart syndrome.[4] Don't underestimate how closely your emotions are connected to your physical body. A new concept of cellular memory indicates that destructive energy patterns are stored in your cells. Chakras, which are energy pathways, are each mapped to different parts of your body and reflect whatever you hold in your consciousness. When you release toxic emotions, the chakras will open up naturally, which removes blocked energy and brings healing to different parts of your physical body. Afterward, you'll feel lighter. Your clarity and life force will return, and your physical energy will expand. Mentally, it will clear your head. Emotionally, you'll feel more at peace. Remember, everything's connected.

Understanding Emotions: Basic Psychological Education

When it comes to emotions, the field of psychology is a profound and comprehensive subject. For now however, let's skip the elaborate psycho-babble and focus on the basics. Emotions are something we all have; they provide meaning, guidance, and enrichment to our everyday lives. Without them, we wouldn't be able to find passion in our work or develop a meaningful relationship. With no emotional desire or attachment, we couldn't keep our families together, maintain friendships, or gain any pleasure from our social networks and service to others—life would be a complete sham or utter monotony. It's through our feelings that we can relate and bond with others, pursue our life passions, and experience intimate growth in our relationships. Emotions allow us to feel our life experiences.

Some people are naturally in tune with their emotions, some are out of touch, and some are completely out of control. Simply put, this means that to varying degrees, we can be *conscious* or *unconscious* of certain feelings. If we suppress our emotions, that doesn't mean they don't exist—feelings can still drive our behaviors, whether we're conscious of them or not. Emotions by themselves are not the problem; rather, it's our inability to deal with them constructively that causes problems. Stuffing them away doesn't help in the long run, nor does projecting or inflicting them onto others in senseless and destructive ways. Numbing them out through addictions such as overeating, excessive alcohol, or drugs doesn't help either. Emotions need to be acknowledged and channeled constructively. This requires *emotional intelligence*.

Emotions that are buried deep in the subconscious are still a driving force in your life, because they'll find a way to manifest somehow. When you continually deny the depth of your emotional pain, you will jeopardize your psychological well-being in some capacity. For example, if you don't flinch after you commit a senseless crime that should be a red flag—something isn't right with you emotionally. By the same token, if you don't deal constructively with emotions such as anger, that's certainly not healthy either. Neglected emotions have a way of dominating your subconscious mind, and that can spell danger. Suddenly, on impulse, a person snaps. A person who murders with no apparent motive or indication is labeled "emotionally disturbed." It's an understatement to say that people can get dangerous when they give their power away to their emotions. Our jail cells are filled with criminals for this very reason. We must recognize, however, that evil can only prevail when the opportunity presents itself. Cops fight the bad guys for a reason. They're fighting out of a reaction to right a wrong and to gain justice from an unjust situation. We can also wage war against evil by being *proactive* rather than *reactive*.

If we're ever going to become a society of healthy self-managers, we need to teach and gain some emotional intelligence. We can acquire this skill by learning to process emotions in an intelligent way, whether these emotions pertain to our self or to others. Though this sounds simple in theory, it can make a world of difference. In today's society, little emphasis has been placed on individuals who exhibit unstable emotional tendencies. This is often contemplated in hindsight, after some unfortunate circumstance occurs. Perpetual increases in technology have led to limited cognitive and social behaviors. Common sense and good judgment gets lost in a complex world.

The importance of providing a new psychological infrastructure that promotes emotional intelligence can't be overstated. What appears to be a psychological paradox or a moral dilemma stems from great uncertainty.

However, by being *proactive* rather than *reactive,* we can prevent many perils that stem from this emotional instability. A *proactive* person who's highly emotionally intelligent won't argue with an insane man, but a *reactive* person who lacks emotional intelligence will go to war. From this vantage point, societies today need greater psychological education, leadership, and accountability in this arena. There are no guarantees that people anywhere develop any sort of emotional intelligence. While a parent's heart may be in the right place, having this good intention alone just doesn't cut it. We've only relied upon indirect measures and clearly, this hasn't worked.

Our education system can quickly determine if someone has a high intelligence-quotient or excels academically, yet it fails to recognize whether this same person is severely psychologically disturbed. There's no educational standard to teach or measure emotional intelligence. By the time children become teenagers, the social pressure of being cool takes precedence over good judgment, and many pay the price for it dearly. Although a few parents do an excellent job of teaching emotional intelligence, this is far from the norm. The majority of parents are faced with time constraints; and some aren't emotionally equipped to help their children at this deeper psychological level. Consequently, emotional development gets neglected, and society pays the price, not only through the increasing obesity rates and staggering health care costs but through many senseless crimes.

The civilization of psychological health has not rightfully evolved. In fact, it has taken a turn for the worse. This subject of emotional intelligence has slipped through the cracks of the entire education system, and to complicate matters, many children are hindered farther due to their upbringing or environment. Some children are naturally endowed with a high degree of emotional intelligence, yet because of severe psychological abuse, they learn to manipulate, hurt, lie, and frighten others instead. When youngsters grow up so emotionally hurt and starved, they create destructive survival mechanisms. Without any sort of guidance or support, they go on to repeat the cycle.

Study: **Youth Now Have More Mental Health Issues**
Published Jan. 10, 2010—By Martha Irvine—AP National Writer

CHICAGO — A new study has found that five times as many high school and college students are dealing with anxiety and other mental health issues than youth of the same age who were studied in the Great Depression era.

The findings, culled from responses to a popular psychological questionnaire used as far back as 1938, confirm what counselors on campuses nationwide have long suspected as more students struggle with the stresses of school and life in general.

"It's another piece of the puzzle—that yes, this does seem to be a problem, that there are more young people who report anxiety and depression," says Jean Twenge, a San Diego State University psychology professor and the study's lead author. "The next question is: what do we do about it?"

Jean Twenge has posed a great question, what do we do about this significant decline of mental and emotional health? No corroborated resolution has emerged into the consciousness of the mainstream to alleviate this psychological burden. It appears that the solution itself is complex and multifaceted. Nonetheless, the logical place to start promoting psychological health is within the public health education system, particularly, by emphasizing this development of emotional intelligence. Fundamentally, the development of one's psychological well-being is an extension of his or her health at large—it's part of optimal health. Once individuals broaden their horizon and expand their knowledge base of what being healthy truly means, then standard health education can begin to evolve respectably. Until this happens, it should come as no surprise that society's psychological and physical health, has hit rock bottom.

As mentioned earlier, men, in particular, suffer regrettably, because they're often encouraged to hide their feelings under a tough, "macho man" exterior. Emotionally, their issues never get dealt with, communication fails, and this results in a tremendous disadvantage to all of society. We must get clear about this matter. Contrary to conventional opinion, feelings are *not* reserved for women. The ability to process our emotions intelligently is a crucial part of psychological health—surely it is not gender-based. We simply can't make progress in developing healthy behaviors if we continue to ignore our emotional well-being. This makes reform in health education all the more crucial; the physical and psychological dimensions of health need equal honor. An evolved civilization should know the difference between being human and being humane.

This tragic lack of emotional intelligence has only fed the health care crisis. We have focused on the detrimental effects of obesity, but failed to address the underlying causes. This of course, has solved nothing. Our emotional well-being is psychological in nature, but it is integral and critical to health! It should not be limited to the offices of clinical psychologists or therapists. Teachers of physical and health education, along with a variety of psychology experts, should begin to collaborate. As partners, their pursuit should be to establish a fundamental protocol to educate people how to develop emotional intelligence. Emphasis should be placed on the outcomes rendered with certain emotions, choices and behaviors. In short, we must teach the value of processing emotions intelligently and that harmful consequences may result from doing otherwise. While we can't resolve deep-rooted psychological issues with a one-shoe-fits-all approach, we can at least, begin to steer people in the right direction. This is an innovative path that needs to be paved with much attention to detail, but it can be straightforward enough to bring people back to their senses.

It's unfortunate that emotional intelligence has been lost. Our children deserve so much more. They should be educated sooner, before they have to pay for the consequences of destructive behaviors. They should have swift access to psychological resources whenever needed. Measures and programs can be instituted to help them individually, along with their families—it's simply a matter of offering and promoting better-quality education, even as we respect the boundaries and rights of families, environments, and cultures. We've reached a critical turning point where it has become necessary to teach emotional intelligence within the school system. In fact, the entire educational path needs to be revamped to promote greater psychological development. We need new measures and higher standards with strict accountability. The time is short, and we must act fast—society's health, both psychologically and physically, has been on the decline. Countless people are in dire need for this type of education. The root cause of obesity and many senseless crimes are psychological in nature—much stems from sheer emotional ignorance and instability, yet this is a preventable epidemic.

Installing a new psychological groundwork throughout the public education system would not only promote emotional intelligence at the local level, it will help bolster the well-being of entire communities. Even small modifications that significantly touch and influence lives will yield results on a larger scale. If one small community concurs with a revised educational standard of emotional intelligence, this can spearhead and facilitate a tremendous shift in psychological wellness. All of this is at the crux of healthy self-management. Building upon this human privilege, individually and collectively, will provide a meaningful resource to many health issues. It will make a dent in true health care reform. This fundamental movement begins within the public school system, but at the same time, we must not neglect the psychological well-being of adults, particularly parents.

Today's busy parents need as much psychological support as they can get. There are ways to provide this support at different levels through local and standardized forums. These can be backed by professional and certified counselors, psychologists, and different types of health advocates. Psychological screening could be offered, and worthwhile incentives could motivate many. Emotional intelligence and wellness could curb acts of senselessness against oneself or others. Lives can change for the better, simply by placing a greater emphasis on this important, yet overlooked dimension of our health. If knowledge is power, then preventing ignorance can thwart many transgressions. By teaching this development of emotional intelligence, societies worldwide can begin to evolve.

To facilitate this process, ask yourself a few questions: Are you open to improving your psychological health? Are you a healthy self-manager of your emotions, or are emotions ruling your life? Do you pay attention—are you even aware of your emotions? There are hundreds of emotions, along with their blends and variations—more subtleties than we have words to describe. What are we supposed to do with them? We need to learn not only how to identify them, but more significantly, how to process them intelligently, and the sooner we do, the better off we will be.

"See to it that no one misses the grace of God and that no bitter root grows up to cause trouble and defile many."[5]

Deal with Emotional Blocks and Issues

Because our emotions are a critical part of our psychological well-being, they need to be recognized and expressed in a healthy way. Emotional blocks are created when we deny our emotions and fail to process them constructively. Deep unresolved emotional issues can be the wedge between our mental well-being and physical health. Let's consider how this might occur. In order to become psychologically well and take care of ourselves, we need to be self-aware. However, if we're not living consciously, then we're already limited in our ability to nurture ourselves. In some capacity, we're emotionally out of touch—unaware of our real needs, fears, strengths, and weaknesses. If we can't make sense out of our world, then we certainly won't know the optimum path to nurture ourselves. From a psychological perspective, this inability may stem from several origins; oppression, depression, trauma, or years of accumulated mental distress and self-neglect.

Irrespective of the cause, the result is the same—our developmental process has been interrupted and in some capacity, we've become alienated from a part of ourselves. Alienation causes fear, which creates walls of self-doubt. This type of self-doubt causes us to live in an uncertain world. We sense something isn't right, but the self-doubt consumes our mind. When we're afraid of the unknown, we may make decisions that go against our better judgment. On some level, we become immobilized. If we're not even aware of our fears, we'll certainly be incapable of facing up to them. This puts us at a greater psychological disadvantage, because a vicious cycle follows, wherein we experience more alienation or disorientation toward ourselves, life, and people.

Facing our fears would definitely be the healthiest thing to do, but instead, we get lost in our own disoriented world. This is the point where many resort to unhealthy or addictive coping mechanisms; they'll turn to whatever is available in hopes of temporarily numbing out the emotional pain. Most people think they can escape from their emotional turmoil through overeating, overdrinking, overworking, smoking, overspending, gambling, or some other addiction. Even though they understand it's unhealthy, they simply find it hard to stop the vicious cycle. Nobody is immune. Emotional anxiety and the addictions that follow affect every social class and walk of life. Prescription drugs and antidepressants don't stop compulsive behaviors. In fact, in some cases, they exacerbate them. Consequently, the psychological health of society continues to suffer immensely as a result of this widespread neglect. It's quite a tragedy. We must start developing emotional intelligence in order to bridge this gap between psychological and physical health.

As an individual, where should you start? Make a commitment to believe in yourself, first and foremost. If you've been consumed with self-doubt for many years, however, then the tendency to trust others may seem more appealing. While it's true we all rely upon one another, we all came into this world alone, and we're going out alone as well. It's important that you learn to trust yourself and become willing to face your own demons and fears. Perhaps you have some very deep-seated, frightening, or ugly emotional issues that you would rather not, face alone. If you sincerely think you need professional help, then by all means get it, but the more work you're willing to do on your own, the more empowered you'll be. This requires courage, honesty, and a lot of soul-searching. Look inward, and seek your higher source of power for help. Sometimes facing your fears *alone* is exactly what you need to do to get over them. Doing so not only improves your psychological health, but it will also improve the quality of your relationships. When you become more self-reliant, then you won't be imposing unrealistic expectations on others and depending on someone else to prop you up. Your emotions need a healthy outlet, to be sure, but the avenue you choose for expression is still up to you.

You're a work in progress, so be patient. Begin to trust yourself and believe that everything will be okay. If you need to rant or punch your pillow, then do it. If you need to take your aggression out physically, go workout—any form of cardio or strength-training exercise will help. If you need a good cry, don't hold back the tears. Maybe you want to talk to a friend or join a support group in a local church. Perhaps you need something more calming; such as time alone in peace and quiet, or prayer. Your emotional issues are your own, and you can begin to find *constructive* ways to deal with them. The operative word here is *constructive*, not *destructive*. Don't do anything that would harm yourself or others. Keep junk food out of sight and don't eat when emotions are running high.

You can start taking responsibility for own psychological well-being. Begin with your own reality—that is, what you experience and what's true for you is not necessarily true for everyone else. As you develop emotional intelligence, you'll discover for yourself what's real, what's right, and what's wrong with that version of reality. It's your prerogative to keep your issues separate from another person's reality. Certainly, a psychologist can help you along this path, but remember, you're on the second rung of the PHS Pyramid—Healthy Self-Management—you should be building upon this principle of self-responsibility. When you accept responsibility and operate from the awareness that everyone has his and her own version of reality, then everything and everyone in your life will become more tolerable. You'll begin to see things in a different light—a much more grounded perspective.

Human beings are interdependent; we depend upon one another for different reasons. However, if you're ever going to be proactive with your health; then you need to gain some autonomy. Nobody can do that for you. This concept itself lies at the heart of the PHS; it means learning how to stand on your own, without constant input or feedback. As you gain your own emotional bearings, you'll come to realize that it's not necessary to get a consensus from the boardroom to make an executive decision about your life. Since healthy self-management is built upon lifestyle management, you're the one responsible for your decisions and behaviors. In a review of a social cognitive theory model regarding behavior modification, *self-efficacy* is believed to be the single most important characteristic that determines a person's behavior change.[6] It's only reasonable that behavior modification requires us to become self-effective. By gaining emotional intelligence, you won't need to turn to food, drugs, alcohol, dysfunctional relationships, or violence as a crutch to support your reality. You'll be able to stand in your own power and truth—with your own energy, love, and motivation.

Here's the Truth:

- **You can be a lot more than you think.**
- **You can do a lot more than you think.**
- **You're a much greater person than you think.**

It's rare to hear the truth because the world is filled with plenty of people who support no agenda but their own. However, in spite of your shortcomings, psychological hang-ups, faults, weakness, and quirks—you are unique and that alone, makes you awesome. This isn't about becoming delusional; it's about you learning to evolve toward self-autonomy. You should understand that all the mistakes, hardships and relationships you experienced in life happened for a reason. There were no coincidences. You were born with a purpose that's different from everyone else. Therefore, you're going to have a different set of experiences. Those experiences can teach you a lot about yourself, so learn to make the most out of them.

Everything in your life is unfolding exactly the way it should, even if you don't understand everything right now. Answers will come in time. Also, keep in mind that there will always be things in life that make no sense to you whatsoever. That's okay—nobody on this earth has all the answers. You can only be responsible to understand your relationship to life, no more or less. If you have kids, it may be your responsibility to teach them, but eventually, they'll have to face their own reality.

Don't get sidetracked—be on guard to keep your focus. This is the primary human challenge. At any step along the way, as you evolve toward autonomy, the process can be interrupted, frustrated, blocked, or diverted. If this happens, part of you will be fragmented, split, alienated, or stuck on a certain level of emotional or mental immaturity. To a tragic extent, most people have already been stranded along this path of self-development. Yet transition is still possible. If a healthy transformation is what we desire, we must accept our personal responsibility in the matter. Whoever accepts the responsibility of thinking, whoever chooses to operate consciously, creates a better world for everyone with whom he or she interacts. The mind is the basic tool of survival for the human species. "That being the case, nothing is more essential for our self-esteem and successful adaptation to reality than valuing sight over blindness and consciousness over unconsciousness."[7]

When you develop emotional intelligence, you take responsibility for those psychological hang-ups you created. For example, one of my clients said, "I know I'm an emotional eater. I eat when I'm bored, and I like to drink when I'm bored too." Even though what she's doing is not good, she's taking responsibility for her behavior—by *owning* her emotional issue. Nothing is more common in moments of acting irrationally than to blank out our awareness. That's why people love to get drunk. They want to escape from taking responsibility for their consciousness, yet they still made a conscious choice to drink. Ironically, their diversion from reality isn't going to help them when they drive drunk and get pulled over. It's one thing to numb out the emotional issue at hand; it's quite another to be aware. When you're not dissociated from your behavior, you can get to the root of your emotional problems. This anchors you in reality and helps you to function more wisely. Review the following list of common emotional issues. If these are left unresolved, they often lead into several common problems.

Common Emotional Issues

- Boredom
- Low self-esteem
- Anxiety-stricken
- Heartbroken
- Lonely
- Alienated
- Fear of failure
- Fear of success
- Depressed or oppressed
- Hopeless
- Insecure

Common Problems

- Addictions: overeating, heavy drinking, smoking, illegal drugs
- Obsessive/Compulsive behaviors: gambling, overspending, overworking
- Troubled or dysfunctional relationships
- Rebellious, delusional, paranoid, prone to acts of violence, trouble with the law
- Anxiety and panic attacks
- Loner—alienated from friends, family and social networks
- Lethargic (chronically fatigued)
- Aimless (lacks direction or goals in life)

The more unresolved emotional issues people have; the more withdrawn and disturbed they'll become. The more disturbed they become; the more destruction they can cause to themselves or within society—it's a vicious cycle. Destructive or cruel people are simply lashing out with the tools they have. Their own issues have become their tools to hurt others in words or actions. When someone has psychological issues that have not been resolved, he begins to feel bad about himself and the tendency to lash out at others increases. By contrast, if someone is emotionally stable, he may be upset over a situation, but he does not need to harass or harm others. Also in some social ranks, individuals are suffering from an unfortunate misconception. They experience enormous pressure to maintain high-society's ideals, but deep down, they're anxiety-stricken. They may not necessarily hurt other people, but they hurt themselves through self-destructive behaviors. There are numerous reasons why we must learn to deal with our emotions more intelligently.

The reality is that we all need support in life when everything is *not so perfect*. If we accept this notion, and use common sense to offer kindness and help to others, then society at large will make strides in developing emotional intelligence. When one person does something kind for another and nobody else is watching, this reflects emotional intelligence because it's not ego-based. Common everyday people can do a tremendous amount of good by offering a few words of encouragement, a complement or affirmation, a nice gesture, a listening ear, or a few minutes of time. Even offering a friendly smile can prevent someone from the hopelessness of suicide. The world today is in desperate need for healthy, emotionally intelligent people. Never take anyone for granted who has served you in the shadows of life.

Conquering Depression

Depression—it's an assignment from the devil. In this life, there are good spirits and evil spirits. These can either help us or hinder us. Therein exists the spiritual world—angels, demons, blessings, and curses. Learn to recognize the difference between these powers and ultimately who governs them—God or the devil. You have a choice.

"This day I call heaven and earth as witnesses against you that I have set before you life and death, blessings and curses. Now choose life, so that you and your children may live and that you may love the Lord your God, listen to his voice and hold fast to him"[8]

If there's an area of your life where you think there's no possible solution, seek God. Don't entertain depressing thoughts. If you think there's no way out, then understand that's a deaf and dumb spiritual force trying to attack you and destroy your hope. Those spiritual forces wreak havoc on your emotions. The devil is the mastermind of driving people into hopelessness. His intention is to "depress" you. If he can take away your hope and joy, he can do a lot more damage when you're depressed. Happy people aren't the one's committing suicide. Conquering depression is like passing a class. Think of the class as an assignment from the devil to test your character. But if God didn't think you could pass the class, then he wouldn't allow you to take it.

In the Bible, Job was given a test. Satan told God that the only reason Job was blameless and upright was because God blessed the work of his hands and put a hedge of protection around him, his household, and everything he owned. Satan said if you take away everything he has, then surely he's going to curse you to your face. *The Lord said to Satan, "Very well, then everything he has is in your hands, but on the man himself do not lay a finger.*"[9]

God allowed Job to be put to the test. Job suffered greatly and struggled with depression. He felt like dying. Remember, positive people aren't always happy, but Job held on to his hope in God. His wife told him to curse God and die, but he rebuked her, "You are talking like a foolish woman. Shall we accept the good God provides and not the bad?"[10] Job was trying to maintain a positive attitude in the midst of depression. Because Job remained faithful, eventually, God restored him and even doubled everything the devil had taken away.

Don't let the enemy try to defeat you with discouraging thoughts. You may be suffering in a certain area of your life, but don't lose hope. Give yourself credit for at least knowing the difference between right and wrong. For example, you know it's wrong to abuse your body with overeating or smoking. In this same respect, thinking negative and destructive thoughts is no different. If it doesn't help you, why do it? Below are a few reasons why you may succumb to discouragement.

- **Everyone else seems to be doing it.** *You think it's "the norm" to think negatively. Likes attracts likes. Learn to limit time with negative people.*

- **Limited skill—it's all you've ever known.** *You developed an ingrained mental pattern of living in despair. This became a way of life, but it's time to move on. Open your mind to gaining new skills. In order to break negative mental patterns, you need to transform your mind-set with new thoughts and positive affirmations. If you can break this one bad habit, you'll be able to conquer many areas of your life.*

- **Payoff—fear versus familiarity.** *You may recognize that change is necessary, but you got comfortable with the pain. The reason you resist change is because you're afraid of the unknown. Be courageous, feel the fear, and move forward anyway.*

Consider Amanda, one of my client's friends who got severely depressed. It was one of the worst days of her life. On October 4, 2011, she was diagnosed with ovarian cancer. A preliminary test had revealed a biopsy of a mass on her pelvic wall, described as the size of a tennis ball. This news was given to her on her daughter's thirty-second birthday. She was furious! What did she do to deserve this? She had performed her due diligence of health checkups. Depression set in as she allowed herself time to grieve. My client wanted to help, so he gave her a copy of the PHS flow chart.

Amanda figured she had nothing to lose, so the next day, she went to work on applying the PHS principles. She took full responsibility for her illness and knew that in her spirit, she was fighting an enemy. Her emotions wanted to pull her down and keep her depressed, but her spirit got in the battle. She even joked that she liked challenges, and this was the Mac Daddy of them all. She was proactive and researched everything she could find on diet and nutrition. She learned that raw green vegetable juices, a vegan diet, and wheatgrass were written up in many cancer journals as miraculous healers. She immediately cut out alcohol, caffeine, soda, dairy, salt, white sugar, and meat from her diet. She started juicing and officially became a vegan. She also started walking every day for thirty to forty-five minutes, regardless of how she felt. She made appointments at cancer treatment centers. She started chemotherapy and enlisted the help of a therapist and Reiki healer to help her work on connecting her body, mind, and spirit. When she was scheduled for surgery two months later, on Dec. 7, 2012, there was no longer a mass the size of tennis ball on her pelvic wall. Only a little was removed from her ovaries. The doctor and anesthesiologist were astonished and were curious as to what she had done.

Amanda could've stayed stuck in her depression. It was a tremendous emotional battle, but her spirit was determined to win. If you don't learn to conquer depression, it will conquer you. You'll have the same old responses to everything and fail to recognize that anything good could result from a tough circumstance. If you're always wired to think the worst, even when positive energy flows to you from other sources, you'll resist it. People talk to you positively, and you think it's just a bunch of hype. Negativity has taken deep root in your psyche, and it will spew out like poison in your interactions. One of my clients likes to call it "stinking thinking."

If you want to pass the "Conquering Depression" class and become a healthy self-manager, then you need to get rid of those stinking thoughts and unproductive behavior patterns. You may have repeated this class over and over, experiencing lots of heartache and pain, followed by more of the same. Basically, you're having a hard time trying to pass the class, because you haven't learned from your mistakes. Life is screaming at you to get your attention, but you developed a knack for repeating the same old emotional issues. To break the pattern, something needs to be changed. Stop reacting in the same way; begin to look for new and different answers. Consider for a moment, that there's a message behind your emotional anguish. When you change your thought patterns, you can elevate this new level of consciousness.

Conquering depression is a belief-based course—it's testing your belief system. Will you step up to the challenge and believe the best, or will you continue to react in the same futile way? The choice is yours. Many people compound their psychological issues because they've failed to conquer depression. A discouraged mind can lead to a twisted one. If the way we think is based on fear, we're already deceived in some capacity. A fear-based mind-set is influenced by lies. In other words, we can deceive ourselves into thinking that good is bad, and bad is good. We must be careful about the thoughts we give credence to and consider what the Bible has to say about lies: "You belong to your father, the devil, and you want to carry out your father's desire. He was a murderer from the beginning, not holding to the truth, for there is no truth in him. When he lies, he speaks his native language, for he is a liar and the father or lies."[11]

This sounds extreme, but if we develop enough fear-based, faulty thought patterns, the results will speak for themselves in devastating ways. Often we just need to change the way we think in order to conquer depression. Everybody will experience high and low points in life— this is a given. So if you prepare to go down in the valleys, as you sometimes will, choose to walk with God instead of the devil. Anticipate problems beforehand. Be proactive regarding the possibility of attending a Conquering Depression class. You may have to be there for a while to learn what is necessary. Gain knowledge from the class, pass it, and move on.

> **"Even though I walk through the valley of the shadow of death, I will fear no evil, for you are with me; your rod and your staff, they comfort me."[12]**

One way to stay depressed is to hold in your anger. There is nothing wrong with being angry. Anger is human; we all have it. However, if it's not identified and released constructively, it becomes a toxic subtle energy. When people deny or repress their anger they could suddenly snap on impulse. When anger hits, it's best to slow down your reaction time and immediately identify the cause. This may be easier said than done, but stop to think about it. There are many reasons for anger; the important thing is to vent your frustrations through a healthy outlet. When you're about to explode, that's probably not the best time to confront the offender. The Bible says, *in your anger do not sin;* this is an emotion we must learn to manage, not deny. Initially, you may need some time alone to rail about the object of your anger. You can do this by yourself, with God, a trusted friend, or a therapist. Then after approximately forty-eight hours; start letting go of your anger. Releasing anger is a process; you can pray to have it removed or vent all your venom in a journal. Learn to breathe your anger out of the emotional energy center and calmly breathe back in.

Aside from anger, depression can have many roots. Some individuals inherited depression genetically. Others experience it when they're lonely and bored or when life doesn't go as planned. Everybody goes through bouts of depression and there's certainly a time to grieve. We shouldn't suppress our painful feelings. There comes a point, however, when it's time to let go and move on. For example, if you're heart-broken over a failed relationship, the tendency to drown in sorrow day after day may be tempting, but good friends won't allow you to mope around for too long. They'll force you to go out, mingle with new people and try to have some fun. Well, that advice shouldn't just apply to getting dumped. Staying busy can become a great remedy to keep depression at bay. When you find your passion in life, this can do wonders to lift your spirit and heal you. It's hard to be depressed when you're doing something you love. Maybe you think you have no interests, but everyone has something that makes his or her eyes light up. We all have special gifts. Try different things in life until you find that special passion. When we pursue something we love, this instantly shifts us to a higher place. It serves as a natural anti-depressant. Also, don't underestimate the power of your social connections. Friends can have a very positive effect upon your mood and well-being, especially those funny ones that always make you laugh.

Life is too short to spend it depressed. We must accept the things in life we can't control. Learn to appreciate everything—even our pain can be a blessing in disguise. For instance, before getting married, I experienced my fair share of boyfriend heart-break. In the midst of all my sorrow, I intuitively tapped into my creativity. Beautiful and amazing songs just poured out of me with hardly any effort on my part, one right after another. If I hadn't been feeling those blues, no symphony or rock-band could've captured the wonder of those lyrics. Everybody can find a productive way to cope with emotional pain. By doing something you love, you'll accomplish more, get healed, and save yourself a lot in antidepressant medication.

The Power of a Positive Attitude

There's tremendous power in a positive attitude. Positive energy has built-in protection against the ravages in the world and those challenges that seem unbearable. One positive attitude leads to another, and this creates more positive energy to spread around. Yes, it's true that sometimes we just need to vent. Remember however, that if you *can* change something in your life, then do it; if you *can't*, then simply accept it. Complaining won't help. Not wasting time over things we can't control will save our energy which can be channeled into something more meaningful.

A positive attitude can be considered a commodity by itself. It's an asset in the balance sheet column of life. The price is intangible, and the reward is beyond measure. When we're positive; we create affirmations of who we are by relinquishing our fears, anger, frustration, insecurities, and resentments. Sometimes we have to deal with these unpleasant feelings, but eventually we can release them. If we continue to harbor these feelings, we become carriers of negative energy. Soon we'll be acting on them or giving off bad vibes.

Losing our positive response to the world and people; means we lose out on many wonderful opportunities in life. For instance, a positive person doesn't typically develop a friendship with someone who's always complaining and miserable. Likes attracts likes. If we are negative, we attract those of the same mind-set—misery loves company. Instead we should accept our life challenges in a positive way. If you encourage yourself daily, this will wage war on negativity. Remember, positive energy has more power in it than negative energy does. Use this power to your advantage.

Here's an example: The Bible tells us in Genesis, that Joseph was sold by his jealous brothers to become a slave in Egypt. Joseph was later unjustly accused of sleeping with his master's wife and put in prison. But Joseph wasn't a complainer; he always put his trust, hope and faith in God. It became clear to the pharaoh that God was with Joseph when he interpreted his dreams. Nobody throughout the land of Egypt could compare to the spirit of discernment and wisdom that was upon Joseph. The pharaoh not only released Joseph from prison, but he put him in charge of his palace, all the people, and the whole land of Egypt. When a famine occurred in the land, his brothers had to submit to him, but they were unaware that it was Joseph. Eventually, the truth came out, and Joseph said to them, "I am your brother Joseph, the one that you sold into Egypt! And now, do not be distressed, and do not be angry with yourselves for selling me here, because it was to save lives that God sent me ahead of you. So then it was not you who sent me here but God."[13]

Joseph maintained a positive attitude. He could have become bitter toward his brothers and jaded about being put in prison when he did nothing wrong. Instead, he didn't waste his time. He made the most out of every situation. He knew his problems happened for a reason, and he put his trust in God. God can do wonders for us when we rely on him.

"For my thoughts are not your thoughts, neither are your ways my ways declares the Lord. As the heavens are higher than the earth, so are my ways higher than your ways and my thoughts than your thoughts."[14]

There are many routes to take in life, so why choose the beaten path that's filled with discouragement and depression? Choose God's highway instead. Know that he'll be with you, even if your car flips over. God calls his angels to watch over you. He gives grace even to people who haven't accepted him as their savior. He watches over all. Think about those times when you sensed the presence of God—an accident was prevented; he saved someone's life that you cherished; you were healed miraculously; that job showed up in the nick of time. These are all moments when God put his hand on your life, whether you acknowledge him for it or not. If you seek God, he'll be there to guide, teach, inspire, and help you. God is all loving, powerful, and merciful. God operates out of justice; he will allow everything to happen to you in proportion to the way you live your life. So keep a positive attitude, and continue to believe in the best.

CHAPTER 8

Healthy Self-Management—
PHS Principle: Regain Balance

The yin and yang principles act on one another, affect one another, and keep one another in place. —Chuang Tzu

Holistic practitioners from different faiths and walks of life reveal they have something in common—all seek a state of balance to achieve optimal health. Chinese medicine illustrates the most important of healing principles; how yin/yang forces must balance to achieve harmony. Muslim doctors have determined, "Health means that the body is in a state of dynamic equilibrium," as Ali ibn Al-Abbas said. Avicenna (ibn-Sina) explained this dynamism of the health balance, saying, "The state of equilibrium which a human being enjoys has a certain range with an upper and lower limit."[1] The Japanese term "Zen" has become very popular, and it's commonly used to describe balance, harmony, relaxation and simplicity.

Holistic health focuses on treating the whole person, by promoting optimum balance to all dimensions of well-being—the mental, emotional, physical, and spiritual. Along these lines, we learned that whenever one of these dimensions is significantly out of balance; it will have an effect on the others. To restore us closer toward optimal health, we need to *regain balance.* This spirit-based principle lies at the heart of the healthy self-management component; it involves reconciling those areas of your inner-self that have become imbalanced. You'll discover that by nurturing your spirit, this will reduce stress and promote your well-being on many levels. Ultimately, it's the power in your spirit that enables you to reach a higher potential, one that brings more fulfillment and balance to your life.

"Everything in moderation" is an often-used expression when it comes to food and alcohol, yet this motto can apply to our entire life. When we're pulled in different directions, if excessive demands are made upon our time, or if unexpected drama throws our life into a tailspin, we must find a way to regain our balance. It's tough to think straight and function effectively when we're feeling overwhelmed and off-center. Unfortunately, so many people have resolved to living in this quasi state of imbalance that it has become a way of life. Yet they do not live with any peace of mind; an unsettled feeling persists on the inside. This lack of inner contentment continues to grow deeper as the day-to-day distractions demand their time and energy. Instead of resolving to find this inner harmony and fill this void from within, they are trapped in a detrimental cycle; some depend heavily on alcohol, food or drugs as a means to cope.

If we expect to gain any sense of balance or composure within our lives, we should start paying some attention to areas where we've put too much emphasis or too little. For instance, if spending so much time at work causes you to neglect your family, this reflects an imbalance in lifestyle management. Or perhaps the opposite is true, you focus so much attention on your family that you make no time for yourself. You learned earlier, that striving to find this balance in your lifestyle is only part of the equation. As part of healthy self-management, seeking your inner balance is deemed of greater relevance, for in the midst of life's storms, it certainly takes precedence. At your core, this deep inner balance represents your spiritual well-being. It can also be referred to as your life-force or inner self. There are no guarantees in life, but when all else fails, you can return to this spiritual center.

You can pull yourself together mentally and emotionally because of this strength that resides within your spirit. Whenever you function from this calm spiritual center, this will support all aspects of your well-being. That's because your spirit is the hub of healthy self-management. As you begin to seek its voice and honor the wisdom of this Great Spirit within, you naturally become a healthier self-manager.

. . . .
Who can find repose in a muddy world? —Lao Tzu
. . . .

So we discover that regaining balance is an interdependent, juggling act. We must manage and balance the external activities of our lifestyle in order to manage and balance our health. For instance, deep breathing and meditation is a wonderful activity that helps to center us, but this won't help if we can't find five minutes to do it. At the same time, when we are restored to this inner state of balance, this will help us to get a better grip on our crazy, busy life.

If we backtrack for a moment into the component of lifestyle management, we will find that many of us struggle to balance our lifestyle. Sometimes, this task seems impractical when life itself, is brazenly unpredictable. We might begin to question if it's possible at all to manage our health when nothing in life is static. The reality is that we all experience different phases in our life journey that require greater time and attention. This doesn't give us a license to neglect our health; it does however, give us more incentive to focus on regaining our inner balance. Think of this principle like a star in the sky—it will shine bright when you seek it and appear dim when you look away, but it's still there. Just because you don't see it, doesn't mean it exploded into oblivion.

The law of karma teaches us about reconciliation. Essentially, it's a moral doctrine of cause and effect; we reap what we sow. This similar type of balancing act affects our health. For example, if you worry a lot, those thoughts are out of balance with your body's natural state of contentment. If you do it enough, your body will give you feedback. Anxious thoughts and emotions don't belong in a healthy body; they get rejected through the manifestation of physical malfunctions, aches and pains, illness and disease. Thoughts carry their own energy and vibration. As you transform your thoughts to line up with a higher frequency, your emotions and spirit will respond accordingly. The more conscious you are of this balanced interconnection, the greater advantage you will have to experience the power behind this principle.

Consider my client, Tami, a twenty-eight year old, registered dietitian and former athlete, who ironically, had been struggling with weight loss for several years. Though she's extremely knowledgeable about nutrition and exercise, nothing seemed to work—she was battling some personal demons. During our initial consultation, she told me it was as if this little devil was on her shoulder, making her do bad things—skip meals, overindulge in pizza, drink, all the things she knew she shouldn't be doing while being at least one hundred pounds overweight. She signed up and scheduled her one-on-one personal training sessions with me, but we both knew she needed more than just a fitness program. I gave her a copy of the PHS flow chart, and this principle of regaining balance jumped out at her immediately. She took it to heart and quickly went to work to find some balance in her inner-self.

She started by watching Joyce Meyer ministries every morning for a half hour, five days a week. She said that it instantly put her in a better mood and frame of mind as she started her day. A few weeks later, I noticed that she was quite calm in her disposition; she wasn't ranting and raving about her typical boyfriend issues. She told me that regaining this sense of inner balance made a huge difference in her overall well-being. Not only did this help her psychologically, but she had found a new strength in her spirit that was greater than food or alcohol. This gave her the willpower she desperately needed to reject those thoughts of temptation and to start becoming a healthier self-manager. After following the PHS for five months, Tami made a significant stride in her health journey; she lost over thirty pounds!

The spirit takes precedence when it comes to balance, because it's the highest source of power available to us. In times of tragedy, people often comment that there's no greater force than the power in the human spirit. This power we experience is a gift deposited to us from our heavenly Father above. Christ or the Divine Spirit is bigger than *any* of our life problems or health issues. If we accept Christ to live in us, his spirit will intercede and help us in our weakness. We discover an inner resiliency that supersedes the here and now. Like muscles that keep our body strong, this spiritual brawn will help to keep us centered. No matter what we experience in our crazy life, that is, the external world, when our spirit is renewed through Christ, we find balance—this is the center of our being. People all over the world refer to God as the Rock of Ages. That's because from the beginning of time, God is the same spiritual source for all—Divine Spirit, Christ, Allah, Yahweh, Messiah, Universal Spirit, Universal Consciousness, and the Alpha and Omega. Call it what you want, when you have this power living in you, this will promote your inner balance.

Perhaps you do not consider yourself a spiritual person. Nevertheless, as you work on becoming a healthier self-manager, this will draw you closer toward your spiritual center. This shift takes place quite naturally, because your internal condition will inevitably improve whenever it's in harmony with the Divine Spirit, that is, your higher source of power. We can certainly see how this occurs within many 12-step recovery groups. People want to get clean from a certain substance abuse problem; (alcohol, heroin, cocaine, etc.) in order to do so; they must straighten out their head and get a grip on their neurotic behavior. If they could do this easily on their own accord they would, but unfortunately they're driven by compulsion. It becomes intolerable for them as their life is consumed with getting the next fix. Only after they wholeheartedly turn their lives over to a higher source of power, do they find the inner strength to overcome their addiction. Until then, there's no serenity in their life.

We must remain cognizant of this need for balance in three key areas: our lifestyle, our inner-self and our physical body. You may recall that the PHS component of healthy self-management serves as a bridge between your psychological and spiritual well-being. It is focused primarily on your inner-self. You can view it as sort of a "health consolidation" with this balanced spiritual condition at the center. In accounting lingo, this means it goes on the front line of your balance sheet—it's an asset that takes all aspects of your *inner* well-being into account. In the process, you may have to make several "inter-health reconciliations." In other words, becoming a healthy self-manager involves reconciling the imbalances of your *inner-self*, whether in mind, emotions, or spirit. Applying this spirit-based principle will help you to get your internal balancing act together. Later, (in the program design) you'll learn how to promote balance in your physical body by eating a well-balanced healthy diet, and exercising regularly.

"All this is from God, who reconciled us to himself through Christ and gave us the ministry of reconciliation. That God was reconciling the world to himself in Christ, not counting men's sins against them. And he has committed to us the message of reconciliation."[2]

Develop Self-Awareness

To regain balance and make progress as a healthy self-manager, you must become self-aware. Remember, lifestyle management precedes healthy self-management, so step back for a moment to determine if you need more balance in your lifestyle. We all go through different phases or seasons in life. The problem is some people get stuck in a season way too long—but they don't realize it. Let's consider the proud parents of a newborn baby. Parents share the same story; life is no longer about them anymore. Certainly, becoming selfless in the baby's early stage is understandable, but plenty of parents get stuck in this same mind-set, long after the birth. With another mouth to feed, they believe this gives them a legitimate reason to perpetually neglect their own health—yet many didn't take care of themselves long before their new arrival.

When their child is eighteen years old, they're still using this excuse for being overweight and unhealthy. It's time to stop the blame game. If you've taken responsibility for your life and health, then it's possible to maintain healthy behaviors before, during, and after childrearing. This truth doesn't minimize the enormity of being a new parent; on the contrary, it should help you gain some sanity if you are one. When the baby is born, of course you need to focus more attention on this transitional phase of your life. Nobody is suggesting that you leave a helpless, crying baby alone so you can go to the gym, flex your biceps while staring at yourself in the mirror and making a loud grunt. Let's get some perspective here.

Still, there comes a point when you realize, it's time to take care of yourself. This is an important moment of self-awareness that shouldn't be discounted. Begin to honor those internal cues. Even as you go about taking care of loved ones, be mindful of how this affects you—pay attention to what you're feeling and doing. For example, if you're a new mother, then after the baby is born, you do not need to continue eating for two. Within a couple months, it's usually safe to resume exercise again. Disciplined moms exercise much sooner, within a few weeks; they know this helps them to de-stress and it restores their psychological equilibrium. This same logic applies to anyone who has experienced an injury. Sure, it takes time to recover, but almost everyone will experience some physical setback over the course of their lifetime. Plenty of people go to the gym on crutches or in casts, and this doesn't mean they're obsessed with exercise.

Developing self-awareness in this sense means becoming cognizant of your needs. Once you recognize those needs, then you can do something about them. Consider my friend, Seth, who in spite of his physical limitations, (he's unable to walk) goes to the gym regularly because this helps him psychologically. He considers the gym not just a great place to exercise, but he also uses it as a social outlet, to catch up with friends and interact with others. Clearly, there are times when we need to back off and let our body heal, but we can usually work around the problem areas. Being self-aware is so crucial because it helps us to recognize which areas of our life and health need more attention or less. This differs from developing emotional intelligence, because it keeps us focused on everything important to us, it's not only concerned with our ability to interpret emotions. If our health is something we truly value, then we must remain conscious enough to honor it. Otherwise, we can easily slip off track into unconscious, harmful behavior patterns.

As mentioned earlier, there's a direct correlation between healthy self-management and a balanced lifestyle—it's a two-way street. If you have balance in your lifestyle, it's much easier to manage and improve your health. Likewise, when you're healthier and you feel more centered, you will function better in life. So this transformation can happen in one of two ways. Either you adjust your lifestyle by carving out a piece of time to focus on your health, or you simply seize a moment to focus on your health and let your priorities shift accordingly. Whichever way you decide, without this self-awareness, you can't regain any sort of balance, because someone or something will always come along to distract you. Here's an example: one of my clients Isabella, had a problem of always running late to her personal training appointments. First it was her kid's fault, then it was her husband's fault, then it was the traffic, then it was the babysitter's fault, then it was another story. Isabella had plenty of sagas and always tried to make her sessions last longer than her scheduled time, or she wanted to reschedule at the last minute. Each time she tried to do this, it wasn't feasible; she reluctantly came in and I ended her session at the regular scheduled time. In the last episode, her training time was cut in half. Then I spoke to her about this problem—she needed to be made *aware* that showing up late was costing her time and money. Isabella couldn't make progress in healthy self-management, because she was still struggling to manage and gain some balance in her lifestyle. Tardiness had become her way of life, but it was only after she became fully *aware* of this problem that she was able to change her behavior. Sure enough, after our talk, she showed up ten minutes early for each training session.

Life has its seasons. Sometimes we have to spend more time in a particular season, but we can still find our way back to center. For instance, you may need to focus more attention on your children, or on getting a new job and relocating, or going back to school, or taking care of a sick family member. Suddenly, in the midst of it all, you notice that a spare tire has settled around your midsection. Somehow, it just seemed to wrap around you, and you aren't sure how it got there. It sounds simple enough, but cultivating this type of self-awareness is exactly what you need. Noticing that spare tire will help you to shift your focus on your health and bring more balance back to your world. Life will test your ability to maintain this balance, and it's up to you not to drift off too far one way for too long.

. . . .

If you drink beer and golf all day long, rest assured your life is in need of some serious balance.

. . . .

Understand Your Attachments

Part of becoming more self-aware involves understanding your attachments. Whenever you have an unhealthy attachment to anything in your life, this indicates an imbalance somewhere else, and it could possibly trigger a destructive habit. Of course, the unhealthy attachment may become the destructive habit itself; or it may lead to another. If you don't reconcile the underlying imbalance in the right way, you may be tempted to mask it by resorting to a vice. Then of course, you end up with another problem. Over time, you could very well become oblivious as to the origin of the imbalance. First, let's make some distinctions about what constitutes healthy and unhealthy attachments. When we pursue our passions and are extremely attached in this regard, we're aligned with our higher self and purpose. Though we may lose track of time consumed with our pursuit, it's passion that fuels our motivation, so this is considered a healthy attachment. It's often said that people who love their work actually never "work" a day in their life.

However, when we do things out of obligation, fears, or mindless routine; this can inadvertently create unhealthy attachments. The difference is that the unhealthy attachment will cause us to take actions that stem from fear, whereas the healthy attachment will cause us to take actions that stem from love. For example, if we stay in a bad relationship simply because we fear the ramifications of leaving, this is an unhealthy attachment. We're not in the relationship because we love the person; we're in it because fear is preventing us from breaking away. In this sense, the destructive habit becomes the codependent relationship itself.

Determining the type of attachment is important, but we must also consider whether that attachment has become excessive. For example, exercise is a healthy attachment, but when it's taken to an extreme, it can become unhealthy. An anorexic woman who works out excessively will only compound her existing imbalances. We need to be able to draw the line between what's a healthy attachment and what's not, what's excessive and what's not. Remember, "everything in moderation" applies to everything in our life. We may love our children dearly, which is clearly a healthy attachment, but if we go overboard by not setting appropriate boundaries, this creates an imbalance that becomes unhealthy for both the parent and child. Review the following list to identify what may be causing or compounding any existing imbalances.

- Unresolved subjective issues: anger, fear, self-pity, shame
- Projective issues: manipulation, control, power, verbal and physical abuse
- Overeating, drinking, smoking, illegal drugs
- OTC drugs, prescription pills, painkillers
- Overworking, constant busyness
- Overly consumed with marriage and/or kids
- Dysfunctional/codependent relationships
- Obsessive/compulsive behaviors or addictions

Anything that's done excessively can give rise to a bad habit. The bad habit is created to compensate for the imbalance occurring elsewhere. In other words, one thing could be used compulsively, in a subconscious way to reconcile another. Most people don't address their real issues because of this tendency to turn to a quick-fix. What they really want to do is offset the imbalance they're experiencing, but the problem with compulsive behavior is that it doesn't work. At best, it is only a short-lived form of relief.

People will either determine how to reconcile their imbalances constructively, or they let them accrue by distracting themselves—through food, alcohol, smoking and other compulsive behaviors. It may be a human tendency to gravitate toward the later, but when this is done in excess, it will only compound problems, because it can numb us out and hook us on something. This is why being self-aware is so important. Mindfulness prevents us from living in denial and getting trapped in harmful behavior patterns.

To develop a greater sense of self-awareness, take a moment to gauge yourself:

- Am I overweight and unhealthy? If so, what drives me toward self-destructive behavior?

- Do I eat or drink whenever I'm lonely, bored or anxious?

- Do I have one or several addictions that I need to face?

- What goals, interests, and passions have I neglected?

- Am I happy with the consequences of major decisions; such as my marriage or relationship, my career choice?

- What issues do I have to deal with as a result of my own self-neglect?

- What are the rewards and risks associated with change?

- What issues do I have control over?

- What issues are out of my control?

- Will I be happy in five years if I stay on the same path?

- Am I being true to myself?

Before you can resolve your problems you must become aware of them. Figure out what triggers these imbalances in the first place. When you become self-aware, you will start to understand the "why" behind dysfunctional behavior patterns. For example, if you're not sure how you gained all that weight, then start documenting everything you eat and drink on a daily basis. Jot down *what, when, how much*, and *why* you eat—that's a step in the right direction. Then if you find out that you eat or drink whenever you feel lonely, then choose to do something else instead; (call or meet a friend, volunteer to help someone, take a walk, pray, read, etc.) If there's an area where you feel you have no control, release it to your higher power. You may need a supernatural intervention, or perhaps you need to make peace with certain situations. Stay proactive and remember the PHS is about empowering you.

Get a Reference Point in Your Life

When performing an exercise that requires balance it's often recommended to focus your eyes on one spot because having this reference point helps to anchor you. This suggestion holds true within our lives and health as well. We can regain our sense of balance by getting a reference point in life. Whenever you feel off center, turn to a source that grounds you. This could be your family, friends, your loyal dog, or any support system—whatever makes you feel right, deep down in your soul. Keep in mind, however, that everything in this world is temporary and therefore, it is subject to change.

Sometimes loved ones aren't available when needed or they may not be equipped to provide the type of support we really need. Regardless of our situation, we can always turn to our higher source of power for help. Ultimately, God is the rock that keeps everything together and everything centered. He's the Alpha and Omega—the beginning and end. This Divine Spirit is the same, no matter where we seek it; whether we discover it in church, in yoga class, or in nature—through the rustling leaves of a woodsy park, along the seashore, or viewing a beautiful sunset. If we remain deeply connected to our higher source of power, we'll always have a reference point in our life.

A fire or natural disaster that destroys our house, a major accident, an illness, the death of a loved one, a divorce, psychological trauma, financial devastation—any unexpected event can throw everything out of kilter and affect the balance in our life as we know it. Some situations in life just push us over the edge. When we "lose it" we lose our inner balance, but whatever knocked us off our center doesn't have to keep us there forever. God is always there to help; he can heal us, bring us back to center and use those heartbreaking experiences for a higher purpose. The Bible tells us that if we hear the word of God and put it into practice, we are like a wise man who built his house on a rock. When the storms come and beat against that kind of a house, it doesn't fall because it has a firm foundation.

Consider Carly, a member of my church congregation. She told me that when she was a child, she was beaten up every day over little things she did wrong in her parents' eyes. Her brothers and sisters also beat up on her and one another. As she describes it, her upbringing was sheer hell and complete chaos. Carly had no control of her environment and certainly no joy in her life. On the surface, she was a child, weak and vulnerable. On the inside, however, Carly was a warrior. She prayed in her heart that she would get out of that awful circumstance and always envisioned a better life for herself. She was applying two PHS principles without even knowing it. By being proactive, she was using her imagination to envision something better for herself, and by relying upon God to strengthen her spirit, she regained her balance internally. Now, as an adult, Carly has many lessons to share. She teaches parents that they don't have to resort to physical or verbal abuse to discipline their children. She also talks about how the power of forgiveness has liberated her life. By allowing God to become her point of reference in life, Carly learned at a young age, how to gain a sense of balance.

We must learn to accept graciously whatever things in life we can't control. Most people want to do their best in life, in spite of problems. The question is how can we take care of ourselves in the midst of life's great challenges? There are different remedies for different situations and different people. The PHS teaches us that we're responsible for figuring out what we need to regain our balance. On the next page, review the list of simple ways to nurture your spirit, and consider what resonates most to you.

Simple Ways to Nurture Your Spirit

- Pray—accept and make peace with your higher source of power
- Make time to be alone, meditate and breathe deep
- Exercise and in particular, do yoga
- Attend a church service or read the Bible
- Practice gratitude daily
- Spend time outdoors in nature
- Listen to "Zen" music – something soft and soothing to the soul
- Get out with friends and socialize
- Take a mini-vacation
- Forgive yourself and others for any harm or wrongdoing
- Help others through community service
- Be creative and pursue your passion
- Clean clutter from your surroundings
- Laugh and find humor in your life
- Spend time with children and pets
- Relax in a hot tub, an aromatic bath, or dry sauna
- Get a deep-tissue foot massage
- Use aroma therapy to energize your environment
- Take a break from technology devices

Only if we recognize what throws us off center can we do something about it. For example, if we work in a field where we're constantly interacting and talking all day, at the end of the day, we may want nothing more, than peace and quiet. On the other hand, if we work from home and never interact with others, perhaps a social night out with friends would be our remedy. Determining what we need to regain balance is our responsibility. Sometimes we know exactly what to do, but other times; we figure it out slowly in phases, through trial and error. It's common for people to block out incidents that have been too difficult to face, but it's important to deal with those situations in order to get healed. While our conscious mind may forget, our subconscious knows—it stores everything. As previously discussed, bitter emotions need to be released so they don't hold us captive. Through the grace of God, all things are possible. He can help us lose the victim mentality over any awful situation we endured. God can restore us and bring us back to our center, because he's bigger than our problems. We don't have to carry our burdens alone.

God won't allow us to experience anything that doesn't serve a higher purpose for our life. Sometimes we don't have the answers or understand how God plans to use those awful experiences. We don't always know why things turned out one way or another, but here's what the Bible has to say about our problems: *"And we know that in all things God works for the good of those who love him who have been called according to his purpose."*[3] Our problems are tremendous growth opportunities. God can take any unfair or seemingly impossible situation and use it to enrich our lives. When the power of God's spirit takes over, anything is possible. We will start viewing all of our problems as blessings in disguise.

Here's an example; after getting married, I moved out of my very peaceful, quiet and functional one bed-room apartment into an old house where everything was backwards and upside down. The hard wood floors creaked in every room and although we tried everything to quiet them down, nothing seemed to work. The bathroom was my biggest nemesis. The toilet flushed backward and it was in an awkward, very tight spot next to the shower faucets, there was no fan, but a window inside the shower adjacent to the surrounding tacky, black and green tile. It was hideous and certainly not a bathroom designed with women in mind. My cool composure was being tested daily between the annoying squeaks and lack of functionality. Needless to say, I was ready to move out and we started looking for new homes in the area.

A couple months later, I was involved in a tragic car accident. It was a three car pile-up. A young man rushing to meet his new boss for lunch was speeding through a red light. He was T-boned between me and another car. I saw my life flash by, as my face headed straight into the steering wheel. It was my time, I thought. The car was completely totaled, but miraculously, I walked away with no whiplash, no broken bones; just a couple scratches on my nose. At that time, we didn't have full coverage on both vehicles, so living in Michigan, (a no-fault state) we were out of a car without adequate reimbursement. This seemed unfair, but in the scheme of things, it really didn't matter. I was just grateful to be alive.

When I finally made it home to the dumpy old house that creaked, I cried tears of joy. I was completely overwhelmed with gratitude just to be there again! It was a blessing. All the issues I had to deal with in that house suddenly became insignificant and faded away. When my spirit was so overjoyed and enamored with life itself, I found a deeper inner peace than ever before. Nothing in this world can give us joy because it's not based on things or conditions. Joy and peace come from the same place. It arises from within, as a state of our being—this is our spiritual center. When the peace of God transcends our human understanding, this will insulate us from our world-weariness.

In spite of our personal viewpoints or religious predisposition, we each have this amazing power in our spirit that we can tap into at any time. If we neglect our spirit that doesn't mean it ceases to exist. Our spirit has an inherent desire to evolve. Being spiritual in this sense, doesn't mean you're someone who goes to church every Sunday. In fact, you could attend all the time and still have no life in your spirit. Conversely, just because you don't believe in God, this doesn't mean you aren't spiritual. What we perceive as spirituality may be goodness that radiates from someone's heart and yet, we may discover that this person has no religious affiliation or ever set foot in a church.

Along these lines, consider what type of person commits a senseless murder. Essentially, it's an act conjured up by an evil spirit. A demon is part of the spiritual world, just as there are angels. Some people are walking around like zombies, feeling no connection whatsoever to their spiritual center, but this merely represents the spiritual state of their existence—it doesn't negate it. Being in a spiritual coma is still a spiritual condition. When people keep accumulating negative, dull energy; their spirit stagnates. It vibrates on a very low dimension. We may pick up some bad vibes or experience a drop in our energy level after being around them. Spiritually, whenever we drift farther away from our higher source of power, we get off-kilter. We must reconnect and allow the Divine Spirit to become our compass—this is how we find our center.

Philosophically, have you ever pondered the breakdown of human existence? Who are we; why are we here, and where do we go after our time on earth? One could say that we're an intricate blend of unlimited discovery, while another might argue; we're nothing but worm-food. The list below reveals several facets shared among humanity. Use it as a reference to help you discover what part of yourself is out of balance.

- **Spiritual**—this is our life force; it allows us to connect to our higher source of power. From it, we can seek God, have fellowship with other like-minded believers, receive healing, and evolve spiritually. Maintaining this divine connection with our higher source of power will keep us centered on the inside.

- **Mental**—this represents our mind-set; it can be nurtured by positive thoughts, affirmations, uplifting spiritual messages, and meditating on God's word.

- **Psychological**—this combines our mental and emotional capacity to process events, reflect, and experience behavioral growth in relation to self and others. This development can take place in many ways through—our upbringing, transition, healing, interacting with others and guidance.

- **Social**—we're designed to be in relationships. We need social interaction to develop friendships, build intimate relationships, work as part of a team, network, and maintain deep connections with family and loved ones.

- **Intellectual**—in order to gain knowledge and grow intellectually, we should continue to learn by keeping our minds stimulated.

- **Physical**—to keep our body in balance and functioning at its peak; we need to maintain a well-balanced nutrition and exercise routine.

When we improve our health and well-being on these different levels, we become more balanced. We function at our best when we are pulled together as an integrated whole. If we attempt to invest time and energy into taking care of our physical body, but neglect what's at our core—we could be wasting our time. By keeping God at the center of our life, our spirit can thrive. He can heal us from the inside and help us evolve in all these dimensions.

From a spiritual standpoint, there's a universal way God wants us to behave. It is simple. We should treat others the same way we treat ourselves.

How to treat yourself:
- Affirm, accept, and respect yourself
- Seek to understand yourself
- Forgive yourself
- Love yourself

How to treat others:
- Affirm, accept, and respect others
- Seek to understand others
- Forgive others
- Love others

Jesus replied: "Love the Lord your God with all your heart and with all your soul and with all your mind. This is the first and greatest commandment. And the second is like it: Love your neighbor as yourself. All the Law and the Prophets hang on these two commandments."[4]

The General Scope: of the Mind, Body, and Spirit

You've learned that this general scope between the mind, body, and spirit has a need for balance. In order to better manage your health, you must learn to recognize the imbalances that off-set this interconnection. Let's say you've been partying hard for the last few weeks. You've had your fair share of brews, brats, pizza, cake, and ice cream. Not only have you consumed too much alcohol, calories, and saturated fat, but you've been missing out on some important vitamins and nutrients. Hypothetically, assume you were to continue down this partying path for several more months. Overindulging in alcohol and junk-food can create an imbalance that affects more than just your physical body. For starters, abusing your body by consuming too much saturated fat can lead to clogged arteries and when your arteries are clogged, this takes a toll on your heart. If your heart has to work harder, this drains your physical energy. Prolonged physical fatigue can lead to a depressed mood and put a damper on your spirit. Now you don't feel like going to any more parties. (You went from party animal to couch potato.) This appears to be somewhat of an oversimplification, but let's look at this connection more closely to see how it can affect your mood, your thinking, and your entire life.

If you lack a critical vitamin or have abnormal levels of minerals and/ or toxic metals in your body, this creates a biochemical imbalance. Back in the 1970s, American anthropologists studied a tribe of Central American Indians, the Qualla, who were known for their violence and premeditated murder. They discovered that the Qualla diets were very poor—high in refined sugars and alcohol and short on basic nutrition. Every tribesman tested turned out to be hypoglycemic. When our bodies and brains are so off balance, counseling has little to offer. "Our prisons today are full of violent hypoglycemics who are paying a high price for uncontrolled behavior. Thus, maintaining constant adequate glucose levels should be one of the most important functions of our biochemical being. Our brains need glucose so that we can think clearly."[5] From a physical standpoint, it's easy to see how this chain of events occurs; chemical imbalances and hormonal changes alter our body's metabolic equilibrium.

Whether we are experiencing excruciating physical pain from an injury, or suffering from an anxiety disorder, any significant underlying tension or imbalance can disrupt this interconnection of the mind, body and spirit. Let's assume you absolutely hate your job. This isn't a matter of having a bad day at work, because every day to you feels like a bad day— some are just worse than others. You get no fulfillment out of your job except for the paycheck, and this comes with a price—your compromised integrity. Each day you grudgingly go in, and experience a tremendous conflict of interest—this throws you off balance psychologically. You may find yourself feeling on edge and uneasy, irritated or short with people close to you. Your family and friends tell you that you're not yourself anymore. Deep down you feel tormented. Staying in this situation has caused you chronic stress, both psychologically and spiritually. Rest assured, if you do nothing to counteract these imbalances, it can erode the quality of your life and health. It starts by eating away at your confidence and self-esteem, because you're doing something that's not lined up with your values. Not only does this job affect your well-being, it takes a toll on everyone around you.

Analyzing the cost/benefit of such a situation is important. If the net effect is negative, this is a clue that change in is order. Just as when a company operates in the negative, if innovative change doesn't occur to recoup the growing loss, it will have to file for bankruptcy. Don't wait for bankruptcy to take your life and health by default. There's always a price to pay whenever we neglect to reconcile an imbalance in our self, whether this is physical, emotional, mental, or spiritual.

Another way we can analyze this connection is to consider someone who has experienced post-traumatic stress disorder (PTSD) as a result of repetitive physical abuse. Unfortunately, domestic violence still runs rampant in today's society and it affects mostly women. Physical abuse usually comes with many forms of cruelty, including psychological, verbal, spiritual and economical. From a physical standpoint, as the body is physically traumatized, the trauma remains in the nervous system, and this shuts down receptor sites to the brain. When the brain is affected in this way, it will affect everything tied to the central nervous system—from every decision to loads of sensory input. Theoretically, when someone experiences consistent and severe bodily harm, trauma gets stored in the cells making them lose vitality. Strong cells that have not been battered would experience a greater shock if they were subjected to the same harm, but could withstand better against the ravages of such attacks. If you were repetitively traumatized through an ongoing series of physical assaults, then from a molecular level, this would diminish the size and quality of your cells. Essentially, you lose life, because cells are the building blocks to life. When your cells shrink or become damaged, it hampers your ability to function. This disturbs your life-force by making functioning in everyday life more labor-intensive.

In fact, cancer research now points to this understanding through the new concept of cellular memory.[6] If you experience flashbacks, suddenly feel demoralized or repressed, or constantly sense a black cloud of gloom and doom hanging over you, this is likely to signify the spiritual trauma associated with PTSD. Certainly, PTSD is not a pleasant experience, but it can help to release stored trauma from within the body. It's possible for trauma to be removed entirely from the nervous system, releasing its hold on the mind, body, spirit, and emotions. Though the time this requires may vary for each person depending on the situation, restoration is possible on all levels. The best way to receive this healing is through the supernatural power of God's spirit. No appointed needed. He alone can intervene and bring redemption. When you accept the awesome power of God to work on your behalf, your spirit can heal. A spiritual rebirth can take place right at the center of your being. Turn to him when you are ready, he's ready to help.

We ought to appreciate the wonders of modern science and medicine. We should pay tribute to the researchers, scientists, and every person who have contributed to society through their pain or illness. Many people question why someone was placed on this earth to suffer an illness and then just die. It's not our privilege to know. Death is a natural part of the life cycle, it can happen to anyone, anywhere, at any time. There's a natural ebb and flow to life that we just can't control. If all doctors knew everything there is to know about health, we could significantly extend our life span. Doctors who are spiritually enlightened and practice modern medicine as well as holistic healing would know when to apply one therapy versus another. There are some who criticize doctors, claiming that they need to stop "playing God," yet theoretically they're walking with God on a daily basis. Think about it, if God ultimately knows when it's our time to go, he can work with or allow that doctor to be influenced in certain ways, to lead to the outcome of life or death. Only God knows when it's our time. Doctors work with God by default, and you, too, have that ability.

Start listening to your body and if you've been traumatized physically, ask God to remove any stored trauma or toxic emotions that got trapped in your cells. Destructive energy that remains in the physical body can manifest anywhere as an illness or disease. When you work in partnership with God and are willing to look deep within your consciousness, he can heal you on any level. Since the mind, body and spirit are interconnected; whenever one dimension improves, there's a ripple effect of reconciliation throughout. It's only natural for God to intervene and heal you. He knows there are some things that doctors and medicine alone can't cure. Doctor's may offer cures from a physical standpoint, but God can heal you psychologically and spiritually. He can mend a broken heart. Miracles are possible with God. Seek him for every challenge you face and every problem that affects your health. Divine inner healing can ultimately lead to restoration in your physical body. For you, this is a simple option; for God, it's a simple solution.

The Power of Influence

The power of influence and the effect it has on your ability to manage your health holds tremendous weight. Other people can have a positive or negative influence on your thoughts, behaviors and well-being. How often do you come across people who have a natural enthusiasm for life and exude positive energy? When they walk in a room, you're inspired by their aura. You want whatever they have to rub off on you. These people seem to glow from the inside. Physically, they look amazing, and you can sense something special, an inner discipline. When you talk with them, you walk away totally energized. Their presence leaves you feeling better about life and yourself. These types of people have a winning spirit and don't allow themselves to get jaded by negativity. They have the Midas touch!

When you surround yourself with positive, confident people your own self-esteem grows. However, it's not so easy to keep your spirits high when you're surrounded by negative, toxic people; aka energy vipers— experts that attack you unconsciously and suck the life right out of you. When I first became a trainer, I had a client who always made me feel sleepy. She was painfully exhausting psychologically, and never had any physical energy. At the time, I didn't know how to protect my energy, so I drank a lot of coffee before I had to train her. It didn't work. I still felt psychologically exhausted after spending any time with her. She drained my spirit.

It's one thing to have honest people in your life who have your best interests in mind. This is different, however, from being around a bunch of killjoys. These types of people will sap your energy, manipulate you and psychologically throw you off balance. Be on guard and don't underestimate the power of their influence. Sometimes their offenses are blatant, but more often than not, they're subtle. If you're not aware of what's happening, then you won't be prepared to neutralize their attacks. However, if you feel off-kilter psychologically, then you can strategically counteract their deterrents, or better yet, remove yourself entirely from their presence.

Let's say you started that weight loss program, and your dietitian gave you recommendations on what to eat when you go out on the town. The friend you're having dinner with doesn't seem to understand, and hurls insults at you for being such a picky eater. Then your friend proceeds to order a huge plate of greasy appetizers, a new round of drinks, and a very fattening dessert. You're expected to dig in and share. Will you maintain control or succumb to social pressure? If you're mentally prepared, you can still enjoy the night without overindulging. If you do go overboard through sheer temptation, then you are responsible for reconciling this slip-up. As a healthy self-manager, you must start to recognize what you need to regain balance. For instance, maybe the following day, you cut back on the amount of calories you consume, or work out a little bit longer. Perhaps you realize that this friend of yours has a hard time respecting your values and boundaries. Perhaps you decide to stop hanging out with this person for a while. (You can always meet up later, in your new skinny pair of jeans!)

The Reality of Stress

Whenever we manage our stress, we bring more balance back to our life. Not all the stress we experience is bad, however. Some stress is beneficial, because it can bring out the best in us, but the stress that overwhelms us and throws everything out of balance is a different story. Everybody will experience dark days. Annoying people will test our patience, injustice occurs in this world and evil shall cross our path. Of this, we can be sure. Nobody said life would be easy, but we still have choices. If we don't face and treat the core causes of unhealthy stress, we can develop noticeable symptoms. These symptoms can become chronic, such as constant anxiety, panic attacks, headaches, and more.

Consequently, chronic symptoms can cause disease, the kind that requires surgery, chemo and radiation therapy, and heavy-duty medications. "According to the American Institute of Stress, between 75 and 90 percent of all visits to primary-care physicians, result from stress-related disorders.

Scientific studies have revealed that there is a link between certain emotions and disease. When emotions release hormones such as adrenaline and cortisol into the physical body, this can cause a damaging effect that can trigger a host of diseases. Depression has been linked to an increased risk of developing cancer and heart disease. Emotions such as anxiety and fear have shown a direct tie to heart palpitations, mitral valve prolapse, irritable bowel syndrome, and tension headaches, as well as other diseases."[7] Stress is a major killer, and the statistics do the talking.

- Approximately 40 million American adults, eighteen or older, or about 18 percent have an anxiety disorder.[8]

- Currently, nearly 14 million Americans (one in every thirteen adults) abuse alcohol or are alcoholic.[9]

- According to the CDC, nearly one in ten of US adults is depressed.[10]

- A 2010 National Health Interview Survey determined that 1.5 million heart attacks occur each year, with 500,000 deaths.[11]

- According to National Center for Health Statistics 2008, about one out of three US adults—31.3 percent—has high blood pressure.[12]

- In 2010, the National Institute on Drug Abuse listed that approximately 7 million persons were current users of psychotherapeutic drugs taken non-medically (2.7 percent of the US population).[13]

  ✓ pain relievers—5.1 million

  ✓ tranquilizers—2.2 million

  ✓ stimulants—1.1 million

  ✓ sedatives—0.4 million

Stress symptoms fall under four main categories:[14]

- **Physical symptoms involving skeletal muscles**—tension headaches, neck aches, back pain, frowning, trembling of lips or hands, grinding teeth, jaw pain, stuttering or stammering, aggressive body language.

- **Physical symptoms involving autonomic nervous system**—migraines, dizziness, difficulty breathing, heart and chest pain, dry mouth, ringing in the ears, enlarged pupils, nervous diarrhea, constipation, night sweats, hives or rashes, rapid heartbeat.

- **Mental symptoms**—anxiety, worry, guilt, nervousness, increased anger and frustration, moodiness, nightmares, forgetfulness, problems concentrating, difficulty making decisions, frequent crying, disorganization and confusion, suicidal thoughts.

- **Behavioral symptoms**—inattention to dress or grooming, more tardiness, rushing or pacing the floor, overreaction to small things, social withdrawal, weight gain or loss, perfectionism, increased smoking, constant tiredness, edginess, increased frustration or irritability, reduced work efficiency, finger or foot tapping, sleep problems, increased alcohol, gambling and overspending, fast or mumbled speech.

When we can't disassociate our own power from the magnitude of our problems, we create unhealthy stress. This stress is created by our own reactions and interpretations. In order to reconcile the imbalances that off-set optimal health, we must find ways to de-stress in mind, body, and spirit. Stress management is a skill everybody needs to learn. Whenever you feel off-center, go back and review the list of simple ways to nurture your spirit. Refer to it as often as needed. In the end, if you follow a path that leads to deep inner peace, that same path will promote greater balance.

- Go with the flow of life, surrender to what you can't control.
- Don't become an obstructive force in the path of peace and justice. Do unto others as you would like others to do unto you.
- Be open-minded. Don't be afraid to expand your understanding and release self-imposed limitations on your psyche.
- Do yoga! Remove restricted energy from your chakras— healing the energy pathways (aka: meridians) can bring balance to your mind, body and spirit.

CHAPTER 9

Healthy Self-Management—
PHS Principle: Develop Healthy Self-Image

Our thoughts and self-perceptions play a critical role in many outcomes of our life. If we're not healthy from a physical standpoint, we may need to delve deeper into our subconscious and take a closer look at our self-image. This principle helps us to make the changes needed from within that allow us to cultivate a more positive mind-set and develop a healthy self-image.

Low self-esteem is the culprit behind a poor self-image. This is a major and complex issue that runs deep inside the hearts and minds of many. When people scurry to outside sources to try to fix something from within, they put conditions on everything—from their job and income, home, car, marital status, children, and appearance. Despite our God-given value and how unique and wonderful we each may be in our own right, for people with low self-esteem, it just doesn't matter—they still feel empty, unworthy, and deficient on the inside.

Misconception about our inherent value as human beings is not something be taken lightly. Left unresolved, it creates self-destructive behaviors and can even lead to violence. (We've all heard of the guy who goes "postal" because he lost his job.) It's true that some sense of our esteem is associated with how we make a living, but jobs come and go—we shouldn't base our entire life perception and value upon them. We can't take our job or any material possessions with us when we die. Nor should our self-esteem be based solely upon our physical appearance, yet numerous women suffer from anorexia nervosa, bulimia, or body dysmorphic disorder—an obsession with cosmetic and surgical makeovers in an attempt to make themselves feel better about how they look.

Self-esteem affects our health because it touches all aspects of our well-being—the mental, emotional, spiritual, and physical. Though much of it occurs in the mind and is ego-based, we can grasp self-esteem through these multiple dimensions to analyze the relevant connection from within ourselves. For instance, from a Christian perspective, when we consider the *spiritual* dimension associated with our self-esteem, we recognize that our real worth comes from accepting Jesus Christ. When we make this amend with Christ, our self-esteem begins to radiate from the inside, not from something outside ourselves, like our fancy set of wheels parked in the driveway. Of course, there's nothing wrong with feeling good about our hard-earned possessions, but we've each been created in the image of God, and we're inherently worthy, regardless of what we have or don't have. If we honor ourselves at this deeper spiritual level, it can prevent a host of problems associated with low self-esteem. Our spiritual condition has a tremendous impact on our self-esteem, yet ironically, it's often an area of great neglect.

We must remain cognizant of how all aspects of our health and well-being are interconnected. We know now, it's not limited to the physical body—how much we weigh or beautifully sculpted muscles—that's an outdated mentality. We need to strike a greater balance between our inner and outer health. At any point, we can choose the lens of how to view ourselves, whether this is through our mind, spirit, emotions, or body.

Before Tami started applying this PHS principle, she had a hard time loving herself, being one hundred pounds overweight. She longed to go back to her former days, when she was a hard-core competitive athlete. During that time, when she was several sizes smaller, she felt good about herself and held a positive self-image. However, she was only viewing herself from a physical standpoint. In order to improve her self-image, she had to change her lens from within; she needed a transformation in her mind-set. She started to renew her mind by listening to Christian messages on a daily basis. This helped her push past those self-depreciating thoughts to gain a much greater sense of her self-worth. It was a mental battle, but every morning, she continued to focus her thoughts on God's word. After several weeks, it finally sunk in—she realized that she was worthy, regardless of her outward appearance. This didn't become an excuse, however, for Tami to remain overweight. Instead, it motivated her to change, because she started viewing her body as the temple of God's spirit. As her self-image improved, her inner spirit started to shine through. Her desire to take better care of herself increased. She joined Weight Watchers and started working out more frequently. In turn, she said that working out made her feel skinnier, which also improved her self-image. For Tami, everything was coming together; she was integrating and expanding her notion of health with each PHS principle she applied.

When we esteem ourselves properly, it's ultimately reflected in the way we carry ourselves. Similarly, as we take care of our physical bodies, we nurture our self-esteem. Whether you realize it or not, your mind-set and the way you see yourself will have an impact on your physical body. To consider this connection more closely, think about how your motivation to become healthy is tied to your self-image. Without the basic desire to become healthy and improve the quality of your life, you probably wouldn't be reading this book. Though this may be obvious now, there could've been a time when you lost all the motivation to be healthy because you simply didn't place enough value on yourself. All your needs fell by wayside. If this sounds all too familiar, forget the excuses.

In one way or another, this lack of motivation was a direct result of your mind-set and the choices you made. You didn't value yourself enough to even allow the thoughts you needed to make your health a priority. Essentially, you created limitations in your own mind, which in turn signified the value you held about yourself. Your health went on the back burner because it wasn't really a priority. Shifted priorities and negligence occurred, whether you were conscious of it or not. When you remain complacent about your own health and well-being, this involuntarily attaches a negative connotation to your self-image. The presumption is that if you don't take care of yourself, then on some level, you don't value yourself enough to do so. It's this diminished self-perception that stops you.

When people make excuses to justify this self-neglect; they're just creating self-made booby traps. Unfortunately, that's part of human nature; we're all susceptible of falling into a mindless coma that robs us of our true values and undermines our self-image. Essentially, this is a subtle and slow process of self-abuse, and countless people are subjected to it much in the same way. It begins by succumbing to self-defeating thoughts; for example:

- Why bother? I've been fat my whole life.

- I'm too busy with a spouse, kids, and job—there's no time to take care of myself.

- I tried to lose weight, but nothing works. I always gain it back.

- Physical activity is not a priority; I'm just not the "exercise type" of person.

Thoughts of lack and limitation develop into mental and emotional blocks, which will reside in your subconscious. This creates the barriers that inhibit you from taking care of yourself. Yet what do these thoughts really say about how you perceive yourself? That you're unworthy, and your health doesn't matter. A poor self-image can sabotage you from doing what's necessary to manage your health.

For many people, a health club is a safe haven. It's one of the most supportive and uplifting places in the world—everybody goes there to better themselves. While initially it does take time for any new member to get acclimated, for people with a poor self-image, it can be a complete nightmare. They're not only intimidated and overwhelmed by all the machines; they feel too self-conscious about their physical body to be seen in public, working out. They sign up with good intentions of getting in shape, but their inhibitions keep them at bay.

Could this be you? Have you ever professed that you wanted to get healthy and lose weight, but on the inside, you just weren't feeling it? If so, that's because the value you placed on your health wasn't genuine. A struggle was brewing which started on a conscious level and ended up in your subconscious. Whatever that struggle was, it created a disconnection between your words and actions. Then, when you finally realize that you're out of shape and unhealthy, your first inclination is to shift the blame.

- I'm too busy to exercise; I have to take Johnnie to soccer practice.

- I have two grown daughters, but I never lost the baby weight. They're the reason I'm so fat.

- My spouse cheated on me, it's his or her fault that I'm so depressed. Food is my only source of comfort.

In reality, it's nobody else's fault. If you progressed from the PHS component of *Lifestyle Management*, you'd know that taking care of your health is your responsibility. This has always been your God-given privilege. You're entitled to establish your own priorities, come up with viable plans, implement time management solutions, and set the boundaries necessary to honor your health. By now, you should understand that neglecting your health doesn't really help your kids or anyone else for that matter. Parents who have a healthy self-image know full well, that taking care of their health is important. This doesn't mean they're being selfish. On the contrary, when they're healthier, they function better as parents and set a wonderful example for their children. Healthy parents teach their children that healthy behaviors need to be part of their lifestyle. They demonstrate this through action, not only words. For instance, they willingly schedule time for physical activity, instead of projecting a negative message that exercise is some kind of chore that interferes with daily life.

If you want to climb up the PHS Pyramid, this means you must stop the cycle of excuses. It is self-negligence that created the barriers which inhibited you from doing what's in your best interest. This all started in your head. There's tremendous power in your thoughts. Don't underestimate how your own perceptions, intentions, and every limiting thought you hold on to, can affect your self-image. In your heart of hearts, you have the answers. You know what issues *you allowed* to hold you back and whatever those issues may be; there's a way to resolve them. Be patient. The PHS is a journey of self-discovery and personal transformation. Enlightenment can occur on multiple dimensions.

Developing a healthy self-image requires your conscious effort. If you remain oblivious, the floodgates will open for chaos to seep into your life—and that's precisely what causes you to neglect your health. For example, let's say your spouse wants to move to a beautiful area that's less populated. Do you just happily pack your bags without considering how this may affect your lifestyle? What if you don't have access to a gym? Will you neglect exercise? Will relocating become an excuse for gaining weight? If you have a healthy self-image, then maintaining an exercise regimen is not something you will leave to chance. That notion alone is fundamental to the PHS; it exemplifies being proactive.

The good news is that you're already in transition toward a healthier you. As you work on changing your mind-set and developing a healthy self-image, you inherently improve your well-being. Be careful what thoughts you allow to enter in your mind—garbage in, equal's garbage out. This is a simple, yet very powerful concept. You create your self-image through your thoughts, and it will attach to your outward appearance.

A Soul Search: The Effects of Self-Esteem

The term "self-image" is often used interchangeably with "self-esteem." Essentially, self-esteem is how you *feel* about yourself. The measure of your self-esteem can be determined by how you *view* yourself—that is your self-image. High self-esteem has a positive impact on your life and self-image, allowing you to make quality decisions and develop healthy relationships. Low self-esteem creates a poor self-image, which makes you feel undeserving of happiness and unworthy to receive anything good in life. It keeps you stuck in destructive behavior patterns and dysfunctional relationships.

Self-esteem issues usually develop in childhood. Unhealthy environments, dysfunctional families, and tough circumstances can deal a harmful blow to our self-esteem at a young age. When we become adults, it's our responsibility to reassess our self-esteem as it relates to different areas of our life. We can evolve beyond a bad upbringing, break free from a dysfunctional relationship, and do whatever is necessary to take care of ourselves. We can cultivate healthy self-esteem through new thoughts and behavior patterns—by making better decisions *for ourselves* and *about ourselves*. Our self-image can change, simply by the power of our choices.

An inevitable part of human nature is that we simply can't please everybody over the course of our lifetime. Everybody will experience some form of rejection. Once we accept this reality, we'll become grounded in our own power and self-worth. We need to stop worrying about what others have to say about us and seek to understand what God says about us.

"For if my father and mother should abandon me, you would welcome and comfort me"[1]

It's been said that what other people think about us is really none of our business. We shouldn't measure our self-worth by somebody else's standards. It's not based on our age, sex, ethnic origin, job, marital or parental status, popularity, or affluence. It's true that our upbringing, society, and the vocations we choose can help shape or influence us in some way. Because we are social beings; some measure of esteem from others is necessary, but our self-image has much more to do with us and the decisions we make about ourselves. The way in which we regard and treat ourselves will speak volumes about what we believe. We must learn to honor ourselves from the inside out.

If your only means of gaining self-acceptance comes from outside sources, you'll end up on the proverbial treadmill trying to keep up with the Jones's! There's no need to wait for someone or something to make you feel worthy; you can feel worthy about yourself right now. Acceptance and self-love must come from a place deep within ourselves. We all benefit from positive reinforcement, but what we each think, feel, and believe about ourselves on the inside, is what will determine our self-image.

In your formative years as you were striving to gain some sense of identity, parents and teachers may have done their best to guide you, but no one is a saint. They may have unwittingly spoken negative words, misguided, mistreated, or even abused you in a way that left a detrimental mark on your self-esteem. If you haven't challenged any false sense of deficiency instilled in you and replaced it with a deep understanding of your self-worth, you'll continue to feel inferior. If you're still feeling a great deal of shame from the past, turn it over to your higher power. Until you let it go, it'll hover like a black cloud over you.

If you've tolerated abuse, trauma, tragic loss, abandonment, or harassment of any kind, you may be prone to suffer from a poor self-image. Whatever anguish or torment you endured deep inside your own soul, the result is the same—your value feels diminished against such assaults. This is only human. You have internalized the situation and started feeling bad about yourself. In a worst case scenario, however, if this inferiority complex is not rectified, it can lead to a dreadful outcome. This is what drives people to commit suicide—they've completely lost sight of their own self-worth. None of us could feel comfortable in our own skin with this faulty, self-perception.

It could take years of therapy to recover from deep-rooted self-esteem issues. Some people attempt an escape route to temporarily block out their pain—overeating, alcohol abuse, and dysfunctional relationships. Others assume a victim role in life, letting people walk all over them, or they go to the opposite extreme and become a bully; they look for a scapegoat—someone to badger and hurl insults upon to divert attention from their own feelings of inadequacy. Clearly, there's a vast magnitude of troubles and ramifications associated with low self-esteem. Counselors, therapists, psychologists, psychiatrists, and psychotherapists are needed for this very reason.

"How can you say to your brother, 'Brother let me take the speck out of your eye', when you fail to see the plank in your own eye? You hypocrite, first take the plank out of your eye, then you will see clearly to remove the speck from your brother's eye."[2]

In essence, your self-image becomes whatever it is you believe about yourself. If you suffer from low self-esteem, you become vulnerable to manipulation. Don't go through your whole life depending *only* upon other people to validate you. Nobody holds all the power, discretion, and emotional maturity to determine what's right for you.

Take Inventory of Your Self-Esteem:

- How do I intrinsically feel about myself?

- Do other people's opinions strongly affect me?

- Can I agree to disagree?

- How do I respond to someone who is overbearing?

- Does my job, spouse, or children define who I am?

- Do I need to insult others in order to feel good about myself?

- Do I have confidence in my unique skills, capabilities, and talents?

- How do I handle rejection?

- Can I recognize the difference between constructive and destructive criticism?

- Can I set clear boundaries to take care of myself?

- How do I view my body, and what do I consider beautiful?

Reflecting upon these questions should help you become aware of what issues might interfere with developing a healthy self-image. In the beginning of this book, I mentioned that the power of the truth can set you free. Love has the truth and power in it; fear doesn't. By its mere application in your life, you will know whether you experienced love or fear, so keep that in mind as you answer the questions. For instance, consider the first question: how do I intrinsically feel about myself? Is your response based on love or fear? Below are two possible responses—the first stems from love and a healthy self-image, and the second stems from fear and a poor self-image.

- I'm a unique and wonderful person with much to be grateful for. I live my life with love in my heart for myself and others.

- I feel ashamed of myself—I'm overweight and unattractive. My life sucks, people are out to get me, and nothing goes right for me.

Our thoughts reflect our choices. We can choose to believe the best for ourselves and for others as well. When we trust and believe the best about people, we send out a very powerful message. When we make ourselves a conduit of love and peace, any attacks against us will ricochet, and this allows us to maintain our own power. Certainly, there are times to be angry. Ironically, however, it's when we relinquish bitterness and replace it with forgiveness that we reclaim our power. We gain more power when we center our lives on love.

A mind-set that's centered on love will produce different outcomes than a mind-set that's centered on fear. As you review the lists below, consider what thoughts pop into your head with each word. For example: *truth versus lies*. A truthful thought would tell you that your health is important—that mind-set stems from love. A lie, on the other hand, would tell you that you're being selfish to spend time taking care of yourself—that mind-set is based on fear. Proceed down each list, and contemplate the differences as this relates to your health. For example, a patient thought tells you it takes time to see results, while an impatient thought would tell you to stop trying if you don't see results immediately.

LOVE	FEAR
Truth	Lies
Patient	Impatient
Growth	Stagnation
Rational	Irrational
Trust	Doubt
Faithful	Unfaithful
Optimistic	Pessimistic
Real	Denial
Considerate	Inconsiderate
Grateful	Ungrateful
Forgiving	Bitter

We are each uniquely made in the image of God. There are people who love us unconditionally in spite of our shortcomings. We are free to receive this love and accept this reality. Even as we are open to receive, we also can deposit love into the lives of others. If we want to reap more love, then we need to sow love. As we do this, life will grant us with the right support and love when we need it the most. Real love comes from our heart; it can't be feigned.

We're all interconnected and designed to give and receive love freely. We're meant to be in relationships and share our life with others. God didn't design us to be loners. As an emotionally stable adult, however, we need to love ourselves *first*, before we can love others in a healthy way. This only becomes possible when we esteem ourselves properly. To transform your mind-set and develop a healthy self-image, you should depend upon God to find your value. When you were created, your identity was shaped by God, not by man.

"God is not a man that he should lie, nor a son of man that he should change his mind. Does he speak and then not act? Does he promise and not fulfill?"[3]

God isn't fickle in his perception of you. If you fail at something, he's not going to kick you to the curb. He loves and cherishes you in spite of your flaws and weaknesses. "For God so loved the world, he gave his one and only Son that whoever believes in him shall not perish but have eternal life."[4] The world can condemn you for the smallest flaw and withhold acceptance for any reason. Despite your best efforts to please others, there's no guarantee you'll gain this approval. Maybe in your job you work very hard and have excellent performance, but your boss says it's still not enough. Maybe you're judged because of your ethnic origin, your age, what you do for a living, your marital status, your choice to be (or not to be) a parent, or your sexual orientation. Remember, it's impossible to please everyone. There are some people who just don't like you—they have no reason; they just don't like you! What then? Don't allow the rejections, perceptions, and judgments of others to cause you to reject yourself. "What you believe has a much greater impact on your life than what anybody else believes."[5]

Without a healthy self-image, you'll go through the majority of your life feeling quite unsatisfied and dejected. Continually striving to gain this approval from others shouldn't be misconstrued with any version of love. That shouldn't be how you seek to nurture yourself and if it is, then you've been looking for love in all the wrong places. Healthy love is unconditional; it's not manipulative and doesn't come with strings attached. Also understand that serving others is wonderful—it's part of our life purpose—but we shouldn't become martyrs. Serve yourself a healthy dose of love *first;* then give to others.

If you learn to view and love yourself the way God does, this will prevent you from the people-pleasing trap. God can set you free from the bondage of trying to prove your worth to others. He can help ground you in healthy self-love. The only thing that sets you straight is a healthy dose of love—for God, for yourself, and for others.

Fixing the Brokenness Within:
Developing Healthy Self-Esteem

Spiritually, we all came into the world with a broken view of ourselves. From a Christian standpoint, low self-esteem originated way back in the Garden of Eden. Before Adam and Eve broke God's commandment, their life was just splendid. They weren't ashamed of being naked; they were whole and had a perfect relationship with God. Sin shattered their self-esteem and altered that connection with God for many generations to come. Now there was a wedge between them and God. They felt broken on the inside when they discovered they had sinned and were naked. Their first attempt at making themselves feel better was to sew fig leaves to cover themselves. This fallen nature made its mark on mankind. It has become a battle to recapture our lost self-esteem ever since.

We need to become whole again by putting our broken pieces back together. The good news is that God is just as *loving* as he is *powerful*, and there is redemption for this original sin through Jesus Christ. When you accept and make peace with Christ, you liberate yourself spiritually. Healthy self-esteem, in its rudimentary form, is nothing but healthy self-love. In order to love yourself in the right way, you must find your intrinsic value in a higher spiritual power. There's a reason for this—we can't gain our self-worth by doing good works, by people-pleasing, or by attaining material gains. We need something much deeper, something that overrides our human efforts.

Here's what Joel Osteen an evangelical pastor of one of the largest growing congregations has to say about one's self-image: "We must learn to love ourselves in spite of our flaws, not because we are full of ourselves, or because we want to excuse our shortcomings but because that's how our heavenly Father loves us."[6] God isn't holding a grudge against you. He loves us in spite of our sins. This is why he gave his only son—to save us from a life of sin that originally separated us from God. That's not an excuse to sin, but Jesus made a provision for it. If we accept Christ through faith, then we can get right with God again. This will help us get rid of our inferiority complex and make us feel whole. On the flip side, if we become condescending in our interactions with others, this indicates we've developed an inflated sense of pride. Once we recognize that we need God in order to view and love ourselves appropriately, it prevents us from becoming narcissistic. We won't end up trying to play God, and that's a good thing. (The world has enough egomaniacs.) If we're fortunate enough to receive God's grace, he can restore us to wholeness.

When we allow God to take his rightful place in our lives, he can transform our mind. God can bring us to our knees, but he also can bring us to our senses. A broken view of our self leads to broken values. Submitting to a higher source of power prevents us from putting our faith in broken values and losing our self-esteem. When we're faced with our own limitations, there's a natural tendency to get down on ourselves. With God on our side however, this allows us to experience magnificent power in our life. We don't have to carry our burdens alone. Accepting Christ can restore our self-esteem.

Reconsider Your Values

- *Abundant life vs. Abundant stuff*: "What good will it be for a man if he gains the whole world, yet forfeits his soul?"[7]

- *Spiritual vs. Material*: "Jesus answered, "It is written: Man does not live on bread alone, but on every word that comes from the mouth of God."[8]

- *Eternal vs. Temporary*: "Do not work for food that spoils, but for food that endures to eternal life."[9]

> "Delight yourself in the Lord and he will give you the desires of your heart."[10]

Self-Image and Self-Talk

The way we talk to ourselves says a lot about our mind-set. Whether we realize it or not, we have conversations with ourselves on a regular basis. Thoughts pop into our heads, and sometimes we agree with those thoughts, and other times we reject them—either way, there's a dialogue going on. Any bantering back and forth counts as self-talk. Before you can change what you say to yourself, you need to monitor this communication. From time to time, stop and listen to what you're saying to yourself—it can make a huge impact on your self-esteem, for better or worse. Maybe you're always talking down to yourself. Every time you make a mistake, do you berate yourself with criticism? This is not something to take lightly; it's very self-destructive.

"The eye is the lamp of the body. If your eyes are good, your whole body will be full of light. But if your eyes are bad your whole body will be full of darkness. If then the light within you is darkness, how great is that darkness!"[11] Do you see yourself through darkness or through light? The first place to begin to develop a healthy self-image is through your thoughts.

> **"For as he thinketh in his heart, so is he."[12]**

Becoming aware of what you say to yourself is half the battle. Once you become aware, then you need to change any negative self-talk. For instance, if you planned to get up early to exercise but slept-in instead, what do you say to yourself? Would you say something like, "I'm so fat and lazy. I'll never lose weight." Or would you say something along the lines of "It was hard getting out of bed this morning, but if I go to sleep earlier, I won't be so tempted to sleep in"? You can't expect yourself to develop a healthy self-image if you judge yourself all the time. That's quite different from correcting yourself. The Bible says we are to speak the truth in love. It should be no different when we talk to ourselves. If you want to develop a healthy self-image, it's absolutely crucial to catch negative self-talk and replace it with positive affirmations. You're free to come up with your own affirmations, but some suggestions are listed below.

Healthy Self-Management Affirmations

- My health is important.
- I deserve to nurture my mind, body and spirit.
- I am worth the time it takes to take care of myself.
- I'm a better person when I've done something good for myself.
- I'm aware of my needs, as well as the needs of others.
- I don't mind putting effort into taking care of myself.
- I determine my weight and how I look and feel.
- I see myself as a physically fit and healthy person.
- I only eat foods that are beneficial for me.
- I don't eat to relieve anxiety, boredom or loneliness.
- I enjoy the exhilaration and benefits of exercise.

God's word tells us to keep our bodies and spirits clean. "Don't you know that you yourselves are God's temple and that God's spirit lives in you? If anyone defiles/destroys God's temple, God will destroy him; for God's temple is sacred, and you are that temple."[13]

Body Image

We've all heard the motto that beauty is in the eye of the beholder, but let's not kid ourselves either. Not everyone can be supermodels, but that shouldn't stop us from getting in our best physical condition. When it comes to our external appearance, we all need grooming and work. Some people just need to stop justifying their carelessness. Although there is something to be said for taking care of your physical body and having some fashion sense, equally important, is what you feel on the inside—your body image.

Some people believe they will be more acceptable if they were in better physical shape, but this won't necessarily help them if they still feel ugly and ashamed on the inside. I know some women who are absolutely beautiful from a physical standpoint, yet they still suffer from low self-esteem and a poor body-image. As we work on improving our physical appearance, this can help us feel better about ourselves, but we should not neglect this beauty-call from within. How we view ourselves—our body-image will determine the measure of our beauty, both inside and out.

Begin to view yourself as beautiful from the inside as you accept and work with what you have on the outside. Your physical body is the only vessel you have to carry you through this life—learn to take care of it. At some point however, you must make peace with your physical body.

"The only limitations on our health, beauty, energy, vitality, and joy come from our own self-created blocks, our own resistance to the goodness of life, based on fear and ignorance. Our bodies are simply a physical expression of our consciousness. The concepts we hold of ourselves determine our health and beauty or the lack thereof. When we deeply change our concepts our physical self follows suit. The body is continuously changing, replenishing, and rebuilding itself at every moment and it has no other pattern to follow in doing so except the guidance to it by the mind. The more we bring our consciousness into alignment with our highest spiritual realization, the more our bodies will express our own individual perfection."[14]

CHAPTER 10

Motivation—
PHS Principle: Set Your Vision

If you set your vision correctly, you'll naturally be motivated. Why? When you learn to recognize and release any underlying, self-imposed limitations, you'll feel like there's nothing in the world you can't accomplish. Remember, you must continue to think proactively in order to use your imagination. In your mind's eye, there are no bounds—you're free to envision the notions and extent of whatever you desire. By creating a mental image of what you want, you'll begin to activate the power of creative visualization. This summons forces from the universe to restore lost hope and leads you to fulfill your expectations and wishes. Thoughts emit their own energy and carry a power that attracts whatever is lined up with that same frequency. This is a universal truth referred to as the "law of attraction." Basically, it means that the inner vision you set for yourself will align you with the natural orders that govern the workings of the universe. This principle has the power to affect every aspect of your health and the entire course of your life.

> "Where there is no vision, the people perish: but he that keepeth the law, happy is he."[1]

Understanding this PHS Component: Motivation

If there were a way to bottle and sell motivation, the supply wouldn't keep up with the demand—nobody seems to get enough of it. The motivation that's needed to develop a healthy lifestyle is a widespread enigma. People from all walks of life today are simply not very motivated to take care of themselves. They get stuck in a rut and there are countless reasons why. Within the PHS hierarchy, there are several lenses from which to view many relevant aspects associated with this worldwide weariness. Each viewpoint presented within this methodology is connected in some fashion to this PHS component of motivation. As you learn about this connection, you'll discover what blocks your motivation, what drives it, and how to fuel it. You'll soon realize that much of your motivation is tied to your vision. Here, you'll have the opportunity to step back, reflect, and gauge your progress along this health journey. As you do, you may find it's necessary to retrace some steps before continuing on the same path. After all, if you plan to reach the top of the PHS Pyramid, you must follow a route that will get you there.

There's always an underlying reason why people lack the motivation to take care of themselves. For example, you may think that the reason your next-door neighbors are obese and out of shape is because they're lazy. Though they could very well be lazy, there's a reason they got that way. Laziness is the symptom; it's not the cause. Something interfered with their intrinsic motivation—a conflict was triggered that obstructed their path. The root cause can be traced back to the first two components on the PHS Pyramid, as conflicts in either *lifestyle management* and/or *healthy self-management*. Though the issues may be different in scope, the majority stem from several common denominators, such as conflicts with time management, failure to take personal responsibility, difficulty processing emotions, lack of inner peace, and low self-esteem. Many people create their own self-imposed limitations through skewed perceptions and faulty interpretations.

In reviewing these initial components on the PHS Pyramid, we can recognize that besides the daily lifestyle struggles that many people face—a demanding schedule, sick kids, mounting bills—there are mental and spiritual blocks that stifle motivation. If you've been gripped by negative thought patterns, this has a dire effect on your well-being and motivation. (*Motivation? What motivation? The couch and a huge bag of potato chips sound perfectly fine.*) Don't delude yourself. Everything you are on the inside—your thoughts, perceptions, and spiritual condition—is aligned and reflected on the outside. This is precisely why it's crucial for people who undergo gastric bypass surgery to be screened and counseled thoroughly. If significant weight loss occurs without healthy behavior modification, it's a setup for failure. Whether we realize it or not, some of our lifestyle behaviors are already on display. Most people lack the motivation to take care of their health because they're still held back by many issues unbeknownst to them. They don't view health through a larger, more accurate lens and consequently, their internal vision becomes impaired.

Society is partly to blame for this impairment. As previously discussed, within our communities and educational systems, the subject of *how* to develop healthy behaviors has not properly evolved. The general population has been in urgent need of this fundamental instruction, yet we've been positioned in a different direction. With the increasing obesity rates, we're quick to acknowledge the need to set weight-loss goals. We also recognize that exercise and good nutrition is part of a healthy lifestyle, but that's pretty much where the discussion stops. Motivation wanes because there's much more missing. Healthy lifestyle behaviors aren't implemented because of a major educational oversight; it has failed to emphasize that health is integrated, that it extends beyond the basic measures of a fitness program or required physical education. We must get our mind wrapped around this concept and begin to teach that health is not just about eating organic veggies, going gluten-free, or doing sprints in gym class; it's not reserved for the elite athlete. In order to motivate people toward healthier behaviors, some transformation must occur in their psyche.

Again, we must reconsider—what is health? We should question the integrity of health education that only promotes health physically, yet fails to acknowledge the whole. We can see the negative effects of this oversight every time we turn on the news and hear about a mass gun-shooting. Clearly, mental health has been on the decline. Shall we continue to discount this integration of the mind, body and spirit? Although we tend to compartmentalize these dimensions, they should each be taken into account as part of a comprehensive health solution.

To expand your perspective, consider this analogy: if you think about pizza, do you think of it solely in terms of bread, pepperoni, cheese, and tomato sauce? No. It's a combination of these parts. Food experts know that to make the best pizza, they need the best ingredients. Personally, you may prefer corner crust, thick or thin, but pizza is still pizza. Likewise, optimal health is a sum of different parts and each part serves an important purpose. We might choose to elaborate on any part, but we should not forget what we are striving for—we must set our vision on this big picture of optimal health.

The World Health Organization has expanded the definition of health to include the mind, body, and spirit. Now, it's time for us to act. We need to accept this revised definition of health, individually and collectively, in order to make any sort of progress. The health and fitness agendas of many societies worldwide still need to evolve. While this appears to be a tall order, it's a necessary and innovative response to the escalating global obesity problem and national health care dilemma. We must go above and beyond trite fitness programs to motivate individuals toward healthy behavior.

The PHS provides an innovative strategy. Through the power of principles, it guides us along a path to develop these neglected sides of our well-being. Only when we expand our vision and start looking in the right direction can we begin to offer some true incentive. For example, just because children eat nutritious meals, we can't presume they're healthy. They could be suffering from psychological or spiritual abuse at the hands of their parents. This harms their psyche and development in many ways, and that can potentially squash motivation for years to come. They could end up spending a lifetime in therapy, and how healthy is that? But if they were exposed to primary truths regarding optimal health within a basic educational model, this would curtail some of the adverse effects of that upbringing. Education would be the spark of hope and provide enlightenment, because learning can occur on a conscious and unconscious level. Psychologically, this would grant them some recourse.

As a society, if we sincerely want to be motivated toward better health, then we need to correct our impaired vision. In this day and age, many individuals are so overwhelmed by information overload and pressured by time constraints they don't know where to start. Yet we are more alike than we are different, so there are many benefits to following a common path. Consider the PHS a road map. It can be referenced and applied anywhere—in the home, schools, health clubs, corporate wellness programs, hospitals, religious organizations, and substance abuse agencies. It reveals a practical methodology to our collective consciousness as it unravels many common issues that block motivation. Within it, we can find both structure and synergy. It compels each of us as individuals, to look within our own consciousness for many answers. We can choose to do this alone or as part of a group. This allows us to keep our issues private, if we so choose—and to progress at our own pace. For some, evolving toward this path of self-discipline may only take a few weeks; for others, it could take months or even years. That's okay, there's no timeline on self-evolvement.

Self-Assess Your PHS Progress

Before going much farther, you must take some time to self-assess your PHS progress. The inspiration to get healthy starts from the bottom of PHS Pyramid. If you're still struggling to gain some motivation then go back, and do your personal homework within those first two tiers—*lifestyle management* and *healthy self-management*. Doing this homework upfront gives you a tremendous advantage. Whenever you're willing to face up to the truth, learn, change, and grow, you'll remove blocked energy from within your consciousness. This will rejuvenate your spirit and ignite motivation. Then you can take that newfound motivation to the next level by setting your personal health and fitness goals.

Doing your homework effectively doesn't mean your life is suddenly perfect; it means you've prepared the way. You've managed to sort through and resolve a bulk of lifestyle or personal issues that could otherwise hinder your progress. For example, maybe you could never find time to exercise, but now you've set aside four one-hour spots during the week. Or perhaps you were gripped with negative thought patterns that sabotaged your self-esteem, but now you've released the limitations of that old mind-set. Maybe you used to turn to food whenever you were stressed, but now you find more constructive ways to deal with your emotions. Being prepared in this sense, means you've developed some proactive, healthy behaviors.

You will feel lighter, have more clarity and sense a new willingness to move forward.

If you need more time however, then continue to deal with whatever lifestyle and personal issues are still bogging you down. Are you still trying to get a grip on that busy, demanding schedule? Revamp your priorities, and set boundaries on your time. Still have some demons to battle? Ask God to help. He can fight your battles and help you transform on many levels. For instance, if you've been harboring bitterness in your heart, God can lead you to forgiveness to release that dark and heavy force from your spirit. He can replace bitterness with deep compassion, fresh insight and new energy.

Whether you need to make a few modifications or many, having a method to follow will keep things on an even keel. Since the PHS is an integrated methodology; you could've started with any component or principle of your choice. However, if you started from the bottom of the pyramid and progressed upward; that should save you both time and trouble. From that starting point, the PHS reconnects you with core values and this helps to build intrinsic motivation. It grounds you with a psychological foundation that can prevent you from setting goals you're not ready to achieve. Preparation is a key to life success.

Remember, no matter what your personal fitness goals may be, the core objective behind the PHS is the same—it's to help you develop the discipline needed to maintain a healthy lifestyle. Nobody really enjoys being unhealthy. Initially, managing your lifestyle so that you can manage your health may not seem realistic; but it's at the crux of the matter. Getting through that hard part, gives you the leverage you need to make progress. The good news is after you've made reasonable progress in managing your lifestyle and yourself, then you'll be good to go. You'll be fired up and ready to start your fitness program. You can set your vision on your mission knowing that when you get with the program, you'll stay with the program!

Though you're in the middle of the pyramid, this doesn't mean you won't backslide or experience recurrent issues. It's just that you'll start dealing with those issues differently. For example, if someone or something got you upset, you know that there is a PHS principle to help you. Perhaps food used to be your only recourse whenever you were upset, but now by being proactive, you change your response. At this stage, you should see those old coping mechanisms for what they're worth. You recognize that emotional eating won't solve your problems, so you just don't go there anymore. Gone are the days when you down a carton of ice cream, a bag of Cheetos, and a box of Ho-Ho's, all in one sitting. That's *reactive* behavior; now you know better. (Besides, it might cause diarrhea!) Instead you are *proactive* and consider better options. First you take a step back to cool off; then you may decide to vent to a friend, release your burden to God or take a walk to clear your head. You may prefer to write your feelings down or hit the gym to release pent-up aggression. Whatever you decide, the old, self-defeating coping mechanisms should be losing their grip as you find new, constructive ways of behaving. You know that if you continue to think proactively, you'll be more likely to behave proactively.

If you do backslide by finding yourself slipping into old behaviors patterns, take a time-out for a few minutes—stay calm, relax, breathe deeply, and slowly count to ten—in that moment, tell yourself it's going to be okay. Don't lose hope. Soon, you'll figure out whatever is necessary to get back on track. Any doubt or disarray that's putting your life in a tailspin will soon lose its hold. Remember you're always the one in charge of your choices and responses, that's part of being proactive. In spite of any situation, you can find constructive options. It's this firsthand intervention that prevents you from repeating the same old mistakes, making excuses, and getting stuck in a rut. This is your privilege. Now you recognize why proactive behavior facilitates your personal growth. You don't react by resorting to vices anymore. Instead, you choose what's better for you, and you do so, without second-guessing yourself.

In order to keep your vision on your mission, you must build upon the lifestyle and healthy self-management skills you already acquired. The personal barriers you've overcome within those initial components can be used to chart your progress. That is what will separate a true lifestyle transformation from a quick-fix and will fuel the motivation that facilitates PHS success. You'll notice growth instead of stagnation. For example, if you've made time for exercise into your weekly schedule, this represents a progressive change in lifestyle management. If you feel more balanced internally, this represents a progressive change in healthy self-management. To monitor your personal growth, just step back and take note of all your improvements.

Take pride in all your accomplishments big or small. You've already begun to blaze a new trail. In whatever way you've gained momentum, be sure to give yourself credit. Even if you had to take a couple steps backward, that's okay. Now however, is the time to keep pressing forward. Remember, you must climb to the top of PHS Pyramid. Set your vision on all your goals and on the apex of the pyramid—***discipline***—that's the ultimate health purpose in all its magnificent glory. Don't lose focus. If you've made it this far, just stay with it. Keep going until you reach the top—you can do it!

For a quick review, let's recap the five PHS components. Recall, the "do it" stems refers to taking care of your health.

Lifestyle Management—*bids you to do it.*

Healthy Self-Management—*frees you to do it.*

Motivation—*inspires you to do it.*

Program Design—*teaches you what to do and how to do it.*

Discipline—*makes you do it.*

. . . .

Obstacles are the things a person sees when
he takes his eyes off his goals.
—E. Joseph Cossman
. . . .

External / Internal Motivation

Marcus Tullius Cicero (106–43 BCE) was a very popular Roman writer, speaker, philosopher, and politician who said it quite well: "It is exercise alone that supports the spirit and keeps the mind in vigor."

When it comes to motivation, let's consider exercise for a moment. Exercise is an amazing activity with numerous health benefits. Physically, it invigorates our internal organs, such as our heart and lungs. It stimulates muscles, lowers blood pressure and cholesterol, improves our flexibility, and so much more. Exercise can also make us healthier in other ways by promoting our mental well-being and invigorating our spirit. Yet despite all its tremendous benefits, if we're not motivated, we just won't do it. What in the world motivates us? Are we driven externally or internally? Where do we start?

Ideally, children should start learning healthy behaviors at the foundation of the PHS Pyramid and progress upward. This naturally aligns them with the *internal* motivation to be healthy. If they can grasp important principles when they're young, they won't have such a hard time later in life. Being exposed to these truths and informed about what lies ahead will help them establish core values. Instilling the right mind-set in children is invaluable in helping them build and sustain motivation. Games or toys can be designed to construct the PHS Pyramid in building-block format to make learning simple and fun. This primes children for success early on, by teaching them to value health sooner, rather than later.

As an adult, if you've embarked upon the first two tiers, you've already worked on clearing the path ahead. You'll know through your own personal breakthroughs what has become a conduit to internal motivation. Also keep in mind, that the PHS is interconnected with optimal health. This means that external and internal motivation can still feed off one another—one type of motivation can potentially lead to another. Therefore, if you chose to start with external motivation, such as the program design portion of the pyramid, this can also be a good idea. In fact, some people may find it more convenient.

Everyone just needs to find the right starting point, depending on his or her particular life circumstance. Consider Joan, who at sixty years old has a very busy lifestyle, while Phyllis, the same age is retired. For Joan, setting a few goals based on external motivation can be a great place to start, as it can have a reciprocal effect—external motivation can land upon the doorstep of internal motivation. Since Phyllis has more time on her hands, she's prone to building internal motivation. First, let's make a distinction between these two types of motivation by referring back to this example for exercise. Since exercise is necessary for good health, begin to think about what naturally aligns you with physical activity. Perhaps you like taking walks, swimming, biking, dancing, or shooting hoops. Whatever that activity may be, because you enjoy it—it feeds your internal motivation. For instance, I spoke with a gentleman recently, who told me he never realized that playing two hours of basketball was exercise. He didn't realize this until of course, he stopped playing and gained thirty pounds!

Some people can get internally motivated just by looking in the mirror. They hit a moment of truth, and that's incentive enough; they simply want to gain the satisfaction of making a positive change in their physical appearance and health. People who are *internally motivated* are commitment-oriented—their vision is intuitively set on the right track. It's aligned with their core values and best interests.

On the other hand, people who are *externally motivated* base their actions on some type of reward or fear. Whether they realize it or not, their vision has been set on something external. The rewards can be tangible (such as money or trophies) or intangible (such as gaining praise or recognition). Or their motivation can stem from fear. For instance, maybe the doctor warned them that if they didn't start an exercise program soon and stop eating fast foods, they wouldn't live long enough to see their grandkids. When you *"have to"* do something because your health is at risk, that's external motivation. External motivation can lead to internal motivation, as long as you recognize the value of making this integrated health transformation. For example, you might start an exercise program because your doctor told you to, but several months later, when you feel so much better, you realize that you actually don't mind exercising. At some point, you made a change in your internal vision, because now you gladly do this of your own accord. Give yourself kudos, because making this transition from external motivation to internal motivation is awesome!

This is your health journey and you can proceed any way you want. If you lose motivation or something isn't working out, simply refer back to the PHS Pyramid. It's designed to build internal motivation because it helps you to get your priorities straight from the start—by aligning you with this core value of health. Ultimately however, your success depends upon your desire, effort, and commitment.

Examples of External Motivation:

- I want to lose weight for my son's wedding.

- My doctor told me that I have to start an exercise program.

- I want to win a weight-loss bet at work because I can score a free vacation.

- My spouse got me a gift to work with a personal trainer; I better show up.

Examples of Internal Motivation:

- I enjoy the physical challenge of exercise and do whatever it takes to honor my body.

- I take time to nurture my mind, body, and spirit because it feels great.

- I enjoy eating wholesome and nutritious foods.

- I take care of myself, because being healthy improves the quality of my life.

View Obstacles as Fuel for Motivation

Everybody will have their fair share of trials and tribulations in life. We don't live in a trouble-free, risk-free world. Some people think that life would be much better if everything was picture perfect, but it sure would be dreadfully boring if there were no challenges in our path. Life is not plastic; it's meant to be lived, and it may get messy and ugly in the process. Time conflicts, interpersonal struggles, personal issues, suffering, and stress happen to us all. That's just life! Although none of this sounds pleasant, we actually need to be challenged to a certain degree, in order to maintain our motivation.

If you can find a path with no obstacles, it probably doesn't lead anywhere. —Frank Howard Clark

This can apply to any dimension of our life. Just ask a guy who's dating two girls simultaneously. Let's assume he finds both physically attractive, but one girl is very busy and seems a bit unpredictable, while the other is available at his beck and call. Who do you think he's going to be more motivated to pursue? Which one becomes more intriguing and gets his attention? Which one does he go out of his way to impress? You get the idea. This is the ironic part of human nature; we always seem to want, what we can't have. That's because on some level, we all thrive on a challenge. So whenever you're faced with a seemingly difficult circumstance, remember that there's always a built-in stimulus. Whatever the obstacle may be; just consider it fuel for your motivation. There's a hidden benefit within and you'll discover it sooner or later.

. . . .

A man does what he must—in spite of personal
consequences, in spite of obstacles and dangers
and pressures—and that is the basis of all
human morality. —John F. Kennedy

. . . .

Create a new vision by viewing any obstacle you experience in life as a catalyst for positive change. It's that proverbial blessing in disguise that offers this true incentive and helps you to grow. You can think of obstacles as a game you want to triumph in. Imagine a few cheerleaders on the sidelines, rooting you on—they want you to win! Winners don't shy away from obstacles; they look for ways to overcome. This is as true in life as it is with any game. Winners might fall, but they always get back up and give it their best shot.

Whenever you're pushed outside of your comfort zone, this has an ironic way of making you a better person. The discomfort that's created beckons you to reach a higher potential. It stretches you to go above and beyond a predictable point. This is why many people thrive upon competition. When they compete and overcome hurdles along the way, victory becomes much sweeter. It creates a rush of adrenaline—there's an energy, and enthusiasm that emanate from reaching new heights and crushing your goals. You can feed off that energy high.

If you harness the law of attraction, you'll discover that you already have everything within you, a built-in mechanism to rise above obstacles. Although we're naturally wired to channel our energy in a positive way, many people have lost touch with this innate tendency. They've allowed discouragement to override this instinct. Yet the drive is still there; it exists deep down in every human soul. Whenever you stifle your potential, you put a halt on motivation—it can rob your soul of a sweet victory.

. . . .

Obstacles don't have to stop you. If you run into a wall, don't turn around and give up. Figure out how to climb it, go through it, or work around it. —Michael Jordan

. . . .

If obstacles will arise, why not accept this fact and be prepared? This is something everyone needs to capitalize on, because in the process of pursuing our health and fitness goals, we're going to encounter some troubles in life. Demands will be made upon our time, and "stuff happens" to the best of us. When you set your vision to rise above your problems however, you can overcome them and become a champion.

Remember, *you alone* are the product of your own decisions, so don't resort to the blame game or the "woe is me" syndrome. Continue to take responsibility for your life and health. If you remain proactive, you'll discover a way to defend what's important to you. It's been said that 100 percent commitment is easy; 99 percent commitment is what's difficult. That's because when you're 100 percent committed, there's no deliberation involved, you'll do what's necessary in spite of your circumstances. What will be your choice? Will you succumb to pressure and get discouraged, or will you set a new vision and precedent for yourself? When it comes down to the wire, your vision will affect your motivation, for better or worse.

Never forget that being healthy is in your best interest. Whenever you do what's in your best interest, you make the world a better place—it creates a positive chain effect. Continue to ask yourself what takes precedence in your life. Are you still paying lip service to your health? Obstacles will arise as they do whenever you set out to pursue anything worthwhile, but if your health is valuable to you, you will set your vision on this mission and find ways to overcome.

. . . .
I've been motivated by overcoming challenge
and overcoming the hurdles and obstacles
that face me. There still is plenty out there
to get motivated by. —Andre Agassi
. . . .

Perhaps your obstacle comes through a demanding work schedule that hardly leaves a minute to spare. When you're proactive you'll find ways to readjust your schedule by focusing on what's really important (your health) and eliminating potential time-wasters such as unnecessary phone calls. You become more resourceful with your time. Maybe you decide to exercise by taking a half-hour walk on your lunch break, or taking a fifteen-minute walk during lunch and another fifteen-minute walk later in the day. If you're employed close to a gym, perhaps you decide to hire a personal trainer for a time-efficient workout, before, during or after work.

Your obstacle might have to do with raising children or being a single parent while trying to make ends meet. Money and time may be very tight, but you can look for unique ways to stay physically active. For instance, you can incorporate exercise with your kids by using them as free weights. Lug them around and play different games to challenge them and yourself physically. You'll burn a lot of calories, stimulate your muscles, and everybody has fun in the process.

Perhaps your obstacle is trying to find some peace and quiet time to nurture your spirit. When you were single and lived alone, it was easy to make time for meditation and reflection, but now you're married, and your spouse works from home—he or she is always talking on the phone. You may have a child that sings or plays an instrument all day. Perhaps your spouse and/or kids pounce on you as soon as you walk in the door after a long, hard day of work. In those moments, it may appear that gaining any such peace is a figment of your imagination, but that's simply not true. If this quiet time is truly important to you, it's not wishful thinking. You can find a way to bring more solace into your life. Create a sacred spot. Maybe you can assign a separate room in the house and put a "do not disturb" or "man-cave" sign on the door. Incidentally, you don't have to be a man to set up a man-cave; women are entitled to a "woman-cave" as well. You can set some ground rules for your family by designating quiet times, or letting them know up front that you need some down-time immediately after work. You may convince your spouse to find a quiet place to work in the house, such as the basement or garage. Whether you only find one hour for peace and quiet, or a few hours per week, you can create a system that works specifically for you. The possibilities are endless—there's always a way to honor your health and well-being.

If you set this greater vision on overcoming obstacles, the doors of opportunity will open. This will add more fuel to your motivation. Don't succumb to small-minded thinking or be convinced otherwise. Whatever area of your life it may be; start viewing your obstacles as opportunities in disguise. It's like exercise to our muscles. When we lift weights, it may hurt in the process, but in the long run, it makes us stronger. People who've never been challenged in life become weak. They tend to take everything at face value because they lack solid coping strategies.

We can view life as the play of opposing forces and cycles. Tremendous beauty is often birthed through deep pain. Any woman who has given birth knows the splendor that follows the suffering. Songwriters or musicians can capture something magical in heartbreak. If we don't rise above our challenges in life, we get complacent; lose our zest, and stifle our motivation. There are plenty of people living lives of quiet desperation. Overcoming life's challenges will keep us motivated.

. . . .
Pain is weakness leaving the body. —Tom Sobal
. . . .

Have you ever realized that most relationships are riveted by a challenge? There are several relationship books that revolve around this notion, such as *The Rules*, and *Why Men Love Bitches*. People always seem to want what they can't have, and others have capitalized on this ideology. To some degree or another, we're all exhilarated by a challenge. We may not recognize this consciously, but it stimulates our senses and prevents us from getting bored. In the relationship arena, nobody really likes boredom. We all want to keep the spark alive. That doesn't mean we should chase cheap thrills or stay in a rocky relationship because it offers an element of excitement or unpredictability. On the contrary, recognizing our need to be challenged might give us new insight into the partners and choices we make. It could help us to realize that we need to end the drama of an unstable relationship. We can ask: why have we attracted this drama into our life, or what makes us gravitate toward such a partner in the first place? Relationships are like a mirror—the challenges they present are often a reflection of something we desire or something we need to learn in order to experience growth.

. . . .
Challenges are what makes life interesting;
overcoming them is what makes life
meaningful. —Joshua J. Marine
. . . .

While we can all benefit from a challenge on some level, we're not all motivated in the same way. Each one of us has a personal threshold. Some people cave under a certain type of pressure, while others may thrive upon it. Likewise, success in life is not defined the same way for all. We each have our own comfort zones, tolerance levels, incentives, and ideas of success. The reality, however, is that we each need to be pushed out of our own comfort zone in order to experience growth. Instead of being resistant, we should welcome this change from time to time, at least a little bit, in order to assist in our own development. If everything was easy, predictable, and comfortable, we'd remain complacent and lose our edge. Such indulgences can short sight our vision and cause us to become desensitized, dull, or delusional. If life offers no incentive, no sparkle of brilliance, then nothing excites us. It's this utter dreariness to the soul that hinders motivation. The fire within your spirit needs fuel to keep burning. Often, it's the very obstacle you try to resist that can rekindle your motivation. Those obstacles are put in your life path to help you grow past the present moment, so that you can be all that you can be. When you're motivated nothing will stop you from progressing forward.

> The difference between school and life?
> In school, you're taught a lesson and then
> given a test. In life, you're given a test that
> teaches you a lesson. —Tom Bodett

Obstacles may seem contraindicative to your motivation and personal growth, but they're not. This very basic point of view has so much power in it. It separates those who have a winner mentality from those with a loser mentality. Winners think differently from losers in that they don't recognize failures as such. Typically, they view all their experiences as valuable lessons.

Think of it another way; the toughest assignments go to the best students. Nobody gets accepted into an Ivy League college without passing rigorous tests and meeting certain criteria. Similarly, life will test you with its trials and tribulations. If you're mentally prepared to make the most out of them, you won't lose motivation. You know it's just par for the course. If you remain proactive, you can overcome obstacles instead of letting them overcome you. Will you keep your vision set on your mission? Will you continue climbing the PHS Pyramid until that mission is complete? The choice and power is always within you.

> Whenever you fall, pick something up. —Oswald Avery

If we can drive this point home within our education system, children can learn how to benefit from overcoming obstacles early in life. Instilling this valuable life lesson can help them to maintain motivation and prevent them from being driven toward senseless behaviors.

SET YOUR VISION ON YOUR MISSION

1. Stay Focused on Optimal Health

Remember, metaphysically, we are more than just our physical bodies. We each give off different vibes or energy. These energy fields are interconnected with our body, both mentally and spiritually. Although the definition of health has evolved through the World Health Organization, much of society is still unaware of what this entails. Many people launch into their weight loss and fitness programs and neglect other dimensions of their well-being. Some people believe that; if they can't see it or touch it, then it doesn't exist.

In particular, the spiritual dimension of health is often overlooked because society subjugates it into a dogma of religious rhetoric and political correctness. This is quite unfortunate, because when we improve our spiritual well-being, this can restore our health and transform our entire life. Just consider our mental institutions and jail cells—they're filled with people who are suffering deeply from a demented spiritual condition. There are plenty of testimonies where hard-core criminals have turned their life around by accepting and making peace with a higher spiritual power. Surely, our spirit needs some time and attention.

Several years ago, before I started using the PHS with my clients, I trained James, an obese, middle-aged man. James worked out exceptionally hard with me twice a week for several months. On top of that, he did at least four days of cardio, as prescribed, tracked on his heart-rate monitor, and met regularly with a registered dietitian. After a couple of months into his program, he made some improvements in his stamina, strength, and cardiovascular endurance, but he didn't lose much weight. We discussed his nutrition habits, and everything appeared to be on track. Months went by, and he still had very little weight loss. Other than a better posture, James didn't look much different. Knowing the law of thermodynamics, I kept pressing him about his eating habits and meetings with the dietitian—I knew something was going on. Then one day in a casual conversation, the truth finally slipped out. He confessed that he never actually changed his eating habits. In fact, after leaving the gym, he ate all the more! He admitted that he had many unresolved psychological issues and problems with his live-in girlfriend. Food was his only source of comfort—his ultimate coping mechanism and crutch. James never turned to God to help him transform in his mind or spirit. He had a dietitian, personal trainer, and metabolic specialist on his side, yet he needed something greater.

We all need more than just a diet and exercise program to achieve optimal health. Although every dimension of our well-being needs attention, this is a matter of personal responsibility. Nobody can force us to seek God, develop spiritually, or evolve in any way. Being addicted to food is similar to being an alcoholic. Alcoholics Anonymous has a twelve-step process to overcome this addiction. Part of that recovery process includes recognizing our need for a higher source of power. After we make a decision to turn our lives over to the care of God, as we understand God, we can overcome our addictions.

James jumped right into the program design portion of the PHS Pyramid, without applying any of the principles in the lower tiers. Had he worked on managing his lifestyle first, he could've made the proactive choice to admit he was powerless over his addiction and to turn this problem over to his higher source of power. Then, working in partnership with God, he could've gained the self-management skills he needed to progress on his healthy journey—up the PHS Pyramid.

Emotional eating is a classic problem, but there still remains a wide gamut of areas to consider. Studies have confirmed that long-standing resentments, stress, and anger can hold toxins in the body that affect the immune system. Researchers of holistic healing attribute cancer to this very problem. Consequently, even without resorting to food, we can throw our body's natural state off equilibrium. Any number of psychological issues can interfere with our body chemistry. If the mind, body, or spirit, are in constant conflict with each other, this can undermine our health in some way. We may turn to psychologists, therapists, spiritual gurus, and holistic medicine for help. The answers we seek may involve a combination of remedies, yet we can only do this if we remain *proactive* and *take responsibility* for our life. These principles are values we must uphold throughout our lifetime. So before going too far, (if you haven't done so already) take a moment to evaluate where you are; on this health journey.

I find personal training very rewarding because it gives me the opportunity to help so many people transform their lives and health. To take what many individuals think is impossible and suddenly make it possible is a wonderful privilege. I've helped people with a biological body age that was initially ten years older become ten years younger. Numerous positive changes typically occur while in the midst of making this magical transition. Aside from the obvious and quite tangible results, such as weight loss and increased muscle tone, many intangible benefits go along with it. Confidence and self-esteem increase, energy levels rise, mental outlook improves, emotional well-being is enhanced, and bad habits are broken. Yet for some people, despite their obvious physical improvements, it just doesn't seem to matter.

Consider Debra, one of my clients. Prior to using the PHS, she took very little pride in her achievements and couldn't accept it whenever she reached new physical milestones. Within seven months, she had reduced her body age by ten years; dropped her body fat from the obese category into the healthy range; improved her cardiovascular endurance, gained strength and flexibility; and lost weight. Yet in the face of all her improvements, she habitually talked down about herself. She was locked into viewing her body and life from the dark side. I asked Deb why she was always selling herself short. She told me it was habitual. She had been harassed for being overweight while growing up and never felt good about herself. She was accustomed to perceiving herself in this way, so in spite of her healthy body weight and new physical appearance; nothing could offer her consolation. She was stuck in destructive mental patterns and needed to change her self-perception. It was baffling to see her physical body significantly transform, yet observe her mind-set lag far behind. Intrinsically, she wasn't healthy, but I knew those deeply ingrained negative thought patterns weren't just going to fade away. She needed to break the negative mental cycle, just like any other bad habit.

When I shared the PHS, Deb realized an important principle had been bypassed in the second tier of the pyramid. She was only going through the motions of an exercise routine, but never developed a healthy self-image. This hindered her motivation and potential to experience optimal health, because she was stuck seeing herself as fat, ugly, and disgusting. For many years, Deb didn't think there was anything wrong with her constant self-badgering and negative thought patterns. After using the PHS, she made a conscious effort to stop viewing herself negatively. She recognized how far she had come along, and started taking credit for all her accomplishments. Finally, a breakthrough occurred; her mind-set and self-image changed. This enlightened perception gave her new confidence and the motivation she needed to rise to a higher challenge. The following summer, Deb completed her first triathlon. When I first met Deb, the thought of conquering a triathlon would've never crossed her mind. After she became a healthy self-manager however, she was able to set her vision on her mission. Now, she's become an inspiration to many people and continues to set higher goals for herself every year.

Like Deb, to gain intrinsic motivation, you may need to step backward before moving forward. Simply turn around to face the 2nd tier of the pyramid—healthy self-management, within it you'll discover your psychological and spiritual condition. If you find yourself just going through the motions of a fitness program, take a moment to reconsider your self-image. There's always a root cause behind a poor self-perception. While the stories may vary, inevitably this originates from one source—fear. Instilled fear gives rise to negative thoughts. Over time, these negative thoughts and perceptions result in deeply ingrained mental patterns that block energy flow.

The expression, "mental block" is fairly common, but this restriction of energy flow can happen anywhere. Wherever mental, emotional, or spiritual energy remains blocked, it's analogous to carrying around dead weight everywhere. These inner barriers or long-standing defense mechanisms are put up to block fear. Any time we experience these blocks, something is lingering and inhibiting our energy or "flow." In yoga, this is referred to as *prana*. Old issues need to be released to bring in new life. Regardless of whatever issues remain unresolved, the law of attraction is still at work. People who view themselves in a negative way will typically give off this same vibe to others. That's because their restricted self-perception needs to be lined up with the same version of their reality. Most people will perceive them in the same way they intrinsically view themselves.

"A cheerful heart is good medicine, but a crushed spirit dries up the bones."[2]

Once while I was in Chicago for a wedding, seated at our table was a gentleman who wasn't particularly handsome. From an appearance standpoint, he was rather an average-looking guy. He wasn't overweight, but he didn't have a muscular, sculpted body either. However, when he engaged in a conversation and smiled, he lit up the whole room. He charmed the pants off anyone in sight. It wasn't just his personality; he had something dynamic and mesmerizing. It was his energy—it was completely electrifying—everyone loved him!

On the other hand, plenty of people have absolutely beautiful bodies, but they're so shallow, egotistical, depressed, or lacking in self-esteem that somehow, they become unattractive. The energy in their spirit is so washed out. Remember our physical body is indeed our temple, but it's also the temporal part of optimal health. This is why it's so important to view yourself in a positive light. If you have a negative self-perception and mind-set, it's toxic. It will pollute everyone around you.

Life has a way of getting your attention. If you become a magnet for attracting miserable people and situations into your life, take heed and learn from these subliminal messages. Something could be lurking in your subconscious and sabotaging your potential. You need to discover what it is and let it go, completely. To gain motivation, your internal vision needs to be aligned correctly with all aspects of optimal health—the mind, body, and spirit. Maybe you accepted false beliefs because you didn't know any better. Well, it's time to move on. When you think proactively, you can release those fears and negative beliefs. Set a new and improved vision for yourself.

"You were taught, with regard to your former way of life, to put off your old self, which is being corrupted by its deceitful desires; to be made new in the attitude of your minds; and to put on the new self, created to be like God in true righteousness and holiness." [3]

Start envisioning yourself as a more enlightened person, radiating with light and positive energy. As many great philosophers have touted, you become who you think you are. Dare to see yourself in this new way. Use your imagination. Seek God. Meditate on positive affirmations daily. Envision being healthy; inside and out. As you begin to align your vision with a new picture optimal health, the demons of despair will flee. You will feel more whole and motivation will rise on all levels. Negativity and notions of self-degradation will dissolve and become a thing of the past. Many beneficial changes will occur, even on subtle levels. Soon, you'll hold your head high, smile, and accept all your gifts graciously.

2. Climbing to the Top of the PHS Pyramid

Doing your homework in the initial stages of the PHS has prepared you for what's ahead. Your mission is complete only after you've climbed to the top of the pyramid. You must reach that highpoint of discipline—where healthy behaviors become a way of life. The initial components, *lifestyle management* and *healthy self-management*, have served as your wake-up call and coach to help get you moving in the right direction. Like good friends that keep you grounded, those building blocks are always standing by, ready to support you. If you successfully applied the principles in the second block of the PHS Pyramid; then you've already met much of your psychological and spiritual objectives of optimal health.

When you are healthier and stronger on the inside, that gives you the advantage of climbing up the pyramid without any major mishaps. There's still more work ahead, but now you can shift your focus to the outer part of optimal health—your physical body. Consider what changes you want to make personally, in your body and fitness level. At this stage, you should be ready to set and pursue your fitness goals. Be realistic. The goals you set should be liberating, not intimidating.

You've already learned that your vision will affect your motivation. Now it's time to start transferring this knowledge into action. Whatever goals you set for yourself, start to visualize them. Creative visualization is a powerful tool that has been tried and tested for centuries. Many people have used it to cure diseases, increase wealth, build fortunes, and attract love. Create mental pictures of the fitness goals you want to achieve. Gather a vision—a quantum outcome—see yourself at the end of each goal. When you move into the next phase of *program design*, be sure to begin with this end in mind.

For example, imagine what your body might look and feel like after you lose weight, or how you would feel once you become stronger. Imagine having more stamina, not huffing and puffing when you climb a flight of stairs. You can visualize lowering your cholesterol and blood pressure to healthy levels, where meds are no longer required. Picture your body perfect, with no disease, no infirmities, and no issues. Just imagine fitting comfortably in your new pair of skinny jeans.

Creative Visualization Techniques

- Use your imagination to envision reaching each goal exactly as you want.

- Focus on all dimensions of optimal health—being healthy in the mind, body, and spirit.

- Use positive affirmations daily to help internalize and focus on your goals.

- Build a visionary board—a poster filled with pictures of what your life will be like when you meet your goals.

- Take a few moments each day to relax your mind in a quiet place.

- Imagine yourself at the end of this health journey; you've reached your fitness goals and climbed to the top of the PHS Pyramid. Now, you are disciplined; healthy behaviors have become part of who you are.

3. Establish and Assess Optimal Health Objectives

Here you have the opportunity to further establish and assess the three objectives of optimal health: being healthy in the mind, body and spirit. This process entails a brief overview of the healthy self-management component and you may find that some of the areas overlap with your personal goals. At this juncture however, you'll discover that assessing the mental and spiritual objectives is not as straightforward as measuring concrete changes to your physical body. Although this is still possible, it is a rather subjective process. That's because the ideology of optimal health itself, must take deeper root before we can measure *all* its dimensions with complete accuracy.

Optimal Health Objective #1: Your Physical Body

The objective in this category is to determine all the changes you want to make to your physical body. Whatever you want to accomplish that will make you look and feel better, improve your overall health and fitness level, or enhance athletic performance. Common goals include losing weight, gaining strength, decreasing body fat, building muscle mass, improving cardiovascular endurance, increasing fat-burning efficiency, developing core strength and flexibility, and sculpting muscles (aka; getting "cut up"). For your physical body, it's best to set "SMART" goals.

<u>SMART</u> Goals are:
S—Specific
M—Measurable
A—Attainable
R—Realistic
T—Timely

Assessing progress in this way is easy. Example: I want to lose ten percent of my body fat in three months. In the next PHS phase—the program design, you'll find the action steps needed to achieve many of these common health and fitness goals.

Optimal Health Objective #2: Your Mental Well-Being

Certainly, your mental well-being is part of optimal health. Earlier you learned why developing a healthy self-image is important and the effect it has on your mind-set. To a considerable degree, mental health can be fostered by a positive mind-set. Aware of this, you might wonder how do you achieve this objective. How do you quantify or measure a positive mind-set? It might mean one thing to you and something entirely different to somebody else. Measuring a positive mind-set is not like hopping on the scale and seeing whether you've lost weight. This is where many people zone out, because they're unsure what all this really means. Does having a positive mind-set mean that one lives his or her life happily for the most part? Can we distinguish a positive thinker through high self-esteem, a good attitude, prosperity, a fit body, quick wit, healthy relationships and deep inner faith? Although these notions appear to be good indicators, there still remains a bit of ambiguity.

The subject of positive thinking itself is still evolving. It was discovered in the 19th century among a diverse and fascinating collection of philosophers, mystics, lay healers and middle-class women. Today it is growing with increasing popularity as more people are discovering the benefits. Many employers require psychological testing to screen potential employees. So certainly, we can measure the effects of one's mind-set through empirical testing, but we can also evaluate it to some extent, subjectively. Perhaps, we can read it on someone's face, experience it from the energy the person gives off, or perceive it through his or her tone of voice in a simple conversation. The way people carry themselves, their behaviors, and attitudes can give us some clues about their mind-set.

Everything in the universe has an energy and vibration. That energy can be created, shaped, and molded by our thoughts. Quantum physics states that our energy flows where our attention goes. In other words, a negative mind-set yields more of the same—a negative outcome. Many people suffer psychologically as a result of this malady. If you're not experiencing optimal health, then take a moment to consider your thoughts. Is your mind focused on illness or health?

. . . .
It isn't what you have, or who you are,
or where you are, or what you are doing
that makes you happy or unhappy. It is
what you think about. —Dale Carnegie
. . . .

Improving your mental well-being requires consistent, conscious effort. Upholding positive thoughts are an internal mechanism that only you can instill—and this is why it can be difficult to measure. Thoughts come and go, and there's no such thing as the "positive-thought police." Nobody but you can prevent you from thinking negative thoughts. Remember in Debra's case, her negative thoughts patterns were so ingrained that she didn't even realize she had them. If you're not sure whether you have this negative mind-set, do some soul searching. Seek God in your quiet time, and ask him to reveal anything that's stifling you. For instance, you might suddenly realize that all the people you associate with are negative (they're always complaining about something). Whenever you limit time with negative people that drag you down, you're taking ownership of your mental well-being. If you spend time with positive people, you will sense better energy and notice something quite different; they're always giving thanks and counting their blessings. Consequently, the law of attraction sends more blessings their way.

It's your responsibility to monitor your mind-set and work on replacing negative thought patterns with new uplifting affirmations. Consider Connie, one of my clients; she realized that much of her struggle with depression was the result of her own negative thinking. Then one day, she came up with a great idea. She made a conscious decision that no matter how difficult her day was, before she fell asleep at night, she would think of three positive things she experienced during the course of that day. Within a couple weeks, her husband noticed a positive change in her attitude. She shared her little secret with him, and he started to do the same thing. Soon, they were sharing their positive experiences with each other and making it a bedtime ritual.

Another way you can improve your mental well-being is by keeping your mind stimulated. Read an interesting book every few weeks, learn new skills, or take a foreign language class to get your mind thinking in a different way. In fact, studies suggest that learning a foreign language can help prevent Alzheimer's. If you make a point to socialize with interesting people in different cultures, this can also have a positive impact on your mental well-being. You can saturate your mind with positive affirmations every night before going to sleep or first thing when you wake up. Practice gratitude. Do whatever is within your power to improve a situation or gain peace of mind. Smile more often. Find humor, and have fun. Nurture your creativity.

Measuring your progress and shifting from a negative mind-set to a positive one is a private matter. It is subjective growth because nobody else really has this power over you. Connie and her husband made a game out of it by determining who could say the three positive experiences faster. When Connie first started doing this alone, her mind-set was so negative that it took her a very long time to think of three positive experiences. When her mind-set became more positive, she became quite adept at it.

With a more positive mind-set, you may recognize improvements in several areas of your life—superior work performance, more sales and opportunities, better relationships. These are all good indicators. Other people may notice as well. For example, with increased productivity at work, you may get a bonus or raise, or be offered a promotion. A mind-set is basically a mental attitude, but the affects can be profound enough to change the quality and course of your life. The answers to the questions listed below can help shed some light on your mind-set.

· ·

The person who sends out positive
thoughts activates the world around
him positively and draws back to himself
positive results. —Norman Vincent Peale

· ·

Basic Mind-Set Questionnaire

1. Can you take a compliment and say thank you?
2. When things go wrong, do you remain calm?
3. Do you give yourself credit for accomplishments?
4. Are you open to constructive criticism?
5. If you get discouraged, do you continue to make an effort?
6. Are you happy for the success of others?
7. Do you acknowledge and appreciate your talents and skills?
8. Do you deal constructively with your feelings?
9. Do you believe it's possible to achieve your goals?
10. Are you grateful for everything in your life?

If you answered yes to fewer than five, you have negative mind-set tendencies. If you answered yes to more than five, you have positive mind-set tendencies. If you have five of each, you have equal mind-sets tendencies.

If you have a *negative mind-set*, you continually focus your thoughts on everything bad in your life. Your energy is directed toward lack and limitation and on what you don't have. You don't think it's possible to succeed at anything, so you give up on your dreams and goals before you even start. You focus on what could go wrong and see only the problems in every situation. You may want to take action on a particular goal but then immediately think about all the ways you couldn't possibly succeed.

If you have a *positive mind-set*, you are grateful for everything you have and will have. You focus on the positive aspects of your life and feel as if you're already healthy, wealthy, and wise. You faithfully take actions that bring about positive change, prosperity, and improvements in your well-being and quality of life. You intend to meet your goals and are excited and happy while working toward them. You see the good in every situation and find ways to stay committed to achieving your goals.

Harnessing the power of a positive mind-set can improve your well-being in several ways. Start envisioning yourself in a new way; imagine being mentally and emotionally stable, free from disease or infirmity, completely healed from an injury, or cured from some nagging ailment. Perhaps you can imagine success as it relates to a specific performance goal, whether you want to compete in a marathon, triathlon, or just break a personal barrier. You can become a champion in your own right. Focus on being healthy, happy, and successful in every way. It's your imagination; use it the way you want.

· ·
You can't depend on your eyes when your
imagination is out of focus.—Mark Twain
· ·

Optimal Health Objective #3: Your Spiritual Well-Being

We are all spiritual beings having a human experience. Previously, you learned how regaining your inner balance is a reflection of your spirit. As we proceed toward our physical goals, we must not forget that following our spiritual path is part of our divine nature—it's aligned with optimal health. In ancient times, this vital force was identified with breath. In Kriya yoga, the breath, life energy, and consciousness are united to become one. When we reach this high state of divine consciousness, it creates a union with the Universal Spirit—God, our higher source of power, whatever we perceive it to be. This high state of consciousness aligns a bundle of divine energies that are meant to free flow through our bodies.

Spiritual gurus, yoga practitioners, massage therapists and holistic healers refer to these energies as chakras. When these chakras are not blocked, we shall reach this higher state of consciousness and can experience perfect health. Whatever energies you allow in your aura will flow to every organ and cell of your body. These energies can affect your health. Unresolved tension anywhere in your consciousness can manifest as a physical symptom in your body. You may need healing in one or more chakras. When you set your vision on perfect health, you can bring this mental picture into your energy configuration—your aura. Positive thoughts can bring healing and wellness to your body, while negative thoughts can cause distress and disease.

Spiritual health need not infringe on the religious aspects of spirituality, although the two can be intertwined. For example, an evil or demonic spirit that provokes someone to commit a heinous crime is certainly not a healthy one. Lack of spiritual health and the inability to control evil urges, often becomes grounds for insanity. If people become spiritually destitute, anything goes. When they lack a moral sense of right and wrong or appear to be without a conscience, then it's only reasonable to presume that their sanity or psychological condition is already at stake. We can ascertain this rather easily. Whether we're religious or not, this logic involves an understanding about the congruity of health—that the mind, body, and spirit need to be aligned. When one part is out of balance, another part will compensate for it. Laws of quantum physics are at work.

If you become depressed, irritable, and impatient from a psychological standpoint—it may be time to nurture your soul. You could be spiritually depleted. Remember, your spiritual well-being doesn't necessarily have anything to do with religion. Many people who are healthy spiritually aren't religious. Likewise, many who profess to be religious are actually quite wicked. If you're still skeptical about this notion of spirituality, follow the universal golden rule: Do unto others as you want done, unto you. The ultimate spiritual law is to love others as you love yourself.

Most people, who are considered to be healthy spiritually, do trust in a higher source of power. Basically, spiritual health can be recognized as having a good relationship with God, with self, with others, with structural systems, and with all of creation. Again, for some, being spiritual involves religion; for others, it does not.

Spiritual Objectives Depend Upon Your Spiritual Condition:

- If you already have faith in God or a higher source of power, you can focus on strengthening this connection, attuning your spiritual senses, and working on separating evil influences from your life.

- If you're unsure what to believe but remain open, God (the Universal Spirit—your higher source of power) is always available to guide you.

To renew your spiritual well-being, you may need to go back and review the chapter on the PHS principle of regaining balance. The objective here is to magnify the potential of your inner energy, to discover your purpose and life-giving essence. Imagine resonating with life. You may experience a free flow of positive energy running through your body. Set your vision on the fruit of the spirit—love, joy, peace, patience, kindness, goodness, faithfulness, gentleness, and self-control. Envision giving good vibrations or developing a deep inner faith in the process of life, finding a new strength and connection in God. In actuality, spirituality is present in all life. It can be recognized in all humankind, animals, and nature, and in the stars and planets. Our entire universe is conscious of its presence.

The law of spiritual quantum physics states that all physical reality is no more than a projection of one's inner reality. In other words, we can't find all the answers in the same way. Since spiritual health is not so easy to measure, you can learn to perceive without words and see past the physical reality of an object; to see clearly its energy configuration. You're entitled to your own perception. To become spiritually healthy, follow the yearning of your own soul. Imagine yourself being the best you can be, shining like a star—vibrant with health, enlightened, and radiant. When your thoughts and energies flow the way they were intended—along your divine spiritual path—you will experience perfect health. When you're spiritually healthy, you will discover that the Great Spirit is present in everyone and everything. We each have separate paths, but we're all connected and one with this same spiritual source.

"Do everything without complaining or arguing, so that you may become blameless and pure, children of God without fault in a crooked and depraved generation, in which you shine like stars in the universe."[4]

Maintain the Right Perspective

If you want to maintain your motivation, you need to maintain the right perspective. So much power could be available to you at times, if you just changed your perspective. For instance, two people can glance at the same picture, or look up into the clouds and see something totally different. Nobody's right or wrong; it's just a matter of perspective. Is your glass half full or half empty? Sometimes however, your perspective has validity, and sometimes it stems from a faulty belief system. This is important to understand, because as you set out to pursue your goals, you must guard against becoming vulnerable to a faulty belief system. One wrong thought or skewed bit of information could throw you off course and create a spiral effect. Once you lose perspective, you won't believe that it's possible to achieve your goals. Discouragement will set in, and all motivation gets lost. Your thoughts carry power in them, and this is exactly what affects your perspective. Those thoughts can drive your motivation for better or worse.

"I am sending you out as sheep among wolves. Therefore be as shrewd as snakes and as innocent as doves." [5]

You need to protect your goals and belief system, just like you protect anything that's valuable to you. When you set out to achieve your health and fitness goals, you already know that the obstacles will come. You can't afford to have insignificant thoughts make you lose perspective. Protect your mind; by holding on to the thoughts that motivate you and discarding the discouraging thoughts.

"And the peace of God, which transcends all understanding, will guard your hearts and your minds in Christ Jesus."[6]

Ironically, after you finally get motivated to make some positive changes in your life, that's usually when the negative thoughts come rushing in full force. It's kind of like the ex-partner who suddenly reappears and wants to get back together after you just started moving on! Yeah, life can be uncanny at times. If you're not careful, those distracting thoughts will weasel their way back into your mind and become a deterrent. Seemingly petty thoughts can get you off track, indeed some can be a highway to hell. A faulty belief system gives you the wrong perspective, and when you're not in the right frame of mind, you'll get discouraged and lose motivation. The best way to prevent falling into this discouragement trap is to change your perspective. Again, thinking proactively can help you nip this problem in the bud. When your perspective is in need of an overhaul, you can shift it from wrong to right by applying three spiritual laws: *hope, faith,* and *love.*

Consider Sophia, she struggled with obesity her entire life. Finally, after many years of accumulated health problems, she was motivated to make a change. She set a realistic weight loss goal to lose six pounds in four weeks. However, after three weeks into her new diet and exercise regime, she hopped on the scale and it hadn't budged. Not one pound. What was going on? She was so motivated before she got on the scale. Now, that scale triggered a flashback of negative thoughts and faulty beliefs. Yet in that same moment, Sophia realized she had a choice. She could either keep the right perspective and stay focused; or she could get discouraged and quit. Much of our success in life is determined by our perspective. Will we proactively choose to think like a winner, or be reactive and think like a loser? The choice is ours.

"And now these three remain: faith, hope and love. But the greatest of these is love."[7]

The Wrong Perspective	Laws:	The Right Perspective
I'll never lose weight; I'm hopeless.	Hope	There's always hope to pursue my goals.
I don't believe it's possible. Why bother?	Faith	Anything is possible and I'm willing to try.
I hate my body and don't care anymore.	Love	My body is a temple, it deserves the best.

Put yourself in Sophia's shoes. Would you let this problem discourage you? Will you lose your perspective and motivation just because you didn't drop a few pounds? In your mind, is health only about weight loss? Do you realistically think your efforts just won't pay off? Given this scenario, losing weight is the goal, but our goals shouldn't grip us with fear and negativity. Remember, obstacles are put in our path to make us stronger. Once we really get that to sink in, then in the process of any pursuit, we'll be able to maintain the right perspective. There could be many reasons why her weight didn't come off.

Maybe something needed to be fine tuned in her diet. Perhaps sodium intake was too high, which created extra water weight. It could possibly be that Sophia's body already shifted slightly in composition from fat to muscle, in which case she's doing great. Perhaps her caloric intake wasn't initially calculated or adjusted properly. Perhaps a label was misread. Maybe the intensity of her cardio program wasn't high enough. Maybe a medication wasn't taken into account. Maybe she forgot about that glass of wine she kept having before bedtime. There are many factors to consider.

We must learn to view our goals as part of a bigger picture. No matter what our goals may be, negative thoughts are not conducive to motivation. The goal is not an end to itself; the journey can be just as rewarding and a lot of fun too. As you proceed, hold on to this thought: *You are divine! Nobody could ever take your place.* The following scripture should give you the right perspective.

"I praise you because I am fearfully and wonderfully made; your works are wonderful I know that full well"[8]

When God made you, he made you entirely unique. Notice what the psalmist is saying—your works are wonderful, and I know that full well. When you appreciate and understand how wonderful you are, you won't condemn yourself with negative thoughts. Many people spend a fortune on therapists when all they need is a fundamental change of perspective. Some don't understand the difference between healthy self-confidence and arrogance. The psalmist isn't being arrogant; he's giving praise to God for his divine nature. Your perspective determines the way you see yourself. Even in your weakest moment, you can view yourself as strong.

"But he said to me, 'My grace is sufficient for you, for my power is made perfect in weakness. Therefore I will boast all the more gladly about my weaknesses, so that Christ's power may rest on me. That is why, for Christ's sake, I delight in weaknesses, in insults, in hardships, in persecutions, in difficulties. For when I am weak, then I am strong.'"[9]

If your perspective is wrong, faulty, or messed up in any way, it's because you allowed garbage information into your belief system. It's like allowing junk mail to infiltrate your head and cloud your judgment. Learn to decipher and discard the thoughts that are worthless, totally irrelevant, or foolish. Nothing can hinder your motivation unless you allow it.

CHAPTER 11

Program Design—
PHS Principle: Nutrition

Developing a Healthy Relationship with Food

Scrumptious, sinfully delicious, succulent, crunchy, smoky, salty, sweet, sour, tart, tangy, tasty, spicy, fiery, buttery, crispy, cheesy, homemade, savory, creamy, heavenly, smooth, rich, nostalgic, comforting, soothing, warm, tantalizing, moist, tender, tempting, mouth-watering, nutritious, satisfying, soulful, melted, whipped, crumbled, decadent, ala mode, topped, stacked high, heart-warming, rich, gooey, chewy, authentic, healthy, gritty, nutty, fruity, juicy, natural, sprinkled, refreshing, flavorful, fresh, wholesome, garden-grown, flakey, steaming hot, made with love, yummy, seconds please. *Bon appétit!*

Whatever way it can be dished up, it can be loved! Everybody has some kind of relationship with food. Like any other relationship, some of these relationships are healthy and others, not so much. Overeating is a common problem, yet deprivation can be equally self-defeating—when either of these behaviors is taken to an extreme, they're bound to fail. While it's perfectly natural to be comforted by food, for many people it becomes a crutch. For others, being deprived from certain foods can trigger an eating-mechanism disorder. Either the desire for the forbidden food increases and causes them to sneak eat it *in excess,* or they end up eating more of everything else, desperately trying to avoid it.

A starvation diet is another setup for failure. If you significantly reduce your caloric intake to the point that your brain can't function, you'll end up feeling dizzy and about ready to cry. That's the hard way to figure out that starving yourself is not a good idea. It will, however, teach you something about your relationship with food. If you got to this point—where you felt like crying—it shows very clearly that your emotions are connected to food. We're not only dependent on food to sustain our body, but it also provides a way to validate our self-essence. Babies cry naturally when they're hungry, because they're helpless and don't know when they're going to be fed next. Over time, without food, we'll all feel isolated emotionally and want to burst into tears.

Food gives us sustenance; it can nourish our body as well as our soul. It has a way to calm us down and soothe us. There's absolutely nothing wrong with thoroughly enjoying food. It's a celebration of our existence and life in general. It also has a way of bringing people together and breaking down barriers. Some people profess that certain authentic dishes, if served to enemies, can even stop wars! Food definitely serves a social purpose. Whether we're taking a client out to lunch, or celebrating a special occasion, eating together is a way we can all connect, because it not only validates who we are, but who others are as well. When shared, food can taste even better. We often associate certain foods with fond memories of our childhood; the tastes and smells can be heart-warming and nostalgic. So rid the notion right now that you shouldn't use food to feel good. You'll always feel good when you nurture yourself properly, and there's nothing wrong with having a natural love for food. Our love for food shows that we can have a deep appreciation for something delightful to the taste buds, nourishing to the body, and gratifying to the soul. We are all emotionally bonded to food by its mere nature, and that's normal, natural, and a good thing.

Do You Eat to Live or Live to Eat?

Like a drug addict or alcoholic, the problem with food comes when we abuse ourselves in relation to it. If we continue to overuse food, it will create great imbalances in our body and wreak havoc on our health and well-being. Just like anything in life, we have to be careful not to go too far in either extreme—moderation is the key. Developing a healthy relationship with food means we learn *what to eat, when to eat,* and *how much to eat.* That doesn't necessarily mean we can't have an extra helping of our favorite dish or that we should pass over Aunt Reida's authentic decadent dessert. It does mean, however, that we should follow proper nutrition guidelines as well as portion control. Nobody likes to count calories, but we must consider the law of thermodynamics—the calories going in need to be offset accordingly, by the calories going out. This is especially important when we're trying to lose weight, but it's also important to set some realistic expectations.

Whether we're trying to lose weight or not, we should try to recapture a more natural relationship with food. For example, there are many people who aren't even in touch with their hunger; they just eat for the sake of eating. Some mistake thirst for hunger and turn to food when in fact, they should be drinking an extra glass of water. Children are naturally in touch with their hunger and thirst, and they also recognize the feeling of satiation rather quickly. Adults seem to lose this innate ability as they get older, but this is very important—we should recognize when we're hungry or thirsty and when we've had enough! A lot of people overeat simply because the portion size served in many restaurants has become outrageous. Many of us grew up believing that we must finish everything on our plate, because it's unethical to waste food when other people in the world are starving. While appreciating food is one thing, eating when we're already full is quite another—this doesn't help anybody who's starving somewhere. Furthermore, it only harms us by making us gain weight and taxing our digestive system. We must learn to set the boundaries necessary to take care of ourselves.

If you don't feel right about wasting food, that's commendable, but instead of overstuffing yourself, save the rest of that meal for leftovers the next day, or ask for a doggy bag when you go out to eat. Feeling thoroughly stuffed after eating is unnatural. If you ate when you were actually hungry, then you should feel pleasantly satisfied when you're finished. It's natural is to experience a sense of emotional relief after eating a nutritious and delicious meal—especially one that's made with love. Food can touch your soul.

Whenever you eat, it should be something that you enjoy, but that doesn't mean your diet should consist of junk food and desserts because you enjoy it so much. Your body needs proper nourishment as well—it needs the right balance of essential nutrients, vitamins, and minerals. That's why gaining knowledge in the area of nutrition is so important. For example, if you come home late from work, completely famished, do you think that eating a box of sugar cookies will suffice? You may think that you can dump whatever you want in your body, but your cells need proper nourishment. When your body doesn't receive the right nutrients, this creates nutritional imbalances. It's possible to be overweight and completely malnourished. In fact, nutritional imbalances could contribute to being overweight, because you're eating all the wrongs things—in the process of trying to feel satisfied, you end up eating more and more junk. If what you eat isn't what your body needs; it will instinctively store the excess calories as fat. When your body is storing excess fat (outside the healthy range), this automatically slows down your metabolism. Compared to a healthy body fat percentage, this means your body won't burn as many calories when it's at rest. Consequently, everything you eat seems to make you gain more weight.

You Are What You Eat

Nutrition plays a huge role in achieving your fitness goals and maintaining a healthy, balanced body. Gaining better education about nutrition is an important part of being proactive—it's your ticket to take charge of your health. When you're armed with the right information, you have the power to make many of your health issues go away. The right nutrition strategy can reduce the risk of disease and illness, improve health and athletic performance, increase energy levels, and accelerate results from exercise by helping to change body composition. Physically, when you feel great, your life will begin to take on a whole new dimension. The benefits should be enough to keep you motivated and disciplined for life.

The PHS Nutrition Program—Getting Started

When starting out, one of the first questions people ask is, "What should I eat?" The answer to this question is divided into three phases.

I. LEARN HOW TO MAKE HEALTHY FOOD CHOICES

The first phase in building a good nutrition plan is learning how to make healthy food choices. This shouldn't be misconstrued as deprivation. Quite the contrary, when you eat healthy, you'll discover it can be absolutely delicious, and you can make up for deficiencies or imbalances in essential nutrients, vitamins, and minerals. When your body isn't deprived of what it actually needs, you'll feel better, have more energy, and be less likely to overeat. Eating a healthy, balanced diet is preventive maintenance. By staying proactive, this will help you to manage your weight and ward off many chronic diseases and health issues.

Mother Nature grants us with an abundant variety of wholesome foods, yet modern civilization bombards us with another set of options. The grocery store can be an intimidating and overwhelming place, with everything from a produce section, a deli, and bakery, to aisles and aisles of prepackaged, processed, frozen, canned, bulk, dehydrated products and more. Then there are different versions of everything—low-fat, low-carb, sugar-free, fat-free, low-salt, no-salt, gluten-free, wheat-free, lactose-free. Everywhere you turn something is vying for your attention or tantalizing your taste buds. You might go in to pick up one item and leave with a whole cart! Beyond the grocery, you could be surrounded by convenience or fast-food chains seemingly on every corner—there's finger-lickin' Kentucky Fried Chicken; Arby's, with the famous curly fries; Burger King, with the flame-broiled taste; Taco Bell; or White Castle sliders for those serious after-hour cravings.

There's nothing inherently wrong with having all these options; we should always have the prerogative to eat whatever we want. However, we should also recognize where to draw the line—eating too much junk or fast food is not conducive to a healthy lifestyle. In reality, it's not these modern conveniences and fast-food chains that are causing the growing obesity epidemic—it's our personal choices and inability to set limits. Parents lead by example. A couple years ago, I received an urgent phone call from Carol, a single mother in her late thirties. She was worried about her daughter Britney, who refused to eat anything except McDonald's deep-fried chicken nuggets. Carol was also overweight herself, but now little Britney had become obese before reaching kindergarten. It was Carol's wake-up call, she was frantic.

Ironically, the first thing I told Carol is that McDonald's is not the one to blame. I asked Carol who had influenced her child to eat fast food in the first place. Did Britney, who was barely five years old, storm out of the house, get in the car and drive to the nearest McDonald's? Initially, Carol was taken back by my bold question, but as our conversation continued, this made her think. Who should be in control here—a child who's having a temper tantrum or a parent? Carol recognized her role in the matter; she had been enabling her daughter and needed to stop. A year later, Carol called again, this time to thank me for being so blunt. Britney was no longer addicted to fast food and nor was she obese. Carol herself also lost weight. As a parent, you set the standards for your family and should recognize how to lay down the proper limits on certain foods. When you think proactively, you always have a choice to eat healthily.

Making healthy food choices stems from one very simple notion—living off the land. Natural foods such as fresh fruits and vegetables should be the staples in any healthy diet. We don't need to live in the country, become Amish, a farmer, a fisherman, or a hunter in order to appreciate these wonders of nature. Perhaps we've become a society so susceptible to influence that we've dismissed this notion. Our primal needs and inner voice of reason has been trampled on by many distracting influences. Let's consider the snack Cheetos, as an example. Have you ever pondered its origin? What the heck is a Cheeto anyway? Okay, you might know that it's an ultra-puffed, curly, twirly snack that can come in a variety of cheese flavors, but what's it made from? Most people don't know exactly what it is, other than it's something that makes their fingers turn orange. The calories are empty with more than half coming from fat. They're covered with artificial coloring and flavoring, and the nutritional benefit is marginal at best. All that information is irrelevant—people will still run out and buy them. Why? It's a matter of personal preference. Some people just like the cheesy taste and texture. Parents might find them a convenient snack for parties—they get a bowl, pop open the package, dump it in the bowl, and *voila*, the snack is ready! Kids love them because they're just one of those fun things to eat. So even if Cheetos are on bottom of the nutrition scale, they aren't going anywhere.

Is it possible to have the best of both worlds? Absolutely! When you make the decision to eat healthily, this doesn't mean you have to blast all the products on the market. There are plenty of reasons people choose to eat certain foods and snacks. (Just consider the Twinkies sweet comeback.) We might base our decisions on taste, budget, availability, comfort, nostalgia, or convenience. A college student on a tight budget knows that Ramen noodles and canned tuna can go a long way. If roasting marshmallows by the bonfire and sipping hot cocoa on a cold winter night makes you feel warm and fuzzy, then by all means you can do it. Authentic dishes are passed down through many generations, and that's why we love them so much. Other times, social pressure affects our decisions. This can be experienced within every culture and social circle, whether through the office party, a family gathering, a special occasion, or a dinner out with friends. Though we're each entitled to our eating preferences, we can stick to a core set of values. In the midst of it all, we can still honor our inner voice of reason and choose to focus on food that we know is healthy.

It's simple. If you make good, quality food choices and eat healthily, you'll feel better. When you feel better, you'll have a natural incentive to continue on this path. Over time, as you cut unnecessary junk from your diet, you won't crave it as much. After eating healthily, many of my clients tell me that the desire for junk food subsides—most of those unhealthy cravings just go away. Of course, it's best to focus on eating wholesome foods, but the beauty of being proactive is that you have options. So use discretion and remember deprivation can backfire. Some individuals have a tendency to overeat when they deprive themselves of a small luxury. Sometimes, a little taste or small portion of something that you've been hankering for can take the edge off. For example, a miniature piece of dark chocolate or a small handful of chocolate-covered raisins might satisfy your sweet tooth.

But take caution; only allow yourself some wiggle room if you don't have a problem with "trigger" foods. For example, if you're craving some potato chips, but you're the type of person who can't stop eating an entire 12-ounce bag, all in one sitting, don't go there. Maybe your trigger food is not the salty crunchy stuff, but your penchant for sweets. Instead of stopping at one donut, you tear through half a dozen; instead of a slice of cake, you eat the whole thing. If that's the case, save the wiggle room for later. First, you need to learn how to gain self-control by delaying gratification. In the initial stages of a nutrition program, some people find it much easier to abstain from certain foods altogether than to have just a little. If this is you, then do what you have to do. Over time, those trigger foods should not be a major cause for concern. Your success, however, depends on you—you must discover what works best for you.

Eat Natural

So what does eating healthy really mean? We should begin by choosing foods that are *all natural*—fruits and vegetables, whole grains, lean proteins, legumes, organic or farm-fresh dairy (in particular, cage-free eggs or yogurt without additives/grass-fed non GMO), nuts and seeds, pure water. For the most part, the less processed our food is, the more beneficial it will be. Think of your food as "naked." That's right; it's bare or stripped down. What you see is what you get—it's devoid of any man-made additives or preservatives. For example, there's a world of difference between a diet cherry soda and a bowl of cherries. Some people are so gullible, they think that sipping a diet cherry soda is better than eating cherries, because it's sugar-free and this will help them to lose weight. They might see a commercial of a gorgeous woman with a beautiful body drinking it and immediately run out and buy a case. Well, to be sure, there's no diet drink of any kind that's going to help you lose weight or make you become physically attractive. One has absolutely no bearing on the other.

Just because something is low in calories or sugar-free doesn't automatically mean it's healthy—or even beneficial, for that matter. On the other hand, those cherries don't pose any confusion, because they're natural. As simplistic as it may sound, it's better to choose what's "natural" than to choose a product that's low-calorie or sugar-free. Natural foods are like the cool shade of a tree—they offer no complication and much protection from the sun's harmful rays. Simple and natural, they're brimming with vitamins, minerals, and antioxidants to protect against free-radical damage and are packed with fiber for good digestion. Fruits can also satisfy a sweet tooth, which can prevent many people from overeating.

By contrast, the sweetener in a diet cherry soda, such as *aspartame*, is unnatural, and the flavoring is artificial. What good is a diet drink? So you spared yourself from consuming excess sugar—in comparison to what, though? A regular 12-ounce can of pop has approximately ten teaspoons of sugar, ranging from 100 to 150 calories. Almost anything else you drink would have less sugar and fewer calories, so you could have just as easily cut back in another way. Why not drink something natural—purified water with lemon, sparkling water, mineral water, distilled water, spring water, or green tea with a little honey or even a bit of natural sugar? These are much more refreshing, thirst-quenching and pure. Many people claim they don't like to drink plain water, yet if they were stranded for days without it, such a false illusion would change quite rapidly. Our instinct for plain, purified water is there, but many people have lost touch with it, simply because they don't drink enough of it. Yet the benefits of drinking pure water are numerous! It provides essential replenishment to every cell of the human body, cleanses our internal systems, and enables chemical reactions to occur. Also, the natural water found in fruit and vegetables is already pure. A glass of 100 percent fresh fruit or vegetable juice can do absolute wonders for your body.

So don't get too hung up on sugar-free or low calories. Diet sodas might stop pop junkies from consuming excess sugar, but there's an apparent price to pay. There have been plenty of debates and lawsuits regarding these sweeteners, aspartame in particular. Coalitions and many petitions have been formed against it. On February 25, 2008, in Hawaii, there was a hearing to ban the use of aspartame. These concerns and controversies alone should be enough to make us skeptical about using it. Ironically, many people gain weight when they drink it and lose weight when they cut it out of their diet. All sorts of other health issues seem to vanish simultaneously as well—headaches, vertigo, sinus problems, insomnia, depression, and anxiety attacks. There have been ninety-two cited problems associated with aspartame. The human body isn't designed to become a toxic waste tank, yet people mindlessly dump all sorts of unnatural junk into their bodies. When in doubt, it's best to stay away from anything that's unnatural. If you simply eliminate aspartame from your diet, suddenly feel better, and lose weight, that should be proof enough. You can't argue with a good thing. Try to get it out of your system—what do you have to lose? Initially, you may have to experience some withdrawal symptoms, but this is necessary to detoxify. Within a month, your body will return to a more natural state and you'll start feeling great.

Now let's go back to the bowl of cherries and consider some of the nutritional benefits. Cherries contain a compound called perillyl alcohol. Michael Gould, PhD, professor of human oncology at the University of Wisconsin Medical School in Madison, says that perillyl alcohol is the about the best thing ever seen for curing mammary cancer in laboratory animals. "Perillyl alcohol belongs to a group of compounds called monoterpenes. Limonene, found in the peel of citrus fruits, is another member of this family. These compounds have been shown in studies to block the formation of a variety of cancers, including those of the breasts, lungs, stomach, liver, and skin."[1] Cherries also contain vitamins C, A, and E. The vitamin E in cherries is of particular interest, since one study of postmenopausal women found that those who consumed the most vitamin E had the least risk of heart disease. And there was an interesting twist. The women who got their vitamin E *naturally*—solely from food—had less risk than the women who were also taking vitamin E supplements."[2]

It goes on to say that it's difficult to get the daily value of vitamin E (30 international units) from food alone except through high-fat cooking oils and nuts, but cherries are a better source. In addition, cherries contain a compound called quercetin, which helps block the damage caused by free radicals (unstable oxygen molecules in the body). This has been shown to significantly reduce the risk of stroke and cancer. Cherry juice also has been used to relieve the pain of gout. Now, it should be clear that eating cherries or drinking cherry juice is much healthier than sipping on a diet cherry soda. There are numerous benefits to eating natural. According to the book *New Foods for Healing*, there are powerful cures in more than one hundred common foods. We can learn to take advantage of their healing properties.

Fruits and Vegetables

Eating lots of fruits and vegetables—preferably organic and raw—can prevent many ailments and bring new life to a diseased body. They are satisfying, energizing, loaded with anti-cancer nutrients, packed with vitamins and minerals and high in dietary fiber. Fruits and vegetables can cleanse and flush toxins out of your cells and significantly strengthen your immune system. For several decades, prominent researchers have closely studied the properties and extensive benefits that different fruits and vegetables bring to the table; (no pun intended).

For a moment, let's zero-in on one veggie in particular: spinach. If you're old enough to remember Popeye, the Sailor Man (a cartoon character) you might have believed that eating lots of spinach would make you grow superhuman biceps. Apparently, Popeye was onto something. While spinach can help in building muscles; it has even more significant powers! Spinach is loaded with good stuff: vitamin A, K, D, E, omega-3 fatty acids, and a host of trace minerals. It has a dozen different flavonoid compounds which can function as anti-inflammatory, as well as anti-cancer agents. A powerful carotenoid found in spinach, Lutein, can help improve eyesight and protect against the diseases of cataracts and macular degeneration.[3] If spinach alone packs such a powerful punch, how much more could we improve our health by capturing all the potent marvels found in fruits and vegetables?

A large and long study conducted through Harvard discovered that a higher intake of fruits and vegetables lowered the risk of developing cardiovascular disease.[4] Other research reveals that vitamin C, as well as the potassium found in fruits and vegetables, is powerful prevention against high blood pressure. Dr Christopher J. Bulpitt, an expert in hypertension, at Hammersmith Hospital in London; gathered a string of evidence confirming that high blood pressure and stroke fatalities are highest among people who eat the least amount of vitamin C.[5] In 1991, a study through the University of Naples in Italy; showed that 81% of patients who were on a high-potassium diet for a year were able to slash their original dosage of blood pressure medication in half. It also indicated that by further boosting their intake of high-potassium foods, 38% of this group was able to stop taking medication entirely.[6]

The studies are numerous and cumulative research is compelling. Fortunately today, more people are cognizant about this crucial role of fruits and vegetables. Several organizations have teamed up while many others are coming together to support this growing initiative—to improve public health and reduce the risk of chronic disease by increasing consumption of these magnificent wonders—fruits and vegetables. This includes the Produce for Better Health Foundation (PBH), the National Cancer Institute (NCI), and the Centers for Disease Control (CDC).

Benefits of Eating Raw

Raw fruits and vegetables have enzymes. "So what are enzymes? Catalysts, explains medical doctor Richard O. Brennan, the essential biological catalysts that make life possible. In fact, enzymes are a form of protein that initiate every biological cell or organ reaction that occurs in our bodies. Like a car without spark plugs, a body without enzymes is dead."[7] Enzymes serve to build, revitalize, and regenerate our cells and systems. The primary function is the digestion and assimilation of nutrients from the food we eat. Raw foods are packed with these health-promoting nutrients, whereas cooking can destroy some of these, depending on how they're prepared. "They are also loaded with their own digestive enzymes that help our body's enzyme force remove and utilize these nutrients."[8] Basically, if food enzymes do some of the work in the act of pre-digestion, this helps to safeguard our enzyme energy. Raw food essentially provides this spark of life that allows our body to conserve its own enzyme energy and redirect it toward maintaining other systems.

> There is more and more acknowledgment by men of science that raw, uncooked food in the diet is indispensable to the highest degree of health.[9] —Richard O. Brennan, DO, MD, *Coronary? Cancer? God's Answer: Prevent It!*

This freed-up energy allows our body to carry out important tasks, such as cell repair and rejuvenation, blocking foreign invaders, and other self-healing processes. Many people discover that they no longer feel tired, sluggish, or lethargic after switching to raw foods. Instead, they gain energy, sleep well, increase mental clarity, and have more digestive regularity (approximately three bowel movements per day).

Gain Knowledge by Being Proactive

Nutrition is a subject of great magnitude. We each have the potential to prevent many diseases and health issues by eating the right foods. There are ways to heal our body naturally and even curtail the aging process through the magnificent healing properties found in certain foods. The nutrients that provide the most antioxidants and help to fight the ravages of cell damage caused by free radicals are: vitamins C and E, beta carotene, and the minerals sulfur and selenium. These can restore youth to your cells, provide protection against many diseases, and reduce the risk of developing cancer. The right foods can be your best medicine. For virtually every physical ailment that exists in your body, there's a corresponding food to help provide special healing power and restoration. For instance, there's a reason Grandma's chicken soup helps you fight those common cold symptoms. A study conducted in 1978 by three lung specialists at Mount Sinai Medical Center in Miami Beach, Florida, discovered that chicken soup helped ease nasal congestion better than both hot water and cold water. The chicken itself contains a natural amino acid called cysteine, which works similar to a drug called acetylcysteine. "Doctors use acetylcysteine to treat people with bronchitis and other respiratory infections." [10]

Whatever health issues you may be facing, be proactive! Do research; read books, go online, talk to professionals in the field, and gather information. Search for the foods that can help heal you naturally. Don't expect your doctor to provide you with any special dietary recommendations. Traditional physicians are not specialized in the area of nutrition and they don't necessarily endorse preventive or holistic remedies. If your physician has conventional methods of treatment, that's okay—everything serves its purpose. You should still seek the advice of your physician with any medical condition.

Ultimately however, it's your responsibility to become proactive with your health. There are plenty of nutrition books and resources backed by holistic practitioners, scientists, medical experts, dietitians, nutritionists, wellness coaches, personal trainers, and so on. You have the opportunity and personal privilege to do your own homework. For instance, many cancer survivors have sought alternative remedies and experienced total remission through this precise method of self-healing.

Our common ground is that we each need to get our own nutrition plan in place. This should follow some general guidelines, but it can also be tailored to meet your individual needs and unique preferences. Remember, what works for you may not work for someone else. For instance, if you're deficient in a certain vitamin, you can choose which foods you prefer to eat that contain that vitamin. Your nutrition strategy should offer a wide variety of healthy food options, and be designed to meet your individual needs, goals and preferences. It can be as unique as you—if you want to eat four peanut M&M's a day, that's your prerogative.

What if you have a boring or rigid diet and eat the same things every day? In general, this isn't advisable, but it depends upon your situation. For instance, if you know you need to stick to a certain number of calories in order to lose weight, and you already have that menu figured out, then it becomes a matter of convenience. You can make exchanges, but if you're a creature of habit, you probably won't. It might be boring, but there's no guess work—you simply follow the plan, and it works. Likewise, if you have a certain disease, such as diabetes, eating certain foods on a regular basis, such as fish and nuts, can be helpful. But obviously, if you're allergic to nuts, this won't help.

While you may need to include or restrict certain food items, it's best to focus on getting a variety of foods. If you're always eating the same things, you may be lacking some important vitamins and minerals. Eating a wide variety of different foods can help you make up for any nutritional deficiencies. To be safe, this is also why taking a good-quality multivitamin is recommended. "The nutrients that people often don't get enough of include folate, vitamin B6, antioxidants, calcium and zinc."[11] Be proactive, and consider what may be missing in your diet. For instance, women who exercise frequently may deplete their iron stores, and vegetarians may not get enough vitamin B12.

You can use food sources to meet many of your specific needs, but you may still need supplementation. Keep in mind that some foods are better absorbed in conjunction with others. For example, iron absorption depends upon bioavailability, or rate of absorption, of the iron. "Meats contain heme-iron, which is a highly bioavailable source of iron."[12] The absorption of non-heme iron found in plant foods, such as leafy greens, legumes, cereals, and whole grains, is significantly enhanced by combining these foods with a source of vitamin C. So don't forget to drink your orange juice! If you take supplements separately, be aware that there are two types of vitamins: water-soluble and fat-soluble. The fat-soluble vitamins—A, D, E, and K—are stored in body fat, principally in the liver, and toxic levels have been found in people who take megadoses of these nutrients. The water-soluble vitamins (B complex and C) are not stored by the body, and any excesses are excreted in the urine. However, if megadoses are ingested, they too can reach toxic levels. "Vitamin toxicity usually affects the nervous system."[13] In particular, vitamins A and B6 are known to produce adverse neurologic reactions when ingested in megadoses.

You can cross-reference your daily intake of vitamins and minerals with the Recommended Daily Allowance (RDA) or the new versions of the RDI or DRI. There are not huge discrepancies, but these later versions may reveal more accuracy. Also if you are taking any medications; be sure to check with a registered dietitian first, regarding potential side-effects that may occur due to the interactions of eating certain foods. I designed the following two charts to assist you in getting the recommended daily vitamins and minerals. This also allows you to choose foods of your preference. However, use caution when making your food choices particularly if you're taking vitamin and mineral supplementation. Symptoms of toxicity can be just as harmful as symptoms of deficiency. When in doubt, focus on getting your nutrients by eating a variety of foods in moderation rather than using supplementation.

VITAMINS

Vitamin	U.S. RDA	Functions	Symptoms of Deficiency	Food Sources
A (carotene)	5000 IU/day	Formation and maintenance of skin, hair & mucous, bone & tooth growth, helps to see in dim light	Frequent colds, respiratory illness, kidney stones, dry skin, acne, night blindness, burning eyes, dull hair	Yellow or orange fruits and vegetables, green leafy vegetables, fortified oatmeal, liver, dairy products, cod liver oil
B1 (thiamine)	1.5 mg/day	Helps body release energy from carbohydrates during metabolism, growth and muscle tone	Mental confusion, depression, fatigue, apathy, anxiety, inability to concentrate, sensitivity to noise, low blood pressure, heart palpitations	Fortified cereals and oatmeals, meats, rice and pasta, whole grains, liver
B2 (riboflavin)	1.8 mg/day	Helps body release energy from protein, fat and carbohydrates during metabolism	Red tongue, cracks in corners of mouth, dizziness, watery or bloodshot eyes, hair loss, brain and nervous system changes, mental sluggishness, depression	Whole grains, green leafy vegetables, organ meats, milk and eggs
B6 (pyridoxine)	2 mg/day	Helps build body tissue and aids in metabolism of protein	Mental confusion, irritability, depression, anxiety, numbness or cramping in hands & feet, insomnia, nausea in morning, anemia, water retention, PMS symptoms	Fish, poultry, lean meats, bananas, prunes, dried beans, whole grains, avocados
B12 (cobalamin)	2 mcg/day (current)	Aids cell development, functioning of the nervous system and the metabolism of fat.	Pernicious anemia, numbness, apathy, neurological changes, poor reflexes, poor concentration, paranoia, poor memory, confusion	Meats, milk products, seafood
Biotin	30-100 mcg/day	Involved in metabolism of protein, fats and carbs	Fatigue, depression, skin disorders, muscle pain	Cereal/grain products, yeast, legumes, liver
Folate (folic acid)	400 mcg/day	Aids in genetic material development and involved in red blood cell production	Anemia, poor digestion, constipation, diarrhea, deterioration of nervous system, apathy, withdrawal, irritability, poor memory	Green leafy vegetables, organ meats, dried peas, beans and lentils
B3 (niacin)	20 mg/day	Involved in carbohydrate, protein and fat metabolism	Fear, suspicion, depression, insomnia, weakness, mental confusion, red tipped tongue, dermatitis, excessive gas, irritability	Meat, poultry, fish, enriched cereals, peanuts, potatoes, dairy products, eggs
B5 Pantothenic Acid	4-7mg/day (current)	Helps in the release of energy from fats and carbohydrates	Fatigue, sleep disturbances, depression, adrenal exhaustion, recurrent respiratory, illness, constipation, low blood pressure, irritability, burning feet	Lean meats, whole grains, legumes, vegetables, fruits
C (absorbic acid)	60 mg	Essential for structure of bones, cartilage, muscle and blood vessels, helps maintain capillaries and gums and aids in absorption of iron	Fatigue, loss of appetite, sore gums, slow wound healing, aching joints, bruising easily, frequent infections, mental disorders	Citrus fruits, berries and vegetables - especially peppers.
D	400 IU/day	Aids in tooth formation, helps maintain heart action and nervous system	Rickets, rheumatic pains, exhaustion, hypothyroidism	Fortified milk, sunlight, fish, eggs, butter
E	15 IU/day (current)	Protects blood cells, body tissue and essential fatty acids from harmful destruction in the body	Restlessness, fatigue, insomnia, menopause symptoms, muscle wasting, liver damage	Fortified and multi-grain cereals, nuts, wheat germ, vegetable oils, green leafy vegetables
K	80 mcg	Essential for blood clotting functions	Bleeding disorders, hemorrhaging	Green leafy vegetables, fruit, dairy and grain products

216

MINERALS

Mineral	U.S. RDA	Functions	Symptoms of Deficiency	Food Sources
Calcium	800-1000 mg/day	Strong bones, teeth, muscle tissue, regulates heart beat, muscle action and nerve function, blood clotting	Leg & feet cramps, anxiety, numbness, tenseness, insomnia, irritability, nervousness, osteoporosis, periodontal disease	Milk, dairy products, sunflower seeds, parsley, almonds, bonemeal, watercress, whole grains
Chromium	10-30 mcg	Glucose metabolism (energy), increases effectiveness of insulin	Diabetes, hypoglecemia, heart disease	Brewers yeast, meats, beef liver, shellfish, whole wheat, rye, butter, oysters, cornmeal, shrimp, corn oil
Copper	2 mg/day	Formation of red blood cells, bone growth and health, works with Vitamin C to form elastin	Anemia, weakness, hypothyroidism	Oysters, Brazil nuts, soy lecithin, almonds, walnuts, beef liver, clams, cod liver oil, lamb, rye, butter, garlic
Iodine	150 mcg/day	Component of hormone thyroxine, which controls metabolism	Weakness, weariness	Seafood, iodized salt
Iron	18 mg/day	Hemoglobin formation, improves blood quality, increases resistance to stress and disease	Anemia, dizziness, weakness, inability to concentrate, poor memory, depression	Meats, kelp, brewers yeast, eggs, green vegetables
Magnesium	350 mg	Acid/alkaline balance, important in metabolism of carbs, minerals and sugars	Memory impairment, insomnia, tremor, weakness, numbness, fatigue, anxiety, personality change, rapid heartbeat, hyperactivity, muscle aches, depression, delirium tremens	Kelp, green leafy vegetables, peas, molasses, whole grains, soybeans, brown rice, almonds, cashews, nuts
Manganese	5 mg	Enzyme activation, carbohydrate and fat production, sex hormone production, skeletal development	Reduced levels of dopamine, slow bone healing, disk problems in back, sore knees due to cartilage damage, impaired glucose tolerance, reduced brain function and inner-ear balance, skipped heartbeats and convulsions	Turnip greens, rhubarb, brussel sprouts, oatmeal, millet, cornmeal, carrots, eggs, pork and lamb, tomatoes, cantaloupe, whole-grain cereals
Phosphorus	1000 mg/day	Bone development, important in protein, fat, and carb utilization	Joint pain and stiffness, lack of appetite	Fish, meat, poultry, eggs, grains
Potassium	2-6 grams	Fluid balance, controls activity of heart muscle, nervous system, kidneys	Muscle cramps, fatigue, weakness, constipation, edema, headache, heart arrhythmia, joint pain	Oranges, dark green leafy vegetables, legumes, avocado, bananas, squash, tomatoes, sunflower seeds
Selenium	50-200 mcg/day	Protects body tissues against oxidative damage from radiation, pollution and normal metabolic processing	Contributes to cancer and heart disease	Butter, smoked herring, wheat germ, bran, liver, eggs, seafood, organ & lean meats, grains
Zinc	15 mg/day	Involved in digestion & metabolism, important in development of reproductive system, aids in healing	Cold extremities, poor peripheral circulation, loss of taste & smell, poor wound healing, lethargy, poor appetite, prostrate problems, ance, toxic copper levels, hypothyroidism	Lean meats, liver, eggs, seafood, whole grains, oysters, lamb, gingerroot, pecans, peas, shrimp, parsley, potatoes

Sources: ACE PT Manual[14] and 7 Weeks to Emotional Healing[15]

II. UNDERSTAND YOUR BODY'S REQUIREMENTS

Your body has a way of communicating to you. Much of the way you feel and function has to do with your diet, whether you find yourself having more difficulty concentrating, or you're being forgetful lately. Earlier, we discussed why fad diets don't work; in particular, because many eliminate an essential macronutrient. You may recall that a macronutrient falls into one of three categories: protein, carbohydrate, or fat. Much of what we eat has to do with our food preferences, belief system, and knowledge base. For instance, some people just don't believe in eating red meat, because they think it's higher in fat than other animal proteins. Fat content, however, depends on the choice of the meat—venison, for example, is very lean. If, however, you just don't like red meat and prefer poultry, that's your choice. We each have plenty of choices. If you choose to become a vegetarian who still eats fish and eggs, that's fine. If you choose to become a vegan, someone who consumes no animal food or dairy—fine again. We're each entitled to our beliefs and preferences, but we should work on getting our facts straight as well. A great place to start is by understanding the purpose that each macronutrient serves in your diet.

Without adequate *protein*, you'll have a hard time building or repairing lean muscle tissue. You will also lack the antibodies that protect your immune system against disease. Without the proper *carbohydrates*, you'll lack energy, be short on fiber, and become deficient in many important vitamins, minerals, and antioxidants. Without enough *fat*, you'll lack the essential fatty acids that are necessary for proper functioning of cell membranes, skin, hormones, and for transporting fat-soluble vitamins. You'll also find it's difficult to stay warm, and you probably won't feel satisfied after eating.

Learning what your body needs, when to eat, and how much depends upon your current physical condition, your fitness or weight loss goals, your resting metabolic rate and activity level. The following summary should be helpful for reference. The percentages are based on the Food and Nutrition Board (FNB).

Summary of Macronutrients and Recommended Percentages

Protein: 10-35%

- helps to build and repair muscle tissue

- major component of enzymes, hormones, and antibodies

Carbohydrate: 45-65%

- provides energy—this is the major source of fuel for body

- provides dietary fibers (for good digestion)

Fat: 20-35%

- chief storage form of energy

- insulates and protects vital organs (keeps you warm)

- provides fat-soluble vitamins

The Percentages

In order for your body to function optimally, you should stay within the recommended percentages for each macronutrient. Based on my work experience, the standard profile appears to be twenty percent protein, sixty percent carbohydrates, and twenty percent fat. However, the percentages listed above can help you design your own eating preference. For example, strength athletes and body builders typically require more protein, which helps them maintain a low body-fat percentage. Endurance athletes, on the other hand, often resort to what's called "carb-loading." They eat foods high in carbohydrates (typically, the day before an event) because this helps them nearly double their muscles' glycogen stores to gain a competitive edge. Everyone is different. Some people feel energized after eating protein, while others feel lethargic as a result. The same is true of carbohydrates— some people feel like to nod off after eating a bowl of pasta; others feel energized. Some people like a little more fat to add flavor to their diet; others are good with less.

Next, it's important to understand the difference in calories. Fat calories can add up fairly quickly because every gram of fat equals nine calories. For protein and carbohydrates, however, there are only four calories per gram. I created a sample menu below to show how to calculate caloric intake, based on a 2,000-calorie diet. Since everybody has individual needs, this is not a diet I recommend particularly for personal use. This menu is intended primarily for educational purposes, to provide you with an overview of calories, grams, and different foods associated with these percentages.

Sample Menu - 2000 Calorie Diet				
1 gram of protein = 4 calories* 1 gram of carbohydrate = 4 calories* 1 gram of fat = 9 calories*				
		macronutrient percent ranges:	10-35%	45-65%	20-35%
Total Calories	**Type of Food**	**Protein**	**Carbs**	**Fat**
150.5	Quaker Oats 'Old Fashioned' (1/2 cup)	5	27	2.5
146	2 large eggs	12	2	10
15.2	1 large egg white	3.5	0.3	0
116	1 med banana	1	28	0
99	1 tablespoon butter (salted)	0	0	11
149.8	1 baked potato	3	34	0.2
140	Starkist solid white albacore tuna (in water) 4 oz	26	0	4
120	Healthy Choice bread (multigrain) 2 slices	6	24	0
121.7	1 cup grapes	1	28.3	0.5
40	2 small cucumbers	2	8	0
16	2 cups shredded lettuce (romaine)	0	4	0
28	1 medium tomato	1	6	0
90	Salad dressing - Good Seasons (lite Italian) 3 tbsp	3	6	6
214.8	medium grain brown rice (1 cup cooked)	5	46	1.2
176.8	4 oz skinless chicken breast (roasted)	35.2	0	4
48	1 cup steamed broccoli	4	8	0
87.9	raw natural almonds (aprox. 11 nuts)	3	3	7.1
84	1 apple	0	21	0
24	1 cup celery raw, cut (aprox. 4-inch strips)	1	5	0
56	1 cup baby carrots	2	12	0
76.5	Dip - 3 Tbsp. hummus (Athenos)	1.5	7.5	4.5
	Grams:	115.2	270.1	51
2000.2	Calories:	460.8	1080.4	459
	Macronutrient Percentages:	23%	54%	23%

III. FOLLOW A NUTRITION PLAN THAT INCLUDES EXERCISE

The Law of Thermodynamics and Your Metabolism

Plenty of people exercise constantly, but don't follow a sound nutrition plan. It should be no surprise that they never reach their weight loss goals. At the same time, some people never exercise, eat a lot of junk and fast food, and don't gain a single pound. What's going on? The people in this later group have a high metabolism. If your metabolism is slow, you probably think that just looking at food makes you gain weight. You're not alone; weight issues are a primary source of vexation for many people. On the scale, it remains an enigma; a vicious cycle of up and down.

Often people get discouraged by stepping on the scale, but losing weight doesn't need to be so difficult. Building your metabolism through the right nutrition and exercise program can help you lose weight, and keep those extra pounds off for good! First, let's turn our attention back to the law of thermodynamics. This law reconciles the difference between the energy going in and the energy going out. This is important to know, because in order to lose weight, the calories consumed need to be offset accordingly, by the calories burned. Like it or not, calories count.

Some people exercise but ruin all their hard work by overeating; others do better with their nutrition but don't exercise. Your metabolism is determined by how efficiently your body burns calories—this is based on your basal metabolic rate (BMR) and your physical activity level. The Harris Benedict formula offers a baseline to determine your BMR, and it has been used by dietitians for years to assist in weight-loss goals. Exercise should be part of this nutrition equation, because it speeds up the weight-loss process and increases your metabolism. The right nutrition and exercise plan can help you to shed those stubborn pounds, reduce body fat percentage, achieve muscle hypertrophy, and improve athletic performance. If you're serious and want to get the best results, then you won't do one without the other. Nutrition and exercise work in sync to push your metabolism up to a whole new level. While it's best to seek the expertise of both a registered dietitian and certified personal trainer in order to achieve specific goals, let's consider how to shed some pounds through a basic diet and exercise program.

Below you will find the Harris Benedict formula to determine your approximate BMR. Another way to calculate your BMR, also referred to as RMR (resting metabolic rate), is through metabolic testing. A test called "caloriepoint" is offered at Life Time Fitness (LTF) facilities and it could be more accurate in determining this number. Once your BMR is determined, you can follow the steps listed for weight loss, or meet with a registered dietitian to assist you in reaching your goals and discussing specific health concerns.

Harris Benedict Formula and Steps for Weight Loss:

- Determine basal metabolic rate (BMR aka RMR)
- Apply activity multiplier (shown on next page) to determine maintenance calories
- Create a calorie deficit through nutrition and exercise

Note:
1 inch = 2.54 cm
1 kilogram = 2.2 pounds

Harris Benedict Formula for Men
BMR = 66 + (13.7 x weight in kilos) + (5 x height in cm) – (6.8 x age)

Example:
You are 25 years old
You are 6 feet tall
Your weight is 220
Your **BMR** is 66 + (1370) + (914) – (170) = **2180**

Harris Benedict Formula for Women
BMR = 655 + (9.6 x weight in kilos) + (1.8 x height in cm) – (4.7 x age)

Example:
You are 32 years old
You are 5 feet 4 inches (162.5 cm)
Your weight is 185 (84 kilos)
Your **BMR** is 655 + (806) + (291) – (150) = **1602**

ACTIVITY MULTIPLIER:

Sedentary (little or no exercise) = **BMR x 1.2**

Lightly Active (light exercise/sports 1-3 days/week) = **BMR x 1.375**

Moderately Active (moderate exercise/sports 3-5 days/week) = **BMR x 1.55**

Very Active (hard exercise/sports 6-7 days/week) = **BMR x 1.725**

Extra Active (very hard daily exercise/sports/physical job) = **BMR x 1.9**

After you calculate your BMR and multiply by the appropriate activity factor, you will have what's called your "maintenance calories." This is the number of calories you need to *maintain* your current weight. If you want to lose weight, you need to create a calorie deficit. The best way to do this is both through diet and exercise, because this will facilitate the weight-loss process. Incidentally, when it comes to weight loss, it's best to set a goal of one to two pounds per week. People in the morbid obese category, however, lose weight faster and may take off a bit more initially. Keep in mind that one pound equals approximately 3,500 calories. How will you plan on burning up 3,500–7,000 calories per week? Below is an example to illustrate:

Let's say your BMR is 1,200 and your activity multiplier is "lightly active," which means you would need to multiple 1,200 by 1.375. This equals 1,650—your maintenance calories. Remember, you need to burn at least 3,500 calories in order to shed one pound per week. You can take a certain amount off the 1,650 maintenance calories and burn the rest in exercise. The critical point to remember when it comes to weight loss is not to go below your BMR; in this case, 1,200. Your basal or resting metabolic rate is the minimum amount of calories your body requires. If you eat fewer calories than this number, your body will go into starvation mode, begin to store fat, and slow down your metabolism. Eventually, this can burn up your lean muscle tissue, and this is definitely not an effective way to lose weight. Here's a better way:

Take 200 calories off the 1,650, which equals 1,450—this is your new daily caloric intake. If you multiply 200 by 7 days per week, you come up with a 1,400 calorie deficit. Since it takes at minimum 3,500 calories to lose a pound, simply subtract: 3,500 − 1,400 = 2,100. This remaining amount of 2,100 calories needs to be burned during the week through exercise. Now you need to divide the 2,100 calories by the number of days you plan on working out and burn that amount or more accordingly. So if you work out five days per week, this would mean you need to burn at least 420 calories in each exercise session. Keep in mind when tracking the caloric burn during exercise that it's best to use a heart-rate monitor. Some of the cardio machines and treadmills tell you how much you burn, but they are not as accurate as a heart-rate monitor. A good-quality heart-rate monitor can also track which zones you train in, which allows you to see how much fat versus glycogen you burn. (I will cover this in more detail in the next chapter.) Regardless of your fitness goals, following a nutrition plan that is combined with exercise will help you achieve the best results.

Basic Nutrition and Exercise Tips

- If you're trying to lose body fat, do cardio on an empty stomach or wait approximately three hours after you eat. This is recommended because the calories that will be burned tend to come predominately from fat, as opposed to sugars. With some exceptions however, particularly if heart rate goes above Anaerobic Threshold—(to be covered in Exercise Chapter.)

- If you're trying to build muscle, eat a small meal approximately an hour or two before weight training. If you've been weight training and reached "muscle failure," eat immediately afterward (within one hour) and be sure to include protein. A whey protein shake is a great way to refuel, because the biological value is high and this helps your muscles repair and recover more quickly. You can build up to 60 percent of muscle mass in this one hour window of opportunity.

- If you want to improve athletic performance and endurance, it's best to load up on carbohydrates prior to cardio training. Mentioned earlier, this technique is often used to help give competitive athletes an edge.

- Whether you did high intensity cardio or reached muscle failure, your body can absorb nutrients more rapidly after a good-quality workout. For best results, be sure to refuel within forty-five minutes (or an hour at most). Many athletes choose foods that are high on the glycemic index to assist with recovery. For every gram of protein, include three grams of carbohydrates.

The nutrition guidelines on the following page are quite common recommendations. While these are generally beneficial, some things need to be addressed individually. For example, if you're a recovering alcoholic, drinking in moderation is not an option; in that case, abstinence is best. Many of my clients start losing weight by just following a few of these recommendations, such as avoiding artificial sweeteners.

General Nutrition Guidelines

- Do not skip breakfast!
- Eat four to six small meals throughout the day.
- Make fruits and vegetables a staple and priority every day.
- Choose food close to its natural state.
- Eliminate or substantially reduce anything that is highly processed.
- Eat foods high in dietary fiber. (For a 2,000 calorie diet aim for 28 grams a day.)
- Restrict *saturated fat* to a minimum of 22 grams per day.
- Drink plenty of pure water (minimum 96 ounces).
- Drink juices from fruits and vegetables, preferably fresh-squeezed.
- Cut back on salt.
- Limit saturated fat and sodium by eating dairy in moderation.
- Cut back on refined sugar, and avoid high-fructose corn syrup.
- Restrict consumption of foods containing gluten.
- Avoid artificial sweeteners, and eliminate diet drinks with aspartame.
- If identified, avoid foods that contain genetically modified ingredients—this poses a risk to our health and environment. (GMO stands for genetically modified organisms.)
- Read labels to avoid products with lots of additives, such as monosodium glutamate (MSG).
- Eat a wide variety of foods.
- Be proactive—plan meals in advance, carry portable snacks, and keep water on hand.
- Cook with your family and have fun in the kitchen.
- Relax and enjoy your meals.
- Snack on raw foods daily.
- Cycle eating around your exercise schedule.
- Consume caffeine and alcohol in moderation.
- Coffee is a diuretic—for every cup, be sure to drink two cups of water.
- Focus on portion sizes.
- If you are full, don't eat just to clean your plate.
- If you're trying to lose weight, jot down everything you eat in food logs.
- Plan periodic fasts. (This may require physician supervision.)

CHAPTER 12

Program Design—
PHS Principle: Exercise

Joining a health club is an excellent way to start your exercise program. Unfortunately, countless people have gym memberships and never use them. I often hear a story as to why this usage falls short. Besides the hectic demands of a busy lifestyle, many individuals confess that they feel out of place and intimidated by all the members who are thin or in great shape. Then I ask, "What's a gym for anyway?" Although it should be obvious, I must reinforce that it's not just for skinny people or those who are buff; it's for *everyone*—all ages, shapes, and sizes. We should never get hung up on comparing ourselves to others. Some people are seasoned vets who've been training athletically for years, and others have never set foot in a gym. None of that should matter.

Consider that most of my clients started training with these similar feelings of awkwardness, but after pushing through these barriers mentally and physically, their outlook changed quite drastically. Now when they come in to work out, they are so confident and focused on doing their own thing, they hardly notice anyone around them. It doesn't matter how old you are or how much you weigh, you can learn what's necessary and do what you need to do. It's never too late to learn. We are each a work in progress with a unique health and exercise history. It only makes sense that each of us will have different needs, goals, and agendas. We each require different programs or methods of training. Whether we need to start from scratch, make modifications, or step up our game, it's all good.

The reality is that most people join a health club in hopes of getting healthy and fit. But what does that mean exactly? While that certainly sounds like a common fitness objective, this may mean different things to different people. However, there are some guidelines to take into consideration.

- **Body Weight**
- **Body Mass Index (BMI)**
- **Body Fat Percentage**

Based on your height, age, and sex, you probably already know what's considered a healthy weight. How does this relate to BMI? Before determining your BMI, you should recognize that all weight is not created equal. If your main goal is to lose weight; consider where this weight loss is coming from—are you losing fat or muscle? Hypothetically, you can drop ten pounds of fat and gain ten pounds of muscle, and your weight will stay the same. However, this would make a twenty-pound shift in your body composition, which means you may lose inches and drop a size or two. The scale serves its traditional purpose, but it doesn't reveal the whole picture. For example, a forty-two-year-old female who's five foot five, with solid muscle, and weighs 140 pounds is going to look *completely* different from an out-of-shape, 140-pound woman of the same age and height who has 35 percent body fat. The same goes for BMI—it's just a baseline measurement. A male body builder can weigh 250 pounds and get measured with calipers showing a 5 percent body fat reading, yet according to BMI, he might be considered obese.

BMI REFERENCE CHART [1]

Weight Category	BMI Range
Normal Weight	19 to <25
Overweight	25 to <30
Obese	30 to <35
Seriously Obese	35 +

BMI = $\dfrac{\text{Weight (kg)}}{\text{Height (m) (squared)}}$

- Convert pounds to kilograms (divide by 2.2)
- Convert height in inches to centimeters (multiply by 2.54)
- Convert centimeters to meters (divide by 100)

Example: Weight = 185 pounds
Height = 66 inches

185/2.2 = 84 kg

66 x 2.54 = 167.6 cm   BMI = 84/(1.67x1.67)

167.6/100 = 1.67 m   BMI = 30.12

If you only focus on weight loss, you may end up disillusioned. Plenty of people lose weight, only to get stuck with a flabby body—that's a sign of muscle *atrophy*. Regardless of how much you weigh, muscle atrophy typically occurs after the age of twenty-five, unless you have a physically demanding job. This is why it's so important to build muscle through a proper strength-training program. Muscle burns more calories than fat, which means this will speed up your metabolism. People who strength train will get better results and burn a higher ratio of calories throughout the day than those who only do cardio. This translates into "Wow, I can eat a cookie and not gain any weight!" (Not a tiny vanilla wafer; I'm talking about those huge, homemade, rich, double-chocolate cookies.) Muscle also increases your bone density, which protects against osteoporosis.

During initial consultations women often say; "I only want to lose weight and get toned, but I don't want to build muscle and get bulky." Then I tell them that in order to get that coveted "toned" look, they actually have to work *very hard* at building muscle. They are shocked to discover that they never get even *remotely* close to training that hard to warrant such a concern. Another common tendency is for people to say, "I want to lose some weight first and then start strength-training." This line of thinking is also counterproductive. Strength training not only expedites the weight loss process, but it focuses on the loss of fat, not muscle. Doing both—the proper amounts of cardio and strength training—will produce the best results in terms of altering body composition.

We each have different lifestyles, goals, strengths, and weaknesses; our daily activity levels vary from one person to the next. For this reason alone, it's best to work one-on-one with a personal trainer to determine what's right for you—I can't emphasize this enough. There are many variables to consider and much to learn in terms of how to alter your body composition and make progress on your goals. Before you start any program, you should have a consultation and undergo an individual health and fitness assessment. In some cases, this may even require a physician's clearance.

Common Fitness Goals

- Weight loss

- Decrease body fat

- Build cardiovascular endurance

- Gain strength—build and sculpt muscles

- Correct postural distortions

- Strengthen core

- Improve flexibility, balance, and range of motion

- Increase agility and improve athletic performance

A certified personal trainer can offer guidance and has the expertise to design a program that is specific for you. You should understand, however, that this entails more than just learning how to use a few machines and repeating the same exercises over and over. This isn't about learning some "routine." It's about training in progressive phases and making individual changes where needed. In fact, the National Academy of Sports Medicine emphasizes this integrated continuum through the OPT (optimum performance training) model. This means we must train from the inside out, by progressing in three basic phases: stabilization, strength, and power. We can cycle through these stages with various intensities as we go through what's called "periodization."

Consider Philip, who told me his main goal was to bench press heavier and build his upper-body strength, yet he had a hunch back and skinny legs. After discussing these problem areas, I told him his postural distortion needed to be corrected, and he shouldn't neglect the lower half of his body either. I recommended that he back off the bench press for a bit. We started doing stabilization training and corrective exercises instead. Part of his program included improving his upper-body range of motion, flexibility, balance, and building his core strength. Remember, the core is the center of gravity for the whole body. After he strengthened those smaller stabilization muscles, which are invisible to the eye, he began to lift heavier and make greater strides in strength training—not to mention that his girlfriend thanked me for his new pair of legs and nice back.

Often, people don't get results for lack of trying, but they get stuck in a training rut. They hit a plateau and stay there until they discover they've been training inefficiently. I always tell my clients that if they leave the gym shaking, that's a sign of a great workout. If they come in feeling comfortable and leave feeling comfortable, their workout probably didn't amount to much. That's not to say it's always necessary to beat yourself up and leave the gym feeling uncomfortable, but for the best results, it's important to challenge yourself in a variety of dimensions.

Essential Fitness Objectives and Considerations

Cardiovascular Training

- *Aerobic Development:* Determining your VO_2max is an important part of your cardiovascular assessment. Simply put, this is a measurement of how efficiently your body can utilize oxygen. The V stands for volume of oxygen (ml/kg/min). This test can be done in five minutes on most treadmills. It's considered a gold standard for heart and lung fitness. The higher the score, the better. A high VO_2 will help burn more calories. For example, two women of the same age, weight, and height might go into a cardio kickboxing class and do the same workout, but the one with a higher VO_2max, may burn 500 calories, while the one with the lower VO_2max, may only burn 300.

- *Aerobic/Anaerobic Endurance:* Your body needs oxygen to burn fat. Aerobic means with or in the presence of oxygen, and anaerobic means without. You can train your body to burn fat more efficiently, so you don't need to spend countless hours in the gym. By improving your aerobic base (AB)—your fat-burning efficiency and endurance—you can maximize the time spent working out in a shorter period of time. How can this be achieved? First, by knowing your specific heart-rate zones, and second, by training in them effectively. Many heart-rate monitors have default sport zones, based on your age, height, sex, and weight. These offer a decent gauge, but a more accurate reading would be to take a metabolic or perceived exertion test to determine your anaerobic threshold (AT, sometimes referred to as lactic threshold). This represents your heart rate at the point where your breathing becomes labored and your muscles burn. Here, your body can no longer meet its demand for oxygen. Knowing this number is the key to unlocking your specific heart-rate zones.

The highest possible fat-burning rate is at the top of your oxygen-sufficient zone, right below AT. If you train at a heart rate that's at or above AT, your body will use sugar, not fat, as a fuel source. That doesn't mean you should never train above AT. If your AT is low, training at higher heart rates will help to drive it up, but it's important to build a fitness foundation as well. Building your AB will not only help you burn more calories, but it'll help you use more fat calories for fuel. Your AT is not a static number; it can change along with your AB, depending upon how you train.

For most people, there are two basic objectives here: one is to get your AT as high as possible; and two is to bring your AB closer to your AT. There are several variables involved in accomplishing this, but without knowing those numbers, and how, or if you were previously training, making those specific recommendations isn't possible. Again, working with a certified personal trainer and/or metabolic specialist can help you make these specific determinations. To find a health club that offers metabolic testing, you can go to the New Leaf website (www.newleaffitness.com). Also, any Life Time Fitness can provide this service for a small charge, even to non-members. This will also include a customized cardio program showing how to train in your specific zones.

- **Why a Heart Rate Monitor?** Using a good-quality heart-rate monitor will help you to quickly test your VO$_2$max, track what zones to train in, record and store all your workouts, show your caloric burn, help you to stay on pace, and so much more. Keep in mind that cardio can be anything you enjoy that gets the heart pumping—walking, running, swimming, biking, cardio machines, or classes. When starting out, shoot for a minimum of three times per week for approximately a half-hour at a time. As you progress, you can increase your duration and/or days and alternate the intensity through interval and zone training by monitoring your heart rate. For example, your heart rate might be between 118 and 128 bpm (beats per minute) for two minutes; then 128-140 bpm for the next two minutes; switching back and forth between these ranges until your duration is over. Depending on your zones, this type of workout (or something similar) is usually recommended with a high, medium, and low intensity; each to be done on a separate day. You can search online for different heart-rate monitors. Polar RS300X is a basic and popular one I recommend to all my clients. If you want more bells and whistles; just visit the polar website at: www. polarusa.com. Another good-quality brand is Garmin; and you can find more options at: www.bodytronics.com.

- **Improving Recovery Time:** As your heart gets stronger, your recovery heart rate will improve. For instance, let's say you just started working out with a trainer, and you did something that made your heart rate skyrocket. How long does it take before you recover and are able to move on to the next exercise? If you have to sit down and take a five-minute break just to catch your breath, then your recovery heart rate needs a lot of work. On the other hand, if your heart rate can drop 20-30 beats in one minute afterward, and you're ready for the next round, that's excellent! Improving this recovery heart rate is another way to gauge your cardiovascular progress.

Recommendations for Stabilization and Strength Training

- Pre-workout fuel: Eat a small meal approximately one to two hours prior to training. Example: half a sandwich and a piece of fruit.

- Always warm up prior to training. This increases your cardio-respiratory capacity, gets the blood flowing to active muscle tissues, and psychologically prepares you for what's ahead. This takes approximately five to ten minutes—it's low to moderate intensity cardio, such as a treadmill or bike.

- Work with a personal trainer to correct postural imbalances, ensure proper form, strengthen the core, and improve balance, flexibility, and coordination.

- When moving into the strength-training phase, work the large muscle groups first, followed by the small muscles. If your small muscles are fatigued, it's going to be a lot harder to recruit the larger ones.

- Make sure to go through the whole range of motion while maintaining proper form. There's a *concentric* phase, where the muscle acts as the motive force—it shortens followed by an *eccentric* phase, where it lengthens as muscle tension is created.

- The intensity: your sets, repetitions (reps), rest, and pace should be determined and closely monitored by your trainer. This depends on your goals and current fitness level, so it's very personal. In general when starting out, one to three sets is recommended, with a minimum of eight to twelve reps, and a thirty-second rest in between. The pace for each rep will also vary depending on goals and the actual program design; usually, about three to four seconds. But don't get too hung up on sets and reps—that's the trainer's responsibility, and there are more ways to train than most people can possibly imagine. For instance, circuit training involves a series of exercise stations, and it can emphasize muscular endurance, aerobic conditioning, muscular strength, or a combination of all three.

235

- If you're looking to reshape and strengthen your muscles, then eventually you'll need to reach what's called "muscle failure." What this means is that you'll reach the point where you just can't do that extra repetition (you may need someone to spot you). Tearing down the muscle tissue is an important part of rebuilding it and making it grow stronger. However, if you've never worked out before, it's best to start out gradually—you'll be sore enough without much effort.

- Cool down and stretch *after* your workout. Many people are under the misconception that they should stretch prior to strength training, yet it's more effective to stretch after the muscles are warmed up.

- Be sure to refuel within one hour of strength training. For every gram of protein, be sure to include three grams of carbs.

- If you're sore the following day, it's always a good idea to walk it out. This helps to remove lactic acid from your system.

Basic Athletic Training

- Train specifically for your activity. Learn from a coach and/or personal trainer.

- Be sure to train in phases (in season/off season).

- Cross-train. Don't over train one muscle group.

- Maintain the proper equipment and athletic gear.

Personal Training Tips

- Start at your own level. Often, you can be more effective by making gradual improvements and slowing down your pace. Don't start out fast and furious.

- Mix things up. Train in different ways with different intensities. This might be swimming one day, biking the next day, running another, strength training another, and yoga another.

- Make sure to eat frequently throughout the day to keep blood sugar stable. Many protein bars and ready-made shakes have the proper balance of macronutrients and only take a couple minutes to eat.

- Hydrate! Drink 64-96 ounces of water daily and more if training heavily.

- Keep food logs. Writing down what you eat helps you to track empty calories.

- Relish in all your improvements, big or small.

- Exercise should be fun! Find a physical activity or sport that you enjoy; this will help with adherence.

- For weight loss, nutrition plays a critical role *along with exercise*. If you exercise religiously but eat back all your calories, the weight won't come off!

Trivia Question: Ever wonder why some people get shredded faster? People born with fast-twitch muscle fibers will typically have quicker gains in muscle hypertrophy, whereas those with slow-twitch fibers tend to excel as endurance athletes.

Basic Training Progressions

In general, it takes at least two months of training to go through what's called "neural adaptation"—that's when your body is responding and adjusting to the new stimuli. In this phase, most people will feel and function better, but it's typically in the third month of training that significant changes can be seen in the mirror. This entails a couple of days of strength training every week, in addition to at least three days of cardio, although these can be done on the same day. However, if you plan to do high-intensity cardio on the same day as strength training, it's best to do it afterward, so you don't burn up any sugar stored in your muscles. Also, remember that it's crucial to eat within one hour of strength training—assuming the muscles are properly stimulated to "muscle-failure." Eating afterward will help to repair and rebuild them. Muscles grow in the resting phase of training, not during. Muscle recovery takes approximately one to two days.

Unfortunately, some people work out every day and over-train the same muscles, doing more damage than good. On the other hand, others go into the gym daily but don't work out hard enough to ever get results. If people know what they're doing, they can work out every day by alternating the muscles groups and combining this with a personalized cardio program. In fact, body builders usually work out twice a day. However, it's not necessary to strength train every day. Most people just need to learn to work out smarter.

We each need to be challenged in order to make any sort of progress. Yet from this vantage point, there's no "one size fits all" approach. It's very important to recognize that the duration and intensity for weight training and cardio will vary, depending on individual fitness levels and goals. For example, when doing a chest dumbbell press, I might hand Sarah a couple dumbbells, each 7.5 pounds in weight, and ask her how it feels on a scale from one to ten, with one being easy and ten being difficult. If she says six or seven, this is a good challenging weight for her to start. On the other hand, Monica, who's the same age and training alongside Sarah, needs to use dumbbells of 12.5 in order to be challenged at the same six or seven intensity level. Similarly, we each have different goals. A body builder is going to focus much more on building muscle and keeping body fat low, while a sedentary person, who is huffing and puffing while climbing the stairs, really needs to work on building cardiovascular endurance. Many people don't realize where they need to start and what they need to focus on before making progress.

This is why a personal trainer is *personal*; he/she will help educate and guide you specifically on how to properly challenge yourself. With the trainer's expertise, your long-term goals can be broken down into short-term steps. He or she can create the best plan for progress, ensure the proper form and significantly maximize your training time. Even if your budget doesn't allow you to work with a personal trainer for several months at a time, try to find a way to sign up for a few sessions to help get you going in the right direction. Most health clubs offer an incentive when you join to start working right away with a trainer. Take advantage of whatever is offered! Too many people claim they can't afford a personal trainer—until they discover that for several years, they've wasted so much time exercising in the wrong way. Working out incorrectly can create more imbalances and limitations in your body. This is unfortunate and unnecessary, when a little knowledge can go a long way.

Generally speaking, one-on-one personal training sessions last for an hour, (although some last half an hour), while your personal cardio sessions can vary in duration and frequency, depending on your goals. For example, if a person is at least one hundred pounds overweight, extremely de-conditioned, and has a very low VO_2max, he/she needs to start slow by building cardiovascular endurance. In that case, I'm going to tell him/her not to worry about heart rate or zone training but to just start by doing a fifteen-minute walk every day for three weeks. For some people, even a five-minute walk on the treadmill can feel like an eternity, but if they get through it, that's tremendous progress. You don't need to get overwhelmed by all the do's and don'ts. It's not necessary to train for a triathlon in order to challenge yourself. Challenging yourself to feel and function better in daily life, gain more energy and not have your clothes feel so tight may be enough incentive. Contrary to popular opinion, not everyone wants to have a "six-pack" (washboard abs). Regardless, we all need to start somewhere and work purposely at achieving our own fitness goals. Even afterward, we each have to work at maintenance. *Nobody* is excused from this responsibility. Those people with beautiful bodies and sculpted muscles have them for a reason—they work at it.

It's always convenient to have access to a health club to target certain muscle groups with ease. However, after you learn how to train properly, you can exercise in the privacy of your own home. Preferences are not right or wrong as long as you do what's necessary. Some people like the gym atmosphere to socialize; others just want to get in and get out. You may prefer to do in-house training, in which case this may or may not involve equipment. There's no need to become a gym rat. After all, who needs the gym when you can break out some dance moves? Have fun! There are plenty of indoor and outdoor ways to incorporate physical activity into your daily life. Fresh air and sunshine can make exercise even more enjoyable. Remember to always warm up before each session, with a cool down and light stretching afterward.

On the pages that follow, you will find selected exercises with pictures, some of these are basic and some are advanced. If you're interested in learning how to engage the muscles properly, make modifications, or perform any exercise with the right form, be sure to seek the assistance of a personal trainer. Whether you want to use a machine or certain equipment such as TRX, discontinue anything if you're uncertain how to perform it correctly. Always take caution to reduce the risk of injury.

Exercise Without a Gym

- Play your favorite music and bust out the dance moves
- Follow a workout video (Example: P90X)
- Walk or run on nature trails
- Swim at a beach
- Mountain biking
- Plank Hold
- All-Four Stabilization
- Air Squats (aim for 20 repetitions per set)
- Jumping jacks, line jumps, frog jumps, jumping lunges
- Basic Pushups: against a wall, girl (on knees)
- Pushup Progressions: off knees, diver bomb, pushup with claps
- Wall Sits: squat with back against a wall; hold pose 45 seconds
- Mountain Climbers
- Pelvic Tilts – (lift leg and add leg circles for progression)
- Basic Yoga Stretches: child pose, down dog, triangle

Exercise that Requires a Machine or Equipment

- Jump Rope
- Recumbent Bike
- Treadmill
- Elliptical Machine
- Walking Lunges with Dumbbells
- One Arm Dumbbell Row
- Dumbbell Chest Press
- Dumbbell Chest Fly
- Lat Pull Down
- Dumbbell Reverse Fly
- Medicine Ball Squats
- Medicine Ball Squats on BOSU Ball
- Shoulder Head Press
- Push-ups: on a bar, Swiss ball, Medicine ball, BOSU ball
- Kettle Bell Swings
- TRX: Low Row, Cross Lunges, Power-Pull
- Mountain Climbers on BOSU ball (either side)

The squat is a classic exercise. This is a great way to target your glutes and the muscles in your legs (hamstrings and quads) without a machine. Place the stability ball against the wall in the small of your back. Stand with your feet shoulder-width apart and dumbbells in hand. Squat down until you reach at least, a right angle. As a rule of thumb, don't let your knees go over your toes.

Dumbbell Squat with Stability Ball (against wall)

Finish

Start

Stand on the Bosu ball with feet shoulder-width apart. Hold the medicine ball by your chest. As you squat down, push the medicine ball out in front of you. This movement will help to build your core, strengthen leg muscles and improve balance.

Medicine Ball Squat on BOSU Ball

Finish

Start

Lunges are a tried and true way to train and great for sports conditioning. It will fire off your glutes, hips, and leg muscles (quad, hamstring and calf) while engaging your core and helping to improve balance. As you step forward with dumbbells in hand, bend each knee to a right angle. Keep your shoulders back and don't let your front knee go over your toe. Switch legs after meeting in the middle in between.

Walking Lunges with Dumbbells

Finish

Start

Middle

Walking Lunges with Medicine Ball Rotation

Take lunges to another level by building even more core strength. While holding the medicine ball in front of you, lunge *first;* then rotate the ball in the direction of your *front* knee. Let your feet meet in between before repeating on the opposite side.

Finish

One-Arm Dumbbell Row

Place your left hand and left knee on a bench. Your right leg should be wider than shoulder-width. With the dumbbell in your right hand, pull this extended arm up to engage your back muscles (lat, upper back and traps). Keep your neck and spine in neutral. Switch sides and repeat.

Finish

This will build your chest muscles and target some parts of your arms. Hold a dumbbell in each hand while lying on a bench. Starting at a right angle, slowly lift the dumbbells up over your chest to form the shape of an upside down "V." To protect your shoulders, don't let your elbows drop past the horizontal line of your body.

Dumbbell Chest Press on Bench

Finish

Dumbbell Chest Fly on Bench

This will work your chest, shoulders and the secondary muscles in your back. Hold the dumbbells in your hands with palms facing each other and arms extended upward. From the top, slowly lower the dumbbells down to each side, keeping a slight bend in your elbows.

Finish

Dumbbell Chest Press on Stability Ball

Make training more functional by doing your chest press on a
stability ball. With dumbbells in hands, sit on the ball; then roll out
until your head is fully supported. Your abs should be engaged and
horizontally aligned with your shoulders and knees. As you lift the
dumbbells up in the direction of an upside down "V," don't let your
butt drop.

Finish

Dumbbell Chest Fly on Stability Ball

Make training more functional by doing your chest fly on a stability ball. With dumbbells in hands, sit on the ball; then roll out until your head is fully supported. Your abs should be engaged and horizontally aligned with your shoulders and knees. With arms extended up and palms facing each other, slowly lower the dumbbells down to each side keeping a slight bend in your elbows. Don't let your butt drop.

Finish

Start

A staple in any exercise program, this will work your lat and bicep muscles. There are different grips depending on your body size and goals. For the medium width, your hands should be aligned with the right angle bend of your elbows. Beginning at the very top of the bar, lean slightly back, keep chin up and bring the bar down toward your collar bone. Be sure to squeeze the shoulders bringing them down and back (pretend you're trying to grab a pencil between your shoulder blades).

Lat Pull Down

Finish

251

All Four Stabilization

This is an excellent way to build your stabilization muscles, strengthen lower back and improve balance. Lift the opposite arm and leg keeping shoulders, butt and feet in line. Hold this pose for approximately 30 seconds before switching sides.

Elbow Plank Hold

A 30 second hold in this position will do more to strengthen your core than 50 crunches done incorrectly. Maintain alignment in the shoulders, hips and knees. Don't let your body sag and make sure to keep breathing!

Straight Plank

This pose will challenge your core and upper body at the same time! Hands should be at least shoulder-width apart and shoulders slightly over your hands. Maintain proper body alignment in the hip and spine. Hold for 20 seconds, or as long as you can with good form.

This is one of the best ways to work your obliques (love handles). Place one hand on a mat with legs and feet stacked. Slowly lift your hip away from the floor lifting your other arm straight up. An easier version is to perform this plank with your forearm on the mat.

Straight Arm Side Plank

This beast of an exercise will work the core, back and arms. In the straight plank position, hold onto a set of dumbbells. Keep your feet wide, lock out your legs for support and lift one arm at a time to row. Try not to rotate hips much or let your butt get out of alignment.

Renegade Row

Finish

Dumbbell Bicep Curl on Incline Bench

Finish

Start with the dumbbells in your hands and both arms extended straight down. Curl each dumbbell up to the point where your bicep muscle is fully contracted. Slowly lower back down and repeat. This can also be done one arm at a time.

Russian Twist

The Russian Twist is an exercise that can strengthen core muscles, and help in sports related activity. Keep your legs is tabletop position while moving the ball from side to side. Repeat 15 times on each side for a total of 30 reps.

Finish

Start

TRX has been a hot trend for several years because it's all core, all the time! Exercises can become more challenging simply by changing the angle of your stance. This start position can be used for the two examples below. The Low Row will strengthen your back and arms in the pull position. The T will build your strength and stability in the rear deltoids and upper back.

Finish

TRX - Low Row

Finish

TRX - T

Start at your desired
angle of difficulty and
move your arms outward
in the shape of a "Y."
Keep the tension even on
the TRX, particularly at
the top. This movement
will help to build strength
and stability in your
shoulders (the rear and
lateral deltoids).

Finish

TRX - Y

Start

Your workout can be done outdoors in the fresh air on a warm sunny day! TRX is portable which can make exercise more convenient and enjoyable. This move will strengthen your back, shoulders and arms. Before using TRX outside, be sure it's secured properly and the surroundings are safe.

TRX - Single-Arm Row (TRX attached to a picnic table)

Finish

TRX - Power Pull on the Bosu Ball

Add the Bosu ball to the TRX Power Pull and this will step up training by challenging your balance. This movement integrates a large range of motion while it works on strengthening your back and core rotational control. With one hand, keep tension on the TRX. As you squat, point down with the other hand and repeat to the start position.

Finish

If you're a beginner to the TRX, perform the suspended plank from the elbow. It's more stable and doesn't require as much core or upper body strength as the straight plank.

TRX - (Suspended) Elbow Plank Hold

TRX - Pendulum Swing

This is a fun way to work your obliques! In the straight plank position, keep legs and feet together as you swing from side to side. Try to go for one minute. This dynamic movement will challenge your core stabilization muscles to maintain control while it puts your upper body to work.

A strong upper back can help protect your shoulders from injury. This will target the muscles in your upper back and shoulder region (rhomboids, middle trap, lat and rear deltoid). Grab a couple dumbbells, stand shoulder-width apart; bend over to approximately a 45 degree angle and flex your knees slightly. With a slight bend in your elbow, bring the dumbbells up in an arc-like path keeping your lumbar spine and head in neutral.

Reverse Dumbbell Fly

Finish

Kettlebell Swing

The kelllebell swing is as ballistic as a standing jump. Done correctly, it will activate the muscles in your glutes, hamstrings and core while getting your heart rate up. Make sure to use a weight that's challenging but not too heavy. Start by holding the kettlebell in both hands. As you squat, keep your chest high and abs engaged. Hinge at the hips and swing the bell back behind you.

Finish

263

Mountain Climbers on the Bosu Ball Flipped

This is a great drill for core, upper body, balance and cardio. In the straight plank position, place hands in the center of the Bosu Ball (blue side down). Alternate legs by moving knees inward toward chest and keeping only one foot on the floor. Try to go for 30 seconds.

Right

Left

Pelvic Tilt

The pelvic tilt can provide some relief to low back pain. It will activate the muscles in your glutes and quads while offering a nice stretch in your lower back and hamstrings. Knees should be shoulder-width apart and feet should be hip-to-shoulder-width apart. Keep the weight in your heels as you lift up. Hold for 5 seconds, slowly lower back down and repeat.

Foam Roller Stretch

A foam roller provides the benefits of a myofascial release (relief of muscle tension) without a big price tag. You can perform a self-massage, break up trigger points and sooth tight fascia while increasing blood flow and circulation. Roll on a foam roller until you find a tender spot. Hold for 30 seconds to release the tension.

Child's Pose

The benefits of Yoga are numerous! It brings
balance, strength and vitality. This in only one
pose, but it's favored by many. The Sanskrit
name is Balasana. (Bala means child.) Shared
by both Yoga and Pilates, this pose helps to
normalize blood circulation, stretch the back
and release tension in the groin and hips.
Kneel on a mat, touch toes together and
spread knees hip-width apart. There are two
possible arm variations. One is to stretch
arms in front of you with palms down, and
the other is to bring arms back (as shown)
with palms facing up. Do whatever feels the
most relaxing and comfortable to you. If
you're not this flexible don't worry, just press
your butt down as far as possible. Relax. This
is a wonderful end to any workout!

CHAPTER 13

Discipline—
PHS Principle: Be Persistent

Self-Discipline Requires Persistence

Congratulations! You've arrived at the much-desired destination: *discipline*. If you followed the path from the bottom of the PHS Pyramid, all the hard work you did in those lower tiers helped get you to this high point. Although you could've fast-forwarded to this section, this is still the toughest component for most people. There's no quick-fix to being disciplined; it's the unmistakable by-product of your *persistence*. This PHS principle will continue to support your lifelong mission to being healthy—and that's the key to discipline.

Many people neglect their health when they're extremely busy, overwhelmed, or struck by some kind of adversity. During those times, you might think that staying committed to your health isn't realistic, but that's simply not true. In fact, that's when taking care of oneself becomes even more important. If you're disciplined, this is still possible. That's because maintaining healthy behaviors involves more than just sweating and grunting in the gym. You don't have to work out 24/7 and eat organic tofu sprinkled with ground flaxseed to be committed to a healthy lifestyle. Good habits go beyond an exercise and nutrition program. Since the PHS promotes health on all levels—mentally, physically, and spiritually—whenever you apply the PHS principles, you honor this commitment. Let's consider some scenarios of how being persistent can keep you disciplined.

How you would respond if you were in a tragic accident and told you would never walk again? There are countless stories of people who in spite of lost limbs or a physical body that shut down, managed to defy the odds. How was this possible? Through their persistence, of course! They refused to settle into discouragement and hopelessness. Instead, they became more determined to overcome—a fight was burning deep down in their spirit. Mentally, they encouraged themselves daily with positive thoughts, and upheld a clear image of themselves walking again. Their persistence in doing what their physical body was deemed unable to do, created the extraordinary. The power in their mind and spirit, along with all their good efforts, brought that image into alignment with their physical body.

Another example of persistence can be seen within an undefeated varsity team. When a coach screams at and criticizes his team, sometimes we may view this as harsh or counterproductive, but if it's done in the right way, it helps to strengthen the players' mind-set. Overcoming mental barriers requires a certain psychological resilience. A stronger mind-set has a positive impact on morale and physical performance; it can make a team more cohesive and determined to win. As they become persistent on victory, this creates the winning spirit they need to go on and compete with greater fervor. Even within a team, we can find this connection—a unity of the mind, body and spirit.

Now, let's assume you were following your exercise and nutrition plan and that everything was going right on track. Suddenly, something unexpected came along and interrupted your routine—a pregnancy, a job loss, an injury, a divorce, a death, relocation, or more work hours. Even just one of these circumstances can significantly alter everything in your life. Will you let that circumstance take you down, or will you persist in taking care of yourself in spite of it? You must realize that nothing in life stays same, but your value to be healthy doesn't have to change. Sure, you may need to adjust your routine, shift some priorities around, or take a time-out temporarily, but that is part of your life journey. It doesn't have to stop you permanently. When you're persistent, you'll find a way to honor your commitment to health. For instance, if you lost your job and need to cut back on spending, this might mean putting your gym membership on hold and jogging outside or doing jumping jacks and calisthenics at home. If you injured your knee and won't be able to run for a couple of months, this might mean doing water therapy and focusing on your upper-body and abs for a while. Whatever the situation may be, there's always a way to honor your health—that's part of being proactive.

Fortunately, you can apply the PHS principles anywhere and anytime. Whenever you're feeling overwhelmed, take a moment to consider which principle rings the strongest for you. If you're not sure which one needs more attention, focus on regaining balance. That spirit-based principle lies at the heart of the healthy self-management component—in the midst of chaos, it helps to keep you grounded. When you find that deep inner peace, it's easier to handle all the other pressures and demands of life. Breathe deep, meditate for a few minutes, and turn to your higher source of power. Remember, your breath connects you to your energy center. A few moments of calm can go a long way. When you're not feeling overwhelmed, you can sort things out and determine your next best step. A new path could unravel and present itself. Be open to walk it.

Most people will agree that if you eat right and exercise regularly, you must be disciplined. However, it's your persistence toward this end that makes you disciplined, not the acts alone. Again, being disciplined in this sense doesn't mean that your life won't change, but your commitment doesn't change. When you're committed to being healthy, there's a mighty force and purpose behind your actions—you're not just going through the motions. Being persistent allows you to adapt to the tides of life without compromising your personal values. When you're able to uphold these values and behaviors in spite of extenuating circumstances, you become disciplined.

Consider Vanessa, one of my clients. She had relocated three times in one year. At one point, she and her husband were living out of a hotel. She was extremely busy, working overtime, and her life felt like a whirlwind— everything had spun out of control. Finally, after the last move, things calmed down—but then she found out she was pregnant! In spite of all the transitions she endured, she applied this PHS principle of persistence. She made a point of investing in her health and told herself that she wasn't going to make excuses. Every night after dinner, she prepared a healthy lunch (usually leftovers) and snacks for work the next day. She also never left in the morning without eating a good breakfast. Although she was exhausted on many days, she found a way to de-stress her physical body.

Sometimes this meant meditating, doing light yoga stretches or a warm bath to calm her frayed nerves. Occasionally, she made it to the gym to do cardio, and other times, she came to see me to do resistance training and her favorite TRX exercises.

Even during that transitional period of upheaval, Vanessa was doing whatever she could to keep her commitment to be healthy. When she found out she was pregnant, she proactively made a decision that she wasn't going to be the kind of mom who blamed the weight gain and muscle atrophy on her baby. Shortly after her baby was born, she was prepared to use the health club's daycare facility and booked her training sessions in advance. When it comes to her health, Vanessa follows all the PHS principles. Her persistence makes her disciplined and her physical body is envied by many.

Any challenging life situation can trigger a backsliding into unhealthy behaviors. Will you allow those overwhelming moments to send you on a downward spiral, or will you remain persistent? This principle reveals a mystery to one of life's greatest challenges—when you're persistent, virtually anything you want to accomplish in life is possible! Aligning yourself with this PHS principle will help you maintain healthy behaviors—and it's a secret of life success!

Success in Life Requires Persistence

If you look at all the successful people throughout history, that's one thing they have in common: *persistence*. Despite repeated failures or setbacks, they went on to succeed. Consider the life of Thomas Edison, a prolific inventor, who shines a light in our path in more ways than one. He didn't create the first light bulb over night, yet he refused to give up, even after many failed attempts. He was persistent and tried over one thousand times before he finally lit the world! Abraham Lincoln is another magnificent example of a man who personifies persistence. Born into poverty, he received very limited formal education, because he had to work to support his family. That didn't stop him from learning; he was an avid reader, and through self-education, he studied to become a lawyer. In time, he earned a license as a formal attorney to practice law in all the courts of Illinois. With a strong desire to make a difference, his legal career propelled him into the political arena. But Lincoln encountered many setbacks, both in his career and personal life. He lost eight elections, failed twice in his business endeavors, and even suffered a nervous breakdown. In 1860, however, his persistence finally paid off—he was elected president of the United States—and to this day, he's considered one of the greatest.

· ·
For now you know one of the greatest principles of success; if you persist long enough you will win. —Og Mandino
· ·

You might recall the Olympic skater Nancy Kerrigan. Everything was going right on track in her life; she was completely on top of her game. In January 1994, however, her entire world changed. She was clubbed in the right knee and severely injured during a practice session. News bombarded the tabloids and TV with heart-wrenching stories of the scandal. Initially, she was psychologically devastated. From a physical standpoint, rehabilitation was no easy task. She needed healing on several levels before she could resume intensive training. Each day that followed was a psychological challenge, but Nancy remained persistent.

Even while she endured great physical pain, the strength in her spirit, pushed her through. In an interview after the assault, she stated that she never worked harder for anything in her life and that the setback made her "want it more." She had been forced to drop out of one competition but recovered in time to compete for the United States in the Olympics in Lillehammer, Norway. She gave a nearly flawless performance and won the silver medal. Nancy clearly has the heart of a champion because she *persisted* in the face of a great tribulation. We might not have the same ambition to compete at that level, but we can still learn a simple lesson from her example. There are countless reasons to give up, but if you want to achieve any goal in your life, you must be persistent.

Persistence is the driving force behind discipline and success in life. Without persistence, nothing would get accomplished. People would have great ideas and start projects, but nothing would come to fruition. If I hadn't been persistent in completing this book, you wouldn't be reading it right now. But between work, school, and planning my

271

wedding, my time was very limited. Nonetheless, every day that I went into work, I brought along my laptop. In between clients, I worked on it at every chance I got—at the library across the street or at the local café. Sometimes, I was only able to get through a paragraph or two at a time, a half-hour here or there, but I continued to use my minutes wisely, knowing that if I stayed with it, eventually, I would finish. Instead of focusing on the enormity of it all, I stayed persistent. This PHS principle kept me on track, making the seemingly impossible, possible. Every little inch you take toward your goals is a step in the right direction. Soon, you'll discover that *discipline* is the vase that holds the water and flowers intact. It makes you do it!

"No discipline seems pleasant at the time, but painful. Later on, however, it produces a harvest of righteousness and peace for those who have been trained by it."[1]

Discipline: doing what you have to do, even when you don't want to do it.

***Webster's* definition of discipline:** training that corrects, molds, or perfects the mental faculties or moral character. a) control gained by enforcing obedience or order, b) orderly or prescribed conduct or pattern of behavior, c) self control [2]

. . . .
We are what we repeatedly do. Excellence, then, is not an act, but a habit. —Aristotle
. . . .

Consider How Persistence Relates to Your Life

Life is cyclical. There will be times when you're depleted or long days when you're strung out or at your wit's end. During those times, you may need to put the brakes on some activities and physical training. Learn to listen to your body; it'll give you messages. How you respond is up to you. Sometimes you need to suck it up and keep going; other times you need to scale it back and slow down. Recognizing what to do and when is relative to your life situation. You don't need a PhD from the Common Sense Institute to use good judgment. For instance, if your foot has been fractured, going for a run is senseless; you need to back off and give it time to heal. There are alternatives. You may decide to focus on upper-body training, back or rowing machines, ab exercises or water therapy. When some people are in pain, however, particularly cardio "junkies," they just don't listen to their bodies. Only when they get to a point where they're completely debilitated do they stop. There's also another type of people who avoid the slightest bit of pain or inconvenience at all costs. They avoid strength training because they might get sore, or maybe they have to get up an hour earlier.

Whether you have a high threshold for pain or a low one, it's best to avoid the extremes. For instance, it's nice to pamper yourself occasionally, but if you get too spoiled, you may expect everything in life to come easy. You may want the perfect body but be unwilling to train hard and do what it takes. Physically, not only will your muscles get weak and atrophy, but you could get soft psychologically as well. Mentally, you'll be less inclined to do what's required to follow your program. Notice what *Webster's* definition says about discipline—it corrects, molds, and perfects our mental faculties. It tells us that we can develop an orderly conduct for our behavior. There's no doubt that when you train your physical body, there are mental benefits. At the same time, if you push yourself too hard and don't know when to back off and give it a rest, you'll burn out. This can apply to anything in life, not just overtraining. It's true that sometimes we need to step up our game, but there are also times when less is more. This is often learned the hard way. Our health will suffer if we push ourselves too far in any capacity. We reach the point of diminishing returns. Living a highly stressful and demanding lifestyle will have its consequences, but unfortunately, in this day and age, the old busy is not the new busy. In fact, the new busy think that nine-to-five is a cute idea.

The great recession of 2008 caused people to be willing to work until midnight and sleep under their desk. Even before that downturn, many people lost touch with their own values and compromised their health. Consequently, knowing when and where to draw the line becomes even more important. How do we make this determination? Part of the answer lies within our personality type. Type A personalities are relentless, impatient, and time-conscious. Often referred to as workaholics, like a Duracell battery, they keep going and going and never seem to run out of energy—but that's just in their nature. By contrast, the type B personalities are easy-going and laid-back; they simply don't have the same drive or sense of urgency as type A. There's also the AB type—a mix of both. There's no right or wrong; it takes all kinds of people to make the world go around.

Being persistent isn't about pushing yourself to the brink of collapse; it's about your tenacity to follow through. Regardless of your personality type, you don't need to drive yourself in the ground with constant training or overwork. Rest is not a sign of weakness; it's a necessary part of the optimal health cycle. Physically and mentally, we all need some down time. Those periods correspond to our life cycles and natural biorhythms. This doesn't mean we should lose sight of our goals.

Many people fail to be persistent because their greater problem is psychological in nature. They succumb to preconceived notions and limitations because that's all they've ever known. For example, if you've been overweight your whole life; you may think that's your destiny. You started your exercise and nutrition program, but then your mother reminds you that obesity runs in the family. She told you to hang it up—you're wasting time. With your persistence, however, you can be the one to break the obesity cycle and set an example for her and others to follow. You don't have to pay attention to negative comments, not from your mom or anyone! Nothing can stop you from sticking to your guns. The choice is yours.

· ·
Ambition is the path to success. Persistence
is the vehicle you arrive in. —Bill Bradley
· ·

Let's turn our attention to the world of fitness and high-octane athletics. We all know that many athletes get injured. ACLs pop, knees get twisted, plantar fasciitis develops, teeth are lost, bones are fractured, ankles are sprained, joints give out, and concussions happen. If there was ever a reason to stop certain physical activities, these are good ones. The pain can be excruciating. Marathon runners eventually kiss those days good-bye, when that knee pain becomes intolerable. It's true that injuries can take a toll on our body over the years. Being persistent in this case isn't about adding more pain to a physically run-down body. As mentioned earlier, rest is important to allow the body time to regenerate and heal. However, the fighting power in your spirit can keep you persistent during those challenging situations.

Athletes are naturally high-spirited and want to win; they know how to bounce back and get in the game. That competitive streak seems to be ingrained in their DNA. You may not be an athlete, but if you've experienced physical limitations, you also can get back into your own game. Start by mixing things up. This might mean swimming one day, yoga or Pilates the next day, and cycling the day after. Maybe you can't sprint as fast as you used to—that's okay. Keep in mind that the biggest room you can ever enter is the room for improvement. Physical setbacks don't have to rule your life and take away your enthusiasm. Modifications can be made to deal with your current issues. If you've been injured, there are effective ways to manage pain or make it disappear altogether. It may be possible to fully recover and enjoy your favorite activities all over again. When you're persistent, you will look for those solutions.

For example, a couple years ago I was suffering greatly from plantar fasciitis. I searched high and low for new insoles. Finally, I found a wonderful pair with the proper arch support and within two days, my chronic pain was gone! Other remedies for this common issue include regular icing (placing your foot on an ice pack) for twenty minutes and alternating by soaking your feet in warm Epsom salts, avoiding highly repetitive movements, switching up your tennis shoes every six months, doing foot towel exercises, getting a professional foot massage, and taking fish oil supplementation. Whatever ails you, don't lose hope. Be persistent. If your mind-set is only focused on the pain of the problem, you'll never discover a solution.

One of my colleagues blew out his knee and came into work one day on crutches. Most people would never consider running a marathon after that type of injury. After all, if you've ever been injured, you're aware that former pain can linger on or revisit from time to time. Nevertheless, running was his passion. He started to rebuild the strength in his legs, one day at a time. It was a long healing process but eventually, he was interval running again. Within the next year, he was training for the marathon. It wasn't until a year later that I noticed his credentials hanging on a wall. I was in awe—he had run the marathon in record time and took first place! He's a champion in more ways than one. He could've got discouraged and allowed that knee injury to hold him back, but he didn't let his mind get in the way. Instead, he was persistent and focused on his *passion*, not on his the *problem*. This allowed him to make a huge psychological leap and overcome the mental barrier attached to his physical setback. Don't let the demons of despair discourage you. Maybe you don't have the desire to run a marathon, but when you're persistent, you won't play Russian roulette with your health.

"Watch and pray so that you will not fall into temptation. The spirit is willing, but the flesh is weak."[3]

You must *fight* to be persistent. Being persistent means you're committed and willing to do whatever it takes to be true to yourself. You're not afraid to work hard. It proves you value your health enough to fight for it.

Being persistent shows your gumption. You're willing to go the extra mile and fight for what you want, whether this is your health or anything else you desire in life. So you must know deep down what's valuable to you. I can preach the virtues of health all day, but you must own this value for yourself. If you stop believing that it's possible or worthwhile to be healthy, that's a choice you make. If you don't have the tenacity to fight for what you want, this means that you don't want it or value it enough. If you're willing to work hard for what you want, anything is possible. Your persistence is needed.

Nothing in the world can take the place of persistence. Talent will not; nothing is more common than unsuccessful men with talent. Genius will not; unrewarded genius is almost a proverb. Education will not; the world is full of educated derelicts. Persistence and determination alone are omnipotent. The slogan "Press On" has solved and always will solve the problems of the human race. —Calvin Coolidge

Many forces will emerge to discourage you. Fear is a constant companion. If it wasn't, there would be no battle to fight. If you need a major health transformation, then prepare to go to war on several fronts. You're going to experience more than your fair share of obstacles. Discipline is necessary to maintain healthy behaviors—that's the bottom line. Any way you slice or dice it, this requires your persistence.

When the Going Gets Tough, the Tough Get Going

Let's consider a common issue that is likely to resurface over the course of anyone's lifetime: depression. This topic was addressed earlier, but it warrants a second review, because it can be a major setback for many people. Depression can strike at any time. As we experience different seasons in life, inevitably, we'll be exposed to situations that trigger depression. Whether we've lost a loved one or we've been plagued by some tragic events, nobody is entirely immune from it. Depression has different roots. It may stem from a negative mind-set, biochemical imbalances, environmental factors, or a genetic predisposition. Yet to a great extent, we can guard against it ruining the quality of life. We can all learn to persist beyond its effects.

> I know that I have the ability to achieve the object of my definite purpose in life; therefore, I demand of myself persistent, continuous action toward its attainment, and I here and now promise to render such action. —Napoleon Hill

Consider Dennis, when he first started training with me, I never gave him the PHS. He was already disciplined and also loads of fun to train. He trained with me twice a week for several months, used a heart-rate monitor to track his cardio sessions, and met with a nutritionist. Then one day, he came in with some bad news—he needed prostate surgery and had to put his training sessions on hold. Six months after the surgery, Dennis came back to resume training, except this time he had a different problem. A month after his surgery, he started having major panic attacks and experienced severe depression. He lost interest in eating, had no sense of self-purpose, and wanted to sleep all the time. This was hardly the fun, hilarious and disciplined Dennis that I knew.

Without hesitation, I gave him a copy of the PHS flow chart. He went home, hung it on his refrigerator, and within a week he began applying the PHS principles. He pinpointed a major area of trouble—his self-image. He knew he had to take responsibility for his well-being and be proactive; otherwise, the depression was going to overpower his ability to manage himself. He courageously did the following:

- Acquired professional psychiatric help to deal with the immediate depression and panic.
- Enlisted a therapist to assist in the discovery of the root causes.
- Went to an anxiety help group for moral support and assistance.
- Challenged his "internal self-talk" and thoughts (such as loser, stupid, can't do anything right) with positive affirmations and examples that disputed them.
- Exercised and allowed me to push him to build up his body/soul and drive the release of endorphins, which overrode the depression and panic.

Today, the old and fun Dennis is back! He's doing well, and through his persistence he's disciplined once again. Depression can happen to the best of us. While it's normal to experience depression in painful life situations, it shouldn't become an excuse for all life's problems. We all need time to grieve and this time varies from person to person, yet in order to become disciplined, we must continue to manage ourselves. Where in our psyche or spirit do we need restoration? Sometimes we can get healed by pursuing our life passion. Our soul can die while we live in a mortal body, yet this is hardly an existence. When we find our purpose and passion, we'll fall in love with life and get healed. Depression evaporates. To this end, we must all persist.

Paradoxically, depression can be triggered by positive events as well, such as getting married or having children. Some women experience post-partum depression. Psychologists say, that it's quite normal to experience some ambivalence during these transitional life periods. Having gratitude for your spouse and family and focusing on the positive ways your life has changed will help. Seasonal depression can set in during the winter months. Special light can be installed, or taking a mini-vacation with lots of sunshine will help. Loneliness may cause depression when we leave our friends and family due to relocation. During those times, make an effort to socialize and develop new friendships. Also finding ways to help others is a great remedy by getting your mind off yourself. Recall that depression that stems from any sort of abuse (such as substance, physical, or verbal) may require professional counseling or a 12-step program.

We must understand the real cause of our depression and find ways to deal with it. As discussed earlier, we'll all attend a "Conquering Depression" class at some point in life. How long you stay in the class is up to you. The paradox is that you need to graduate from a depressing class with a positive attitude. You can't move on unless you have the right understanding. If you find yourself needing to repeat this class over and over, the pain of depression is trying to teach you something. Life is giving you an assignment, be persistent in finding the right solution.

"For our struggle is not against flesh and blood, but against the rulers, against the authorities, against the powers of this dark world and against the spiritual forces of evil in the heavenly realms. Therefore put on the full armor of God, so that when the day of evil comes, you may be able to stand your ground, and after you have done everything, to stand."[4]

Spiritually, consider what you're up against: the enemy of your soul wants to keep you down and depressed. To break out of this depression trap, you may need to develop some new skills—particularly, the fruit of the spirit. It's easy to see from the list below what has the power to help you or harm you.

Fruit of the Spirit
Hopeful
Forgiveness
Faith in God
Gratitude
Positive mind-set
Open and willing to change
Humble

Fruit of the Enemy
Hopeless
Unforgiving
No faith in high power
Ungrateful
Negative mind-set
Stubborn and resistant to change
Rebellious

No matter what situation you experience in life or how unbearable the pain may seem, everything happens for a reason. It may seem that the pain is insurmountable; it swept over you like a big wave, and now you feel about to drown. Don't lose faith. Pain is a great teacher in life. God allowed it to happen. He's in control and much more powerful than any awful situation. Give him credit, and continue to believe in the best. It takes a lot of integrity to benefit from this principle.

"Consider it pure joy, my brothers, whenever you face trials of many kinds, because you know that the testing of your faith develops perseverance. Perseverance must finish its work so that you may be mature and complete, not lacking anything."[5]

When you get to the end of your rope, tie a knot and hang on. —Franklin D. Roosevelt

Keep the Hope . . . Keep Your Joy

To remain hopeful is a decision. If you lose hope in any area of your life, you can't expect to accomplish much. You'll lose your resolve. Stay hopeful, and you'll persist. Even if you only have a glimmer of hope, fan the fire—don't blow it out. Keep the hope alive, and keep believing in the best, in whatever you want—you'll have nothing to lose. Hope gives you the mental courage you need to overcome fears and to go for what you want. It keeps you persistent. Discouraging thoughts will put out the fire of hope, while encouraging thoughts ignite it. If your health is important to you, nothing will hold you back. You'll keep the hope alive.

When we keep our hope, we can keep our joy. This is our natural state. Consider children; they're naturally filled with joy. We can learn a lesson from them. On Christmas Day, they don't always get what they want, no matter how much they hoped for it. They also might be sad when they discover that there is no Santa Claus. But children are resilient; they bounce back quite rapidly. They live in the moment. They're filled with so much life and enthusiasm that they keep their joy alive effortlessly. Much of our adulthood bears a striking resemblance to our childhood. We don't always get what we want in life, but there's no need to be hopeless. We can lighten up.

Laughter is good medicine; it can cure us from many ailments and diseases. Studies have shown that laughing releases toxins and improves the entire immune system. Some people have a knack for finding the humor in each and every situation. We thoroughly enjoy these people because they make us laugh and always put a smile on our face. When we keep our joy, we keep our sanity, our peace and our health. You don't need to wait for certain events to make you happy. You can be happy right now! When you're grateful for life and everything you have, there's always a reason to smile. Stay hopeful and find some joy and enthusiasm in your life. "Do not grieve, for the joy of the Lord is your strength."[6]

"Be joyful always, pray continually, give thanks in all circumstances, for this is God's will for you in Jesus Christ."[7]

Closing Thoughts:
Find the Healer Within

This has been your personal journey of learning, discovery, and self-empowerment. Whether it was one component at a time, one principle at a time, one day at a time, or one step at a time, you've finally made it through. Now it's your time to take charge and put it all together. Your journey continues. Always remember, when you're proactive, you're in control of your life and health—this is your solution. The PHS principles are always with you. Hold them close to your heart. Accept that your body is your home, and it must be loved. How will you treat it? What foods will you digest? Will you drink pure, uncontaminated water? Will you exercise regularly? Will you make time to relax, breathe deeply, and meditate? What will be your thoughts? How will you deal with your emotions? Will you remain calm in the midst of the storm? Will you be an example of discipline to others? All these choices are yours.

Whatever you project in your mind and spirit will manifest in your body. All illness reflects a disconnection of our spiritual connection to God. Health and beauty resides deep in your soul. If you stay connected to the Great Universal Spirit and don't lose faith, you will find there's a great healer in you. Believe this is possible, and you can do whatever you wish to heal yourself.

Addendum:
A Personal Prayer

In Romans 10:9, the bible says that if you confess with your mouth that Jesus is Lord and believe in your heart that God raised him from the dead, you will be saved. Open your heart to this opportunity. In your own words, you can make this personal prayer in faith. Ask him to heal your heart, your mind, and your spirit. If you accept Jesus as your savior, you have made peace with your higher source of power—know that the Father, the Son and the Holy Spirit are all one. This is the same universal spirit for all.

REFERENCES

Scriptures taken from New International Version are marked NIV - Copyright © 1973, 1978, 1984 by International Bible Study - Library of Congress Catalog Card No. 73-174297

Scriptures taken from King James Version are marked KJV - Copyright © 1988 Christian Heritage Publishing Co. Inc.

Scriptures taken from The Living Bible are marked TLB - Copyright © 1971 Tyndale House Publishers

Scriptures taken from the Amplified New Testament are marked AMP - Zondervan Bible Publishers - Copyright © The Lockman Foundation, 1958, 1954 (Library of Congress Catalog Card No. 55-5388)

Chapter 1

1   NIV Heb 11:1
2   NIV Eph 2:8-9
3   NIV Jn 8:32
4   NIV Jer 29:11-13
5   NIV 1 Tim 6:12
6   NIV Jn 17:17
7   NIV Jn 14:6
8   NIV Jn 18:37
9   NIV Php 4:8
10 NIV Jn 7:37-38
11 NIV Jn 4:32
12 NIV Jn 6:35
13 TLB 2 Cor 6:16

14   TLB 2 Cor 7:1

15   TLB Isa 35:3-6

16   TLB Heb 12:12

Chapter 2

1   Today's Debate:Suing won't make kids thin. USA TODAY. February 20, 2006: 10A

2   Chris Marino; Exercise ETC. Review of exercise related research - CDC reports higher obesity numbers for 2008: July 15, 2009

3   Number of fat people in US to grow, report says: Organization of Economic Cooperation and Development (OECD) September 23, 2010

4   Here's the good news- US No longer fattest nation, February 11, 2011 - report from OECD 2010: Matthia's Rumpf - (source good.is)

5   Only half of worried Americans try to manage their stress - Study: Many overeat, smoke to feel better by Kate Schuler USA TODAY. February 23, 2006:13B

6   Ibid.

7   Ibid.

8   Obesity is a Key Link to Soaring Health Tab by Nancy Hellmich USA TODAY. July 28, 2009

9   Gunn P., Eileen. Healthy Returns. Experience Life. March 2006; vol.8 issue 2: 43-46.

10   Ibid.

11   Health spending rises at blistering pace:USA TODAY. February 22, 2006:B1.

12   Gunn P., Eileen. Healthy Returns. Experience Life. March 2006; vol.8 issue 2: 43-46.

13   New Foods for Healing by Selene Yeager and the editors of Prevention Health Books copyright © 1998 by Roland Press, Inc. p.312-313

14   http://www.nationmaster.com/graph/hea-obe-health-obesity

15   January 1998, the Executive Board endorsed this proposal of the Special Group and adopted resolution EB 10 1.R2 recommending the World Health Assembly to modify the preamble of the Constitution accordingly [15].

16   Effects of Negative Emotions on the Heart can lead to cardiac problems, Feb 11, 2009 - Mercy Health Care Plans Web Site www.mercyhealthplans.com/wellness/healthheadlines/090211.aspx accessed April 1, 2010

Chapter 3

1   Today's Debate: Childhood obesity. Suing won't make kids thin. USA TODAY February 20, 2006:10A
2   Ibid.

Chapter 4

1   'Philips Index for Health and Well-being: A global perspective'. Webwire November 11, 2010 http://www.because.philips.com/livable-cities-award. Amsterdam, The Netherlands – Royal Philips Electronics (AEX: PHI, NYSE: PHG)
2   Now Studio-Bach Remedies; http://www.nourhy.com/services/bach/

Chapter 5

1   Stephen R. Covey. The 7 Habits of Highly Effective People; Copyright 1989
2   Merriam-Webster, Incorporated. Merriam-Webster's Collegiate Dictionary, Eleventh edition; Copyright 2003
3   Covey R. Stephen. The 7 Habits of Highly Effective People; Copyright 1989. Part two:private victory; Habit 1-71.
4   Ibid.
5   NIV Mt 26:39
6   NIV Heb 12:2-4
7   NIV Lk 23:34
8   NIV Heb 12:7
9   NIV Heb 12:11
10   Covey R. Stephen. The 7 Habits of Highly Effective People; Copyright 1989. Part two:private victory; Habit 1-71.

11   NIV Jas 2:26

12   NIV Pr 4:6-7

13   NIV Pr 3:13-15

14   http://www.hsph.harvard.edu/nutritionsource/omega-3

15   Lifelab – Riskpoint/testing done by Life Corp through Life Time Fitness

16   Ibid.

17   Http://www.whitehouse.gov/the-press-office/2010/10/04/presidential-proclamation-child-health-day

18   NIV Ps 127:3-4

Chapter 6

1   Webster's dictionary and thesaurus-New Revised Updated Edition, Nichols Publishing Group; Copyright 1999

2   Branden, Nathaniel PH.D. Taking Responsibility; Fireside Rockfeller Center; Copyright 1996; 13

3   Ibid. p. 10

4   NIV Ro 14:12

5   Branden, Nathaniel PH.D. Taking Responsibility; Fireside Rockfeller Center; Copyright 1996; 13-14

6   Munroe, Myles Dr. The Principles and Benefits of Change; Bahamas Faith Ministries International; Copyright 2009; 151

7   NIV Mt 11:29-30

8   NIV Heb 4:12-13

9   NIV 2 Co 8:12

10   NIV Pr 31:27

Chapter 7

1   National Center for Health Statistics. Health, United States, 2006. With Chartbook on Trends in the Health of Americans. Hyattsville, MD: 2006, p. 38

2   NIV Mt 19:26

3   Immune System Ailments. Self Empowerment and Development Centre website. Http://www.iempowerself.com/59_immune_system_ailments.html. Accessed 11 Aug 2012.

4   Aurigemma, Gerard P. Acute Stress Cardiomyopathy and Reversible Left Ventricular Dysfunction. Cardioogy Rounds. 2006; Vol.10(Issue 10).

5   NIV Heb 12:15

6   Bandura, Albert. Social Cognitive Theory of Self-Regulation. Http://dx.doi.org/10.1016/0749-5978(91)90022-L. Accessed 11 Aug 2012.

7   Branden, Nathaniel PH.D. Taking Responsibility; Fireside Rockfeller Center; Copyright 1996; 101

8   NIV Dt 30:19-20

9   NIV Job 1:12

10   NIV Job 2:10

11   NIV Jn 8:44

12   NIV Ps 23:4

13   NIV Ge 45:4-5

14   NIV Isa 55:8-9

Chapter 8

1   Khayat, M.H., Sprituality in the Definition of Health The World Health Organization's Point of View (1998), available at www.medizin-ethik.ch/publik/spritiuality_definition_health.htm

2   NIV 2 Co 5:18-19

3   NIV Ro 8:28

4   NIV Mt 22:37-40

5   Larson, Joan Mathews. 7 Weeks to Emotional Healing. Ballantine Random House, 1999. p. 235

6   Kim et al (2010). Nature. 467(7313):285-290. http://www.ncbi.nlm.nih.gov/pmc/articles/PMC3150836

7   Colbert, Don. Stress Management 101. Thomas Nelson, 2006. vi-viii.

8   Kessler RC, Chiu WT, Demler O, Walters EE. Prevalence, severity, and comorbidity of twelve-month DSM-IV disorders in the National Comorbidity Survey Replication (NCS-R). Archives of General Psychiatry, 2005 Jun;62(6):617-27

9   Alcoholism Statistics. Alcohol Addiction Web Site. http://www. alcoholaddiction.info/alcoholism-statistics.htm. Accessed Feb 24, 2012.

10   Hainer, Ray. CDC: Nearly 1 in 10 US adults depressed. http://thechart. blogs.cnn.com/2010/10/01/cdc-nearly-1-in-10-u-s-adults-depressed/. Accessed Feb 24, 2012.

11   Heart Attack Statistics. Allheartattack.com. http://www. allheartattack.com/statistics.php. Accessed Feb 20, 2012.

12   National Center for Health Statistics. Health, United States, 2008. Hyattsville, MD: National Center for Health Statistics; 2008.

13   Topics in Brief: Prescription Drug Abuse. NIDA (National Institute on Drug Abuse). http://www.drugabuse.gov/publications/topics-in-brief/prescription-drug-abuse. Accessed Feb 24, 2012.

14   Nathan, G. Ronald, Ph.D., Staats, E. Thomas, Ph.D., Rosch, J. Paul, M.D. The Doctor's Guide to INSTANT STRESS RELIEF; Copyright 1987. p.7

Chapter 9

1   TLB Ps 27:10

2   NIV Lk 6:42

3   NIV Nu 23:19

4   NIV Jn 3:16

5   Osteen, Joel. YourBest Life Now: 7 Steps to Living at Your Full Potential. New York. FaithWords, 2004.

6   Ibid.

7   NIV Mt 16:26

8   NIV Mt 4:4

9   NIV Jn 6:27

10   NIV Ps 37:4

11   NIV Mt 6:22-23

12   KJV Pr 23:7

13   NIV 1 Co 3:16-17

14   Gawain, Shakti. Creative Visualization. A Bantam Book / published by arrangement with New World Library; Copyright 1978

Chapter 10

1   KJV Pr 29:18

2   NIV Pr 17:22

3   NIV Eph 4:22-23

4   NIV Php 2:14-15

5   NIV Mt 10:16

6   NIV Php 4:7

7   NIV 1 Co 13:13

8   NIV Ps 139:14

9   NIV 2 Co 12:9-10

Chapter 11

1   Yeager, Selene and the editors of prevention health books. New Foods for Healing. Copyright 1998 by Rodale Press; 183

2   Ibid. p. 184

3   http://www.naturalnews.com/026273/spinach_cancer_brain.html

4   http://www.hsph.harvard.edu/nutritionsource/vegetables-full-story

5   http://www.foods-healing-power.com/fruits-vegetables-blood-pressure.html

6   Ibid.

7   Brennan O Richard. http://the basicsofanything.com/the-basics-of-healthy-eating-why-raw

8   Ibid.

9   Ibid.

10   Yeager, Selene and the editors of prevention health books. New Foods for Healing. Copyright 1998 by Rodale Press; 190

11   American Council on Exercise. Personal Trainer Manual. 2nd Edition Copyright 1996, p. 134

12   Ibid. p. 138

13   Ibid. p. 136

14   Ibid. p. 135, 137

15   Larson Mathews, Joan, Ph.D. 7 Weeks to Emotional Healing. Ballantine Random House, Copyright 1999

Chapter 12

1   American Council on Exercise. Personal Trainer Manual. 2nd Edition Copyright 1996, p. 185

Chapter 13

1   NIV Heb 12:11
2   Merriam-Webster, Incorporated. Merriam-Webster's Collegiate Dictionary, Eleventh edition; Copyright 2003
3   NIV Mt 26:41
4   NIV Eph 6:12-13
5   NIV Jas 1:2-4
6   NIV Ne 8:10
7   NIV 1 Th 5:16

INDEX

increases the risk of, 2
management, 101
as a mental symptom, 147
releasing, 119–20
unresolved, 102, 132
anorexia nervosa, 131, 149
antibodies, 218–19
anticancer agents, 211
antidepressants, 110
antioxidants, 208, 213–14, 218
food sources of, 64
anxiety
emotional, 109, 113-14, 146
facing children, 24
leads to, 5, 65, 90, 145–46
link to hormone deficiencies, 28
and mental health, 106, 147
preventing, xvi, 163, 209
and risk to health, 102, 141, 145–46
treatment of, 48, 64, 278
arteries, 18, 26, 141
arthritis, 102
relief for rheumatoid, 64–65
artificial sweeteners, 225–26
aspartame, 209, 226
athletes
competitive, 150, 224
elite, 35, 167
endurance, 219, 237
and food choices, 225
and injuries, 275–76
strength, 219
athletic performance, 24, 189, 204, 221, 224, 231
athletic training, 21, 24, 236
Atkins diet, 17
attitude
and mind, 48, 186, 190, 192
positive, 116, 120–22, 279, 191
aura, 144, 194. *See also* energy
autism, 23

autoimmune diseases, 64
autonomic nervous system, 147
Avery, Oswald, 181

B

Babe Ruth, 91
Bach Centre, 48
Bach, Edward, 47–48
balance
to achieve optimal health, 123
in chakras, 5, 147
as a common fitness goal, 231, 235
(*see also* exercise; *to improve balance*)
in diet, 19, 128, 139, 205
and inner peace, xvi, 46, 138, 147, 166
in inner-self, 126–27
as integration of mind, body, spirit, 4–5, 99, 127, 140
internal, 135, 171
in life/lifestyle, 46, 94, 96–97, 124–125, 127–30, 134, 145
of macronutrients, 237
part of healthy self-management, 127, 269
in physical body, 127, 139, 204
psychologically off, 141, 144
and spiritual well-being, 127, 194
bariatric surgery, 60
basal metabolic rate (BMR), 221–22. *See also* resting metabolic rate (RMR)
battle
against obesity, 31
emotional, 117
against fear, 277
mental, 4, 150
of personal demons, 93, 102, 170
of poor self-image, 160, 162

resting metabolic rate (RMR), 218,
222–23
restoration, 2, 45, 143–44, 213, 279
rewards, 77, 120, 133, 174
risk
of cancer, 12, 65, 146, 210, 213
of cardiovascular disease, 211
of diabetes, 12, 65
to environment, 226
factors, 102, 174
of fad diets, 16–18
of heart disease, xvi, 12, 25, 65, 146,
210
and high blood pressure, 65
of injury, 240
in life, 91
reducing, 63–64, 204, 210, 211–13,
240
of stroke, 25, 65, 210
Rock of Ages, 127
Roosevelt, Eleanor, 55
Roosevelt, Franklin D., 281

S

salt, 65, 117, 205, 226
satiation, 203
self-control, 94, 195, 208
self-discipline, 169, 267
self-discovery, xvii, 46, 100, 153
self-efficacy, 111
self-esteem
assessing, 154–57, 169
and childhood, 154
as dimension of well-being, 23, 61,
150, 184
lacking in, 61, 142, 186
low, 113, 149–50, 154, 156, 164, 166
and personal accountability, 87, 112
and physical body, 151

and positive mentality, 144, 189–90
restoring, 160-162, 184
self-image
assessment of, 149–50, 155, 157, 278
improving, 150–54, 159–63, 184–85
and PHS methodology, 39–40, 45,
66, 149
and self-esteem, 154–57
self-imposed limitations, 3, 147,
165–66
self-responsibility, 85, 87, 97–98, 111
serotonin, 28
shame, 54, 132, 155
Shaw, George Bernard, 68
Sinha, Rajita, 12
sleep
before, 191
better, 64, 212–13
deprived of, 72, 82
disturbance, 66
poorly, 25
as primary requirement, 28
problems, 147
SMART Goals, 189
smoking
addiction, 11, 109, 114
chain, 97
as an imbalance, 132, 147
quitting, 43, 56–57, 66, 97
and risk of cancer, 65
and social pressure, 85
Sobal, Tom, 179
social cognitive theory model, 111
social connections, 120, 139
social eating, 32, 207
social networks, 103, 114
social order, 21, 84
social outlets, 129, 136
social pressure, 85, 105, 145, 207
social well-being, 25, 120

Please send inquires, feedback or share stories of how the Proactive Health Solution has helped you to the following email address: proactivehealthsolution@gmail.com